MAPPING METHODS 2
Step-by-step guide
Experience Maps
Journey Maps
Service Blueprints
Affinity Diagrams
Empathy Maps
Business Model Canvas

2nd Edition

Robert A Curedale
Copyright © 25 January 2017 by Robert A. Curedale
All rights reserved. Published by Design Community College Inc.

The publisher and author accept no liability, regardless of legal basis. Designations used in this book may be trademarks whose use by third parties for their own purposes could violate the rights of the owners. The author and publisher have taken great care with all texts and illustrations in this book. The information contained within this book is strictly for educational purposes. If you wish to apply ideas contained in this book you are taking full responsibility for your actions. There are no representations or warranties, express or implied, about the completeness, accuracy, reliability, suitability or availability with respect to the information, products, services, or related graphics contained in this book for any purpose. Any use of this information is at your own risk. The author has made every effort to ensure the accuracy of the information within this book was correct at time of publication. The publisher and author do not assume and hereby disclaims any liability to any party for any loss, damage, or disruption caused by errors or omissions, whether such errors or omissions result from accident, negligence, or any other cause.

All rights reserved. No part of this publication may be reproduced, distributed, or transmitted in any form or by any means, including photocopying, recording, or other electronic or mechanical methods, without the prior written permission of the publisher, except in the case of brief quotations embodied in critical reviews and certain other noncommercial uses permitted by copyright law. For permission requests, write to the publisher, addressed "Attention: Permissions Coordinator," at the address below.

Design Community College Inc.
PO Box 1153
Topanga CA 90290 USA
info@dcc-edu.org
Designed and illustrated by Robert Curedale
Cover color graphic and artwork designed by Robert Curedale
ISBN-10: 1-940805-37-6
ISBN-13: 978-1-940805-37-5

MAPPING METHODS 2

Step-by-step guide

**Experience Maps
Journey Maps
Service Blueprints
Affinity Diagrams
Empathy Maps
Business Model Canvas**

2nd Edition

Robert Curedale

Published by Design Community College Inc.
Los Angeles https://dcc-edu.org

CONTENTS

INTRODUCTION   12
1. 20th century design vs 21st century design
2. Growing use of mapping terms among half a trillion words in books scanned by Google
3. Companies that apply strategic design methods are more successful in business
4. Overview of the methods described in this book
5. Experience maps
6. Journey maps
7. Service blueprints
8. Empathy maps
9. Business model canvas
10. About the author

01 SERVICE DESIGN   17
1. Growing use of the term service design
2. Largest us private employers 1960 vs 2010
3. Private sector employment
4. 1948 To 2010 % of total private employment
5. The growth of services
6. The evolving focus of design practice
7. Bells stages of economic development
8. Preindustrial society
9. Industrial society
10. 1900 To 1950
11. Postindustrial society
12. Why service design is one of the
13. Fastest-growing areas of design
14. Servitization
15. Types of product service systems
16. Why servitize?
17. Strategic rationale
18. Challenges for servitization
19. Implementing servitization
20. From goods-centered to
21. Customer-centered solutions
22. Service industry growth in China
23. Percentage of China's GDP from services 1970 to 2030
24. Why design services?
25. The design ladder
26. The design ladder in relation to success in export
27. Average growth in turnover
28. Storytelling
29. The big questions
30. Story structure
31. Narrative
32. An effective story
33. Plan your story
34. Audience
35. Context
36. Focus on what's important
37. Be visual
38. Ask for feedback from your audience
39. Challenges
40. Effective design balances
41. People's needs, business needs, the best technology and consideration of the environment
42. Human needs
43. Shoshin
44. Service design spaces
45. Spaces for creative work

Haworth recommendations
46. Tacit knowledge
47. Qualitative research
48. Questions to consider
49. Thinking styles
50. Abductive thinking
51. Deductive thinking
52. Inductive thinking
53. Critical thinking
54. Design thinking
55. Divergent and convergent thinking
56. Research triangulation
57. Primary research
58. Secondary research
59. Why use mapping methods?
60. Craft a better user experience
61. Improve your business performance
62. Design ethnography
63. Some disruptive trends
64. Diversity
65. Empathy
66. Experience design
67. Human needs
68. Segmentation
69. Personas
70. Origin of personas
71. Persona template
72. Types of personas
73. Primary personas
74. Secondary personas
75. Stakeholders
76. Exclusionary personas
77. Biographical information
78. Persona exercise

02 APPLYING MAPPING METHODS IN YOUR ORGANIZATION 75
1. Moderating groups
2. Roles
3. Assistant moderator
4. Moderator
5. Group behavior
6. Constructive group behaviors
7. Destructive group behaviors
8. Intervention
9. Time management
10. Keep the interview on track
11. What methods did you use to research your customers?
12. Which internal departments were represented in your mapping team?
13. Use the interview guide
14. Do not rush the discussion
15. Moderator skills
16. Building rapport
17. Listening to discussion participants
18. Teams
19. Diversity
20. Who sponsored your most recent mapping project?
21. Empowerment
22. Facilitation
23. Which research method was most effective for journey mapping?
24. Collective intelligence
25. Which software tools have you used to create journey maps?
26. Cross pollination
27. Cross-disciplinary collaboration
28. Everyone contributes
29. What methods did you use to research your customers?

03 DESIGN SPRINTS 94
1. Google sprint
2. What is a Google sprint?
3. Who invented the Google sprint?
4. The process
5. Google sprint schedule-3 days
6. Design and architectural charrettes

7. 1.5 Day mini-charrette
8. 2.0 Day design charrette
9. 4.0 Day architectural charrette
10. 0.5 Day product charrette
11. 0.5 Day UX charrette
12. Application of multiple
13. Design sprints on a project

04 THE DESIGN PROCESS 105
1. The design process overview
2. The design process in detail
3. How to plan a design project
4. Smart goals
5. Service planning & strategy
6. How customers select a service provider
7. Guidelines for successful service design
8. Service strategy differentiation
9. Service strategy focus
10. Service package
11. Warming up
12. Points to consider
13. Why do warming up exercises?
14. When to do warming up exercises
15. Discovery
16. Discovery phase
17. The discovery process
18. Synthesis phase
19. Actionable insights
20. User need or pov statement
21. Point of view statement
22. What is an insight?
23. When do you have a significant insight?
24. Actionable insights
25. Insights recognize relationships
26. Ask thoughtful questions
27. Look for emerging patterns
28. Understand the action and behavior
29. Insight tool
30. Sam/ think feel do framework
31. The point of view statement
32. Make your own POV statement
33. Reframing the problem
34. Reframing matrix
35. "What if" and "how might we" questions
36. Goal forming exercise
37. Point of view exercise
38. The ideation phase
39. Why is innovation necessary?
40. What is good design?
41. What is universal design?
42. Universal design guidelines
43. Dieter rams ten principles of "good design"
44. 50 Phrases that will prevent you from beating your competitors
45. Brainstorming
46. Who invented brainstorming?
47. Preparing for brainstorming
48. Create a strategy
49. Choosing a technique
50. Refreshments
51. Facilitating
52. Rules for brainstorming
53. Post-it voting
54. Group review
55. The space
56. Methods of arranging ideas
57. Types of brainstorming
58. Focus your ideas
59. Some useful materials for brainstorming
60. Innovation is a numbers game
61. Evaluating an idea
62. Physical product
63. Industry criteria
64. Marketing criteria
65. Product criteria

66. Checklist for environmentally responsible design
67. Prototyping
68. When to prototype
69. Service laboratory
70. On-site when
71. Not real end users
72. Real end users when
73. Use mock-ups when
74. Real props when
75. Real employees when
76. Artificial employees when
77. Low-fidelity prototyping
78. Challenges
79. Low fidelity prototyping resources
80. High fidelity appearance prototypes
81. Challenges
82. Prototyping services
83. Service staging & roleplay
84. Service blueprints & experience maps
85. Storyboards
86. Other techniques
87. Validation
88. Validation process
89. What to test
90. How many to test
91. Diagnostic evaluation
92. Summative testing
93. Design the test
94. Where
95. Scenarios and tasks
96. Tips for writing scenarios
97. Writing tasks
98. Select data to capture
99. Qualitative data
100. Success paths
101. Recruit participants
102. Recruitment ideas
103. Screener
104. Compensation
105. Validation space
106. Schedule participants
107. Stakeholders
108. Script
109. Questionnaires and surveys
110. Pre-test survey
111. Post-task survey
112. Trial run-through
113. The test session
114. Facilitation
115. Task failures
116. After the session
117. Analysis
118. Recommendations
119. Recruitment script
120. Recommendations
121. Recruitment script
122. Screening script
123. Scheduling
124. Participant recruitment screener
125. Think out load script
126. Alpha testing
127. Duration
128. Team requirements
129. Output
130. Goals
131. Identifying risks
132. Risks may include
133. The team
134. Process
135. Iterations
136. Beta testing
137. Why create a beta?
138. Objective
139. Private beta
140. Public beta
141. Team
142. Output
143. Data analysis
144. Coding
145. Clustering
146. Themes
147. Name the themes
148. Types of themes
149. Display the data visually
150. Validate your findings

151.	Triangulation		195.	Launch plan
152.	Reporting		196.	Key activities
153.	Test plan		197.	Pre-launch
154.	Scope		198.	Mid-launch
155.	Purpose		199.	Go live
156.	Schedule & location		200.	Launch
157.	Time		201.	Post-launch plan
158.	Equipment		202.	Post-launch stages
159.	Participants		203.	Post-launch
160.	Scenarios		204.	Did you meet your goals?
161.	Metrics		205.	Measure success
162.	Quantitative metrics		206.	Some success metrics
163.	Roles		207.	What could be improved?
164.	Implementation		208.	Define the next vision
165.	Why		209.	A simple pitching statement
166.	How			
167.	Finalize your design			
168.	Pitch & commit			
169.	This pitch will help build external partnerships			

05 BUSINESS MODEL CANVAS 160

1. Who invented it?
2. Google trends shows the growing
3. Popularity of the business model canvas
4. Business model canvas exercise

170.	Sign off from stakeholders
171.	Authorize vendors
172.	Deliver
173.	Launch activities
174.	Service
175.	Legal
176.	Product proposition
177.	Product development
178.	Customer experience
179.	Marketing
180.	Marketing communications
181.	Lead generation
182.	Internal communications
183.	Demo
184.	Pricing
185.	Channels pricing
186.	Pricing structure
187.	Pricing tools
188.	Pricing analysis
189.	Channels
190.	Channel strategy
191.	Channel plans
192.	Channel stock
193.	The pitch
194.	Launch process

06 AFFINITY DIAGRAMS 167

1. Jiro Kawakita and affinity diagrams
2. Why use affinity diagrams?
3. History of affinity diagrams
4. When should we use affinity diagrams?
5. Strengths
6. Weaknesses
7. Use an affinity diagram when:
8. Do not use an affinity diagram when
9. Process
10. Affinity diagram exercise

07 EMPATHY MAPS 181

1. What is empathy?
2. How long does it take?

3. Why
4. Challenges
5. Resources
6. How
7. Empathy map exercise

08 EXPERIENCE MAPS 192
1. Elements of an experience map
2. History
3. Why
4. A map helps you
5. How
6. Multi-channel map
7. Emotional journey map
8. Experience map exercise

09 JOURNEY MAPS 218
1. A customer journey map
2. Features
3. Common journey phases
4. Why
5. Benefits of journey maps
6. How
7. What do you typically include in journey maps?

10 SERVICE BLUEPRINTS 224
1. Elements of a service blueprint
2. Why
3. Lynn Shostack and service blueprints
4. How
5. Service blueprint exercise
6. Connecting the boxes

11 GLOSSARY 247

12 INDEX 268

13 ONLINE PROGRAMS 285
1. DCC workshops
2. Other DCC titles

14 BIBLIOGRAPHY 293

20TH CENTURY DESIGN | 21ST CENTURY DESIGN

INDIVIDUAL DESIGNERS

DESIGN TEAMS

PRODUCTS

SYSTEMS OF PRODUCTS, SERVICES AND EXPERIENCES

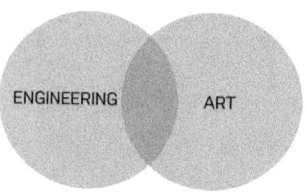

ENGINEERING — ART

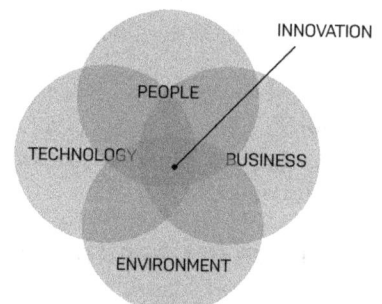

INNOVATION — PEOPLE — TECHNOLOGY — BUSINESS — ENVIRONMENT

DESIGN INSPIRATION FROM IMAGES OF THE WORK OF 20 FAMOUS DESIGNERS IN EACH DESIGN DISCIPLINE

3D DESIGN SKILLS
SKETCHING
MODELMAKING
CAD

DESIGN INSPIRATION FROM RESEARCH AND THE UNMET NEEDS OF-END USERS

4D DESIGN SKILLS
IDENTIFYING UNMET NEEDS
EXPERIENCE MAPS
SERVICE BLUEPRINTS
INTERVIEWING
SCENARIOS
CO-DESIGN
VALUE NETWORKS

ABOUT THE AUTHOR

Rob Curedale was born in Australia and worked as a designer, director and educator in leading design offices in London, Sydney, Switzerland, Portugal, Los Angeles, Silicon Valley, Detroit, and Hong Kong. He designed or managed the design of over 1,000 products as a consultant and in-house design leader for the world's most respected brands. Rob has three decades experience in every aspect of product development and design research, leading design teams to achieve transformational improvements in operating and financial results. Rob's design scan be found in millions of homes and workplaces around the world and have generated billions of dollars in corporate revenues.

DESIGN PRACTICE
HP, Philips, GEC, Nokia, Sun, Apple, Canon, Motorola, Nissan, Audi VW, Disney, RTKL, Governments of the UAE, UK, Australia, Steelcase, Hon, Castelli, Hamilton Medical, Zyliss, Belkin, Gensler, Haworth, Honeywell, NEC, Hoover, Packard Bell, Dell, Black & Decker, Coleman and Harmon Kardon. Categories including furniture, healthcare, consumer electronics, sporting, housewares, military, exhibits, and packaging.

TEACHING
Rob has taught as a full time professor, adjunct professor and visiting instructor at institutions including the following: Art Center Pasadena, Art Center Europe, Yale School of Architecture, Pepperdine University, Loyola University, Cranbrook Academy of Art, Pratt, Otis, a faculty member at SCA and UTS Sydney, Chair of Product Design and Furniture Design at the College for Creative Studies in Detroit, then the largest product design school in North America, Cal State San Jose, Escola De Artes e Design in Oporto Portugal, Instituto De Artes Visuals, Design e Marketing, Lisbon, Southern Yangtze University, Jiao Tong University in Shanghai and Nanjing Arts Institute in China.

AWARDS
Designs that Rob has managed and designed have been recognized with IDSA IDEA Awards, Good Design Awards UK, Australian Design Awards, and a number of best of show innovation Awards at CES Consumer Electronics Show. His designs are in the Permanent collection of the Powerhouse Design Museum. In 2013 Rob was nominated for the Advanced Australia Award. The Awards celebrate Australians living internationally who exhibit "remarkable talent, exceptional vision, and ambition." In 2015 Rob was selected with a group of leading international industrial designers to provide opening comments for the International Congress Of Societies Of Industrial Design Conference ICSID in Korea.

INTRODUCTION

I have created this book to help spread the word about a new and better way of designing almost anything. Through my unique connectedness to over 1.2 million designers in the on-line groups that I established I hope to influence the culture of design. What I have learned from thousands of conversations with global designers and more than 1,000 design projects that I have been engaged in, I would like to pass on to you. I believe that empathy and teamwork are the best hope we has for a brighter future. This is the most recent of thirty books that I have written about innovation and emerging design practices. It is intended to be a useful guide for all people practicing design and I hope will contribute something positive to the culture of design.

There are by one estimate about 30 billion chairs in existence. In the 20th-century design and advertising were about making people want things. With the methods in this book you can design more than a nice looking chair. You can design and implement an innovative chair that deserves to exist because it is better than those billions of chairs and because it meets a human need and will drive a profit for your business.

In this book are described the most powerful tools available to craft a superior experience for your customers and end users.
These powerful and flexible methods are collectively known as design mapping methods. They can be used to optimize the design of goods, services, architecture, spaces and interactions and to plan business strategy. The service sector makes up nearly 70% of most western economies, yet most people are often frustrated by their service experiences. Customers choose products and services that deliver the best experiences. Designing your customer's entire experience is key to differentiating your designs from competitors in an increasingly crowded competitive marketplaces.

Companies that excel at customer experience grow revenues 4-8% above the market."
Source: Bain & Co.

Mapping builds consensus across your organization with stakeholders, to positively impact your entire organization and your bottom line. I believe that these core strategic tools will become required skills for every working designer in every field of design.

My organization, DCC also provides on-line classes. You can review the full list of publications and classes on our web site www.dcc-edu.org

Organizations that focus on journey optimization perform dramatically better than those that do not.
- 10 to 15% Greater revenue growth
- 15 to 20% lower cost to serve
- 20% greater customer satisfaction
- 20 to 30% more engaged employees"

Source: McKinsey

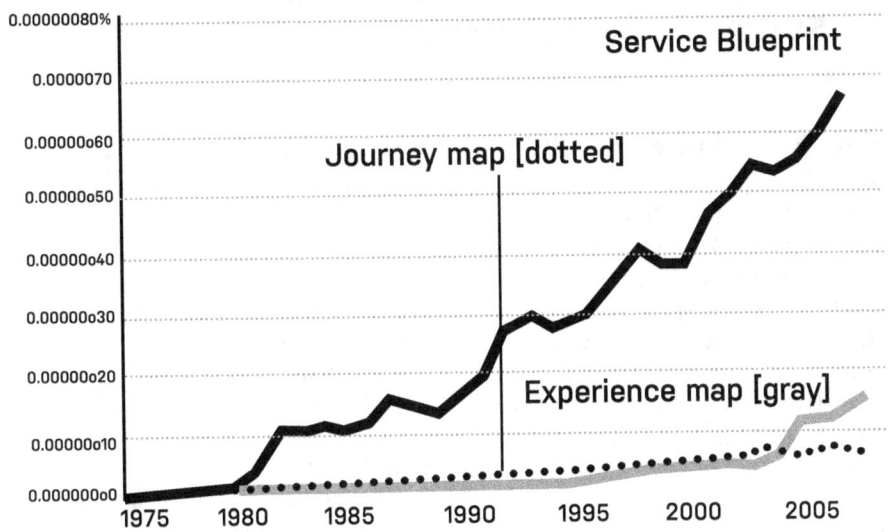

Source: Based on data from Google Ngram viewer

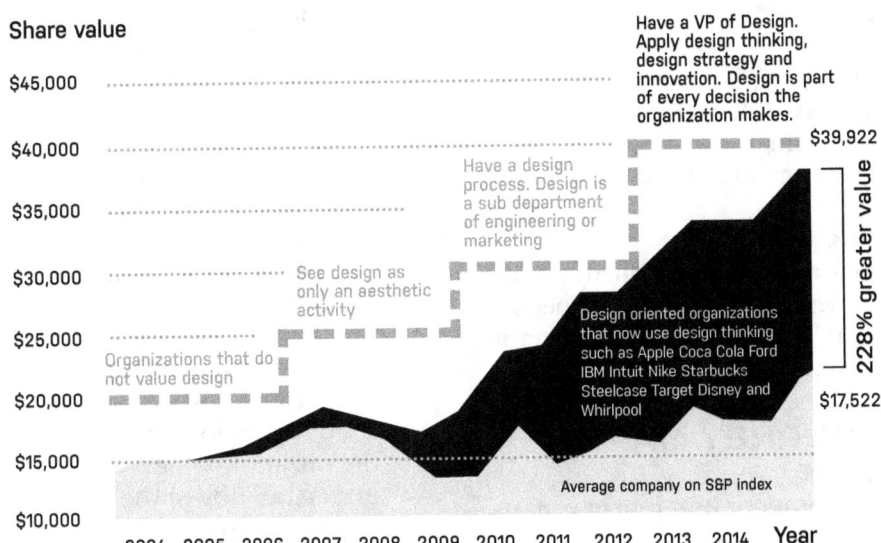

Source: Copyright © Design Thinking Process and Methods 4th Edition, Robert Curedale, 2018
https://dcc-edu.org/product/design-thinking-process-methods-4th-edition Adapted from combining data from studies by DMI Design Index, UK Design Council, Pottsdam University, and Danish Design Center Design Ladder.

INTRODUCTION 13

OVERVIEW OF THE MAPPING METHODS DESCRIBED IN THIS BOOK

EXPERIENCE MAPS

WHAT
Experience maps visualize the end-to-end experience that a person goes through. An experience map provides an understanding of the process that every type of target customer goes through and is not specific to a particular persona or user segment.

FEATURES
1. It is not tied to a specific product or service.
2. Offers a general perspective not specific to a particular persona or user segment.
3. Activities are described in chronological order from left to right.

WHY
1. To understand a general human experience.
2. To create a baseline.

WHEN
Before a customer journey map to describe a general perspective. Can be used an any point in the design process.

JOURNEY MAPS

WHAT
Customer or user journey maps focus on a specific customer's interaction with a product or service. Best used when you are focused on a specific target such as the journey for one type of target persona or one specific product, service, or product or line.

It is a visualization of a particular persona journey in order to accomplish a goal tied to a specific business or product.

FEATURES
1. Based on a specific persona, product or service.
2. 4 lanes: phases, actions, thoughts, mindsets/emotions.
3. It reflects the user's point of view:
4. Omits some process details.
5. Activities described in chronological order.
6. One map per persona or user segment.

WHY
1. Used for understanding customer needs and pain points.
2. Used to identify specific customer journey touchpoints and the quality of experiences in relation to those touchpoints.
3. Used to develop one organization-wide understanding of the customer journey.

WHEN
After an experience map to

describe a specific persona or customer segment perspective. Can be used an any point in the design process.

EMPATHY MAPS
WHAT
An empathy map is a tool used to describe and create empathy for a particular persona's perspective. It helps create a shed understanding of one persona or user segment in order to make better decisions.

FEATURES
1. Four areas. Says, Thinks, Feels, Does.
2. Created from user's perspective.
3. Not chronological or sequential.
4. There is one empathy map for each persona or user type.
5. Best for relatively short experience durations such as 30 minutes rather than a complex end to end experience.

WHY
1. Used to create empathy for users.
2. Used to help in creating alignment for decision making.

WHEN
May be used before an experience map or if available resources are more limited.

SERVICE BLUEPRINTS
WHAT
This technique was first described in an article in the Harvard Business Review in 1984 BY Citbank executive Lynn Shostack based on techniques used in computer programing. A service blueprint visualizes the structure of a service or experience.

Service blueprints are a useful tool to understand the elements of a service or experience that are omni channel, or require coordination of multiple departments. May be used to improve an existing service or plan a new service.

FEATURES
May include lanes describing customer actions, customer action phases, value propositions, channels, customer relationships frontstage employee actions, backstage employee actions, support processes, revenue streams, resources, activities, partnerships, and costs. Lanes are divided into sections by a line of interaction, a line of visibility and a line of implementation.

1. Based on a specific service.
2. Four main lanes: customer actions, frontstage actions, backstage actions, and support processes.
3. Reflects the organization's point of view.
4. Focusing on the service provider and employees

5. Does not include the emotional perspective of the customer.
   6. It is chronological from left to right.

WHY
   1. Used to uncover and eliminate weaknesses in the service.
   2. Used to identify opportunities for improvement
   3. Used to develop one organization-wide understanding of the service structure.

WHEN
   1. After customer journey mapping.
   2. When planning service improvements.
   3. When designing new services.

BUSINESS MODEL CANVAS

WHAT
Business Model Canvas is a strategic management tool for describing new or existing business models. The Business Model Canvas was initially proposed by Alexander Osterwalder.

FEATURES
It is a graphic template with nine elements describing a value proposition, infrastructure, customers, and finances.
The canvas provides nine key business elements to plan and understand vital parts of a business. It helps understand the big picture.

WHY
   1. A hands-on tool for understanding, or developing a business model.
   2. Illustrates potential trade-offs.

The individual elements help in the process of understanding of a business' full scope, while the layout encourages thought about how the pieces integrate.

WHEN
Use Business Model Canvas when you want to describe business model of your business or pivot it. Your business model canvas should be reviewed periodically as the factors may change over time.

01
SERVICE DESIGN

SERVICE DESIGN

Service design is an emerging competence for all designers who are serious about their careers. Service design is about making services desirable, efficient and usable.

We are immersed in services every day. We use the Internet, watch television, travel, shop, drink coffee and eat at restaurants, use government services, and we go to movies.

> *As services are intangible, difficult to standardize, and co-produced while they are delivered/consumed, the core starting point of the service design approach is to be human-focused. You must engage with the hearts and minds of people if you want to design successful and popular services.*
>
> Dr. Geke van Dijk,
> Strategy Director
> STBY London & Amsterdam

Employment in service industries in the US has grown from around 60% of overall employment in the 1950s to around 90% today. 75% of GDP is generated by services. Over the last 50 years, the United States has evolved from an economy based on creating goods to one based on providing services and service experiences.

The U.S. is now a post-industrial, services-based economy. Between 1995 and 2005, the US economy lost 3 million manufacturing jobs and created 17 million service sector jobs. Service providers and retailers employ about six in seven of the nation's workers. The majority of developed countries' gross national product is already derived from services. And the majority of employees work in services businesses. In 2013, the United States accounted for $662.0 billion, or 14 percent, of global services exports and imported $431.5 billion of services.

> *Deindustrialisation—the shrinkage of industrial jobs is popularly perceived as a symptom of economic decline. On the contrary, it is a natural stage of economic development. As a country gets richer, it is inevitable that a smaller proportion of workers will be needed in manufacturing. The first reason is that households need only so many cars, fridges or microwaves, so as they become richer they tend to spend a bigger chunk of their income on services, such as holidays,*

health and education, rather than on goods.

Second, it is much easier to automate manufacturing than services, replacing men by machines. Faster productivity growth than in services means that manufacturing needs fewer workers. In turn, as workers move into more productive areas, this gives a boost to overall productivity and hence living standards."

The Economist

Services are transforming all design industries. Service design requires new skills for designers. Services are not tangible and physical and services change over time. Service design puts customers at the center of the design process. Designers who do not have the skills to discover and design for unmet needs of end users are replaced by designers who have those skills.

> *Businesses planned for service are apt to succeed. Businesses planned for profit are apt to fail.*
>
> Nicholas Murray Butler

Design is no longer about only the aesthetics or surfaces of things. Today designers create diverse and complex systems of experiences of products, services, spaces and touchpoints – the people, information, products and spaces that customers encounter.

Service design can be used to redesign an existing service to make it better, or it can be used to create a new service. Most companies realize that by designing not just the product, but the system of services, and experiences they can add value and maximize profit.

In this edition are the practical methods, processes, and tools that service designers use.

Learn here how to understand your customers' service journey, how to develop new services and how to prototype and test your ideas for real customers in the most efficient and effective way possible.

> *Traditionally, service design had been characterized by the lack of systematic method for design and control." As a result, new services were usually developed by trial and error: in the absence of a detailed design there was no metric to gauge whether the service was complete, rational, and fulfilled the original need."*
>
> G. Lynn Shostack,
> Designing Services That Deliver
> -Harvard Business Review.

Service design is a broad field that involves many disciplines, management, technology and an understanding of people.

Service design uses many methods and techniques. During the discovery phase methods are used to understand the unique perspectives of the customers who will be using the services. In the synthesis stage other methods are used to make sense of the initial research and to generate insights which will be explored during the ideation phase of service design.

> *Society is no longer based on mass consumption but on mass participation. New forms of collaboration such as Wikipedia, Facebook, MySpace, and YouTube are paving the way for an age in which people want to be players, rather than mere spectators, in the production process.*
>
> Charles Leadbeater

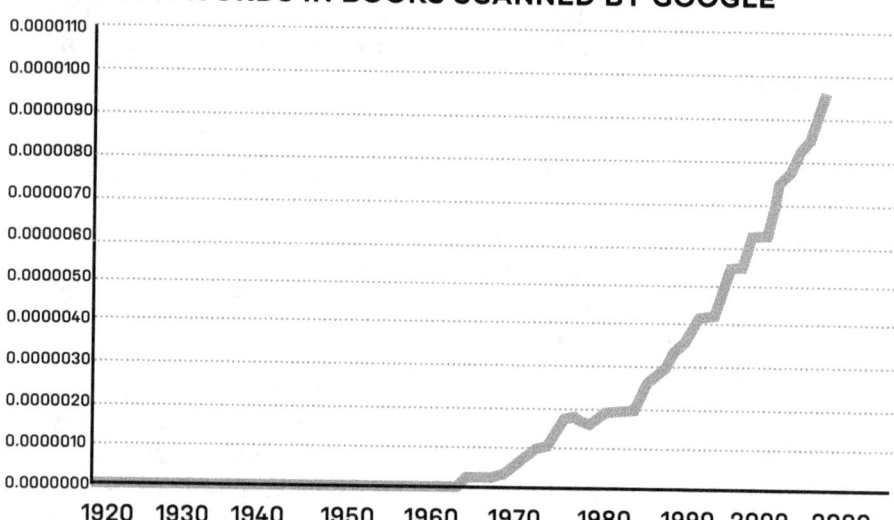

GROWING USE OF THE TERM SERVICE DESIGN AMONG HALF A TRILLION WORDS IN BOOKS SCANNED BY GOOGLE

Source: Based on data from Google Ngram viewer

LARGEST US PRIVATE EMPLOYERS

1960

GOODS PRODUCING
GM
Ford
General Electric
US Steel
Esso
Bethlehem Steel
ITT
Westinghouse
General Dynamics
Chrysler
Sperry Rand
International Harvester

SERVICE PROVIDING
Bell System
Sears Roebuck
AP

2010

GOODS PRODUCING
HP
PepsiCo
General Electric

SERVICE PROVIDING
Walmart
Kelly Services
IBM
UPS
McDonald's Corp
Yum
Target
Kroger
Home Depot
Sears
Bank Of America
CVS Pharmacy

Source: New York Times

PRIVATE SECTOR EMPLOYMENT
1948 TO 2010 % OF TOTAL PRIVATE EMPLOYMENT
Source: Bureau of Economic Analysis, National Income and Product Accounts

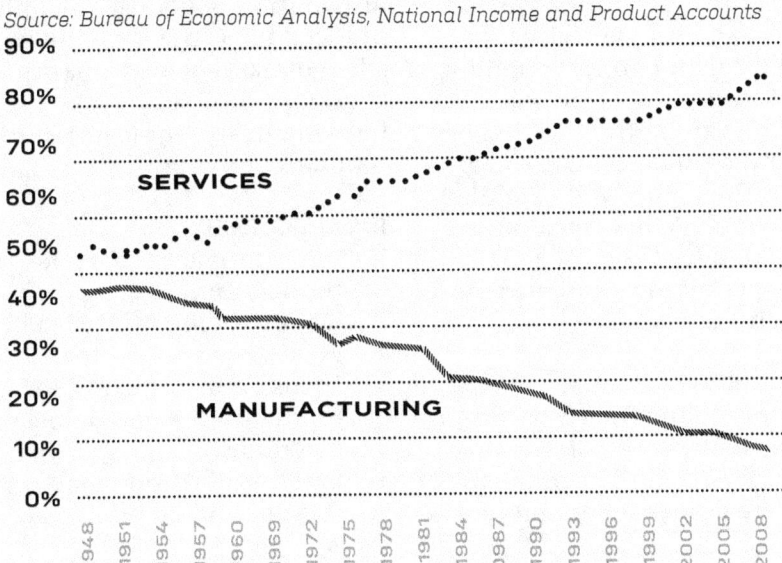

THE GROWTH OF SERVICES

WHAT
A.G.B. Fisher proposed a model for economies of primary, secondary, and tertiary industries. Primary production is defined as agriculture, fishing, forestry, hunting, and mining. He concluded that as income rises demand shifts from the primary to secondary and then to tertiary sectors. Sociologist Daniel Bell proposed a model in three general stages. Preindustrial, industrial and post-industrial societies.

PREINDUSTRIAL SOCIETY
The principal activities are agriculture, fishing, forestry, and mining. Technology is simple, and productivity is low. People depend on their bodies to get things done. Success depends on nature, the climate and on soil quality. The social unit is the family and extended household. People seek only enough to feed themselves. Many people are employed in household services.

Before 1900 in the US.
1. More than 80% workforce in Agriculture sector
2. Service occupations mostly were domestic servants and sailors
3. Family relationships and tradition important.
4. Education and innovation are not important
5. Quality of life dependent on nature

INDUSTRIAL SOCIETY
The dominant activities are associated with the production of goods. Economic and social life has become mechanized and more efficient. Productivity is improved. Focus on optimization. Division of labor is further extended. Technological advancements support constant improvement of machines. The workplace is where men, women, materials, and machines are organized for efficient production and distribution of goods. The unit of social life is the individual in a free market society. Quantity of goods possessed by an individual is an indicator of his standard of living

1900 TO 1950
1. Important activity goods production.
2. Quality of life measured by goods.
3. Focus on maximizing the productivity of labor and machines.
4. Extreme division of labor
5. Dehumanizing jobs.

THE EVOLVING FOCUS OF DESIGN PRACTICE

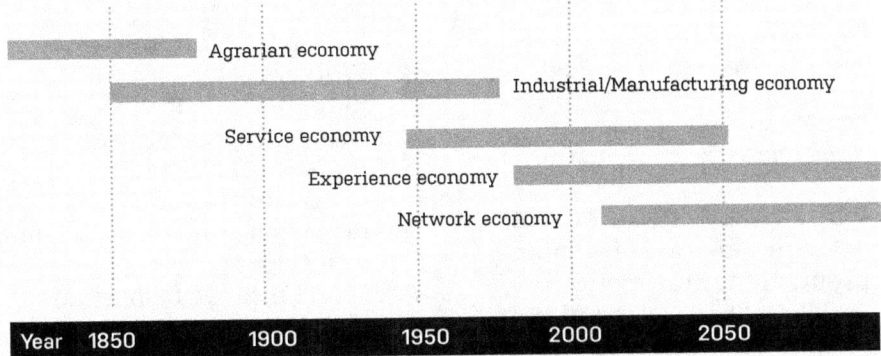

Adapted from a framework proposed by Brand and Rocchi 2011 in a Philips Design document entitled "Rethinking Value in a Changing Landscape".

BELLS STAGES OF ECONOMIC DEVELOPMENT

SOCIETY	PRE-INDUSTRIAL	INDUSTRIAL	POST-INDUSTRIAL
Game	Against Nature	Against fabricated nature	Among Persons
Predominant Activity	Agriculture, Mining	Goods, Production	Services
Use of Human Labor	Raw Muscle Power	Machine tending	Artistic, Creative, Intellectual
Unit of Social Life	Extended Household	Individual	Community
Standard of Living Measure	Subsistence	Quantity of Goods	Quality of life in terms of health, education, recreation
Structure	Routine, Traditional, Authoritative	Bureaucratic, Hierarchical	Interdependent, Global
Technology	Simple hand tools	Machines	Information

This framework was first proposed by sociologist Daniel Bell

6. "Manual workers" outnumber "white collar workers."

Source: Adapted from: Theories Explaining the Growth of Services http://www.informit.com/articles/article.aspx?p=2095734&seqNum=4

POSTINDUSTRIAL SOCIETY

Activities focused on service production, information and knowledge. Networks of people. The central character of economic life is the professional. Higher education a prerequisite to entry into postindustrial society. The quantity and quality of services are indicators of standard of living. The inadequacy of the market mechanism in meeting service demands leads to the growth of government.

Expansion of services is needed for the development of industry and distribution of goods. Expansion of service industries. The percentage of money devoted to food declines. Increments in income are first spent for durable consumer goods, such as housing, automobiles, and appliances. Further increases in revenue are devoted to services such as education, healthcare, vacations, travel, restaurants, entertainment, and sports.

AFTER 1950

1. Service-producing industries increased from 50% to 80% of GDP in US.
2. Health, education, & recreation measures of quality of life.
3. Service experiences dominate economic value.
4. Workers value based on judgment, creativity & theoretical reasoning
5. Increase in efficiency of agriculture and manufacturing releases labor to services.
6. Workers move from rural locations to cities.
7. A decrease in investment as a percentage of gross domestic product in high-income industrialized countries.
8. A rise in per capita income.
9. Deregulation.
10. Demographic shifts.
11. An increase in international trade.
12. The symbiotic growth of services with manufacturing.
13. Advances in information and telecommunication technologies.
14. People pursue more sophisticated needs (Maslow "hierarchy of needs)

Source: Adapted from Service Management: An Integrated Approach to Supply Chain Management and Operations Cengiz Haksever and Barry Render 2013

WHY SERVICE DESIGN IS ONE OF THE FASTEST-GROWING AREAS OF DESIGN

INDUSTRY % SHARE OF TOTAL EMPLOYMENT

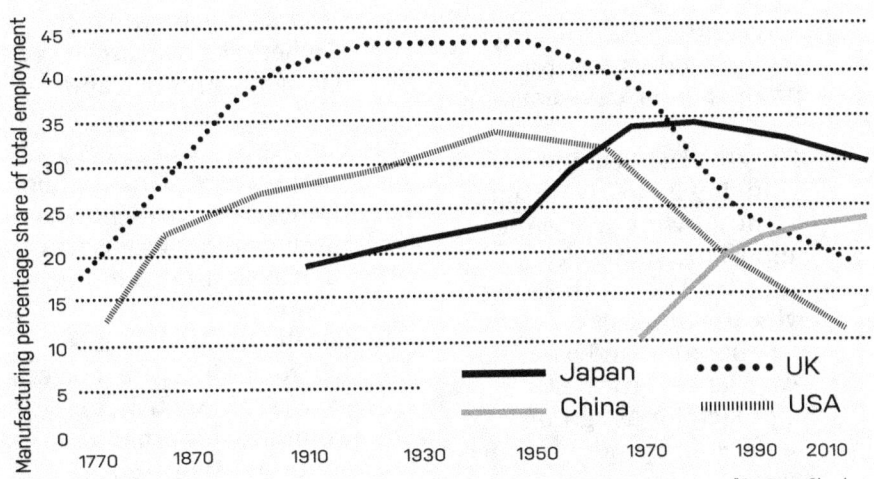

Adapted from "China's Future in the Knowledge Economy" by Peter Sheehan
ANote: scale condensed before 1900

DISTRIBUTION OF US LABOR FORCE
1840 TO 2010 % OF TOTAL WORKFORCE
Source: Bureau of Economic Analysis, National Income and Product Accounts

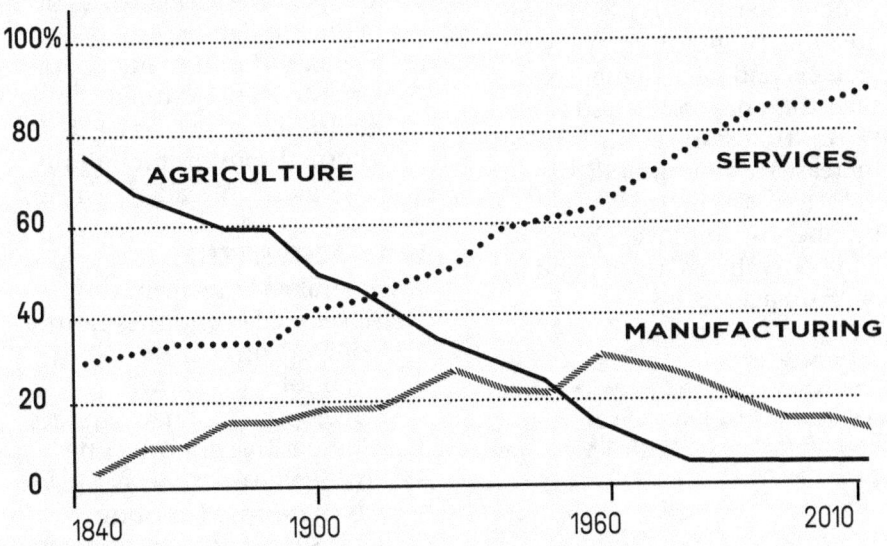

SERVITIZATION

WHAT

Servitization is a shift from selling product to selling product-service systems.

The growth of Design Thinking is closely linked to the growing economic importance of service industry. Design Thinking with its emphasis on team collaboration and user experience is the best approach for designing services and product service systems.

A study of 50,000 servitized and non-servitized French firms between 1997 and 2007 concluded that servitized firms are more profitable, employ more workers and have higher total sales than non-servitized firms. "Firms that start selling services increase their profitability by 3.7% to 5.3%, increase their numbers of employees by 30%, and boost their sales of good by 3.6% on average."

Source: Matthieu Crozet & Emmanuel Milet The effect of servitization on manufacturing firm performance 2015 Universite de Geneve

TYPES OF PRODUCT SERVICE SYSTEMS

1. Product Oriented: This is a where the consumer has a tangible product, and services, such as maintenance contracts, are provided.
2. Use Oriented: This is where the service provider owns the product and sells services, such as sharing, pooling, and leasing.
3. Result Oriented: This is a where products are replaced by services, such as, for example, voice-mail.
4. Solution-oriented: For example, selling a promised level of heat transfer instead of radiators.
5. Effect oriented: For example, selling a promised temperature level instead of selling radiators
6. Demand-fulfillment oriented: For example, selling a guaranteed level of thermal comfort for building occupants instead of heaters."

WHY SERVITIZE?

1. Manufacturing firms in developed economies cannot compete on cost.
2. Technology is allowing the development of new services.
3. Competitive opportunities.
4. Installed base. For every new car there are 13 existing. 4 chairs for every person in the

world. 15 aircraft for each new aircraft.
5. Services have a large potential for growing profits. Grows revenue streams Additional revenue from existing customers.
6. On average manufacturers report a growth in services revenue of 5 to 10% per year.

Source Aston Centre For Servitization Research.

7. Better cash flow.
8. Environmental benefits. De-materialization and investment in cleaner technologies.
9. Selling a Solution, in Addition to a Product:
10. Greater Financial Stability:
11. Stronger Customer Retention Rate:
12. Industrial Internet of Things growing in Importance.

Source: What is Servitization and Why Should Manufacturers Care?

STRATEGIC RATIONALE
1. Lock in customers.
2. Lockout competitors.
3. Increase differentiation.
4. Customers want services.

Source: Professor Andy Neely University of Cambridge

CHALLENGES FOR SERVITIZATION
Challenges include:
1. Leadership support
2. investments to develop and implement services and solutions.
3. Mind-set and capabilities of the organisation to selling and delivering services and solutions
4. Defining and creating a clear strategy.
5. Creating organizational infrastructure.
6. Develop capabilities for designing and delivering services.
7. Creating an organizational culture with the values supporting service design and delivery, including customer orientation, flexibility and innovation.
8. Coordinate and align the development of new products. integrated with new services
9. Involve customers in the process.
10. Create the necessary flexibility and adaptability to enable customization.
11. Formulate attractive value propositions through better understanding of customer needs.
12. Ensure that the quality of service provision lives up to customer expectations.
13. Develop trustful relationships
14. Manage the geographical and cultural distances in a globally distributed network of service partners.
15. Lock out competitors.
16. Increase differentiation
17. Customers want services.

Source: Driving Competitiveness Through Servitization A Guide For Practitioners Avlonitis, Frandsen, Hsuan & Karlsson

SERVICE DESIGN 27

IMPLEMENTING SERVITIZATION FROM GOODS-CENTERED TO CUSTOMER-CENTERED SOLUTIONS

	Manufacturing Solution	Service Customer-centered Solution
Underlying Business logic	Products	Solutions
Customization	Standard product	Customizable
Integration	Low	High
Scope	Narrow	Wide
Delivery process	Transactional	Relationship
Outcome	Functioning product	Value for customers
Design driven	From manufacturer forward	From customer backward
Physicality	Tangible	Intangible
Output	Goods	An experience
Production	Produced	Co-produced
Consumption	Transferred and used	Consumed as produced
Dimensions	Length breadth height	Experience and time

Source: adapted from Filippo Visintin Aalto University 2012

SERVICE INDUSTRY GROWTH IN CHINA

SERVICES NOW ACCOUNT FOR A HIGHER PERCENTAGE OF GDP THAN MANUFACTURING

In the first 11 months of 2015, China registered 3.9 million new companies, up 19 percent, with more than four-fifths in services, according to the State Administration for Industry and Commerce.

China's service sector now employs more than 300 million people, the largest share of the country's 775 million workers. The fastest growth has been in low-end jobs in retail, restaurants, hotels, and real estate. Over the last five years, education and government jobs, most of which are filled by college graduates, have fallen from a little less than half of total service employment to a third or so. Finance's share has also fallen, says Albert Park, professor of economics at Hong Kong University of Science and Technology. "The higher-skilled sectors—telecoms, information technology, computers, finance, and business services—are still not a large share of the total service industry," he says. "And while some are growing, they aren't growing very quickly."

Source: China Trumpets Its Service Economy - Bloomberg
https://www.bloomberg.com/news/articles/2016-01-28/china-trumpets-its-service-economy

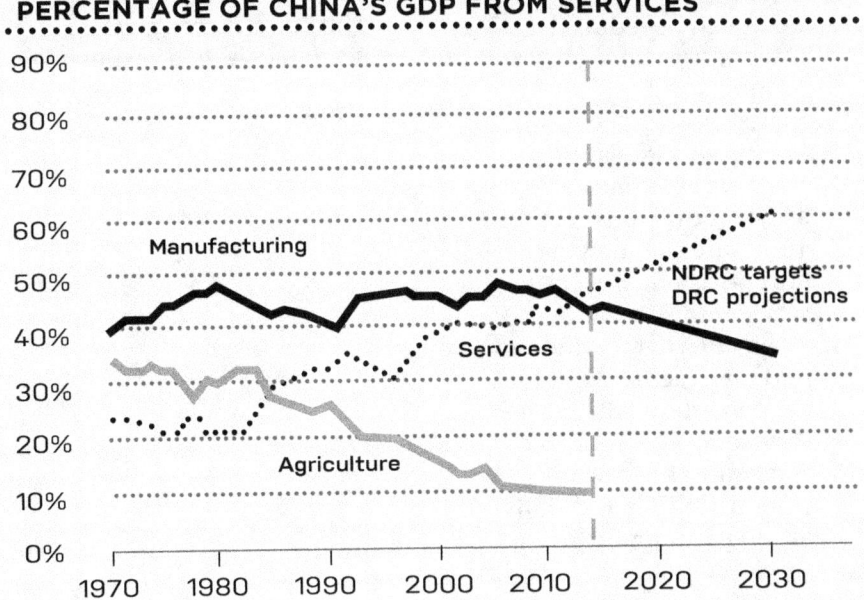

PERCENTAGE OF CHINA'S GDP FROM SERVICES

Source: Adapted from EIA

SERVICE DESIGN

WHY DESIGN SERVICES?

The reasons to design services are varied:

1. To give an organization an understanding of changing market needs and desires.
2. To create more value with existing resources
3. To create more effective services
4. To create more efficient services
5. To create higher quality service experiences
6. To differentiate services from competitors
7. To better align services and brand.
8. To plan future service offerings
9. Costs can be reduced, by integrating the service and products
10. Increasing service revenue.
11. Improved forecasting.
12. Improve customer satisfaction levels.
13. To ensure that new services are consistent with other services.
14. To ensure that technology and management systems are consistent with new services.
15. To ensure that roles responsibilities and skills are able to support new services.

> *Service design is exploring the interconnectedness of people, work-flows, tools, and products to create systems, offerings, interactions, and experiences.*

Meredith DeZutter
Service designer at the Center for Innovation at the Mayo Clinic in Rochester, Minnesota.

> *Service Design is not a new specialist design discipline. It is a new multi-disciplinary platform of expertise. Born in design thinking it integrates various fields of expertise.*

Moritz

SERVICE DESIGN NETWORK MANIFESTO

In 2004, the Service Design Network was launched by Köln International School of Design, Carnegie Mellon University, Linköpings Universitet, Politecnico di Milano and Domus Academy to create an international network for service design academics and professionals. In the first joint manifest of the network, Service Design and its approach was described in the manifesto "[Service Design] is an emerging discipline and an existing body of knowledge, which can dramatically improve the productivity and quality of services.

Service Design provides a systematic and creative approach to:
1. Meeting service organizations' need to be competitive
2. Meeting customers' rising expectations of choice and quality
3. Making use of the technologies' revolution, that multiplies the possibilities for creating, delivering and consuming services
4. Answering the pressing environmental, social and economic challenges to sustainability
5. Fostering innovative social models and behaviors
6. Sharing knowledge & learning

The Service Design approach is uniquely oriented to service specific design needs and is rooted in the design culture. The Service Designer contributes crucial competencies. The Service Designer can:
1. Visualize, express and choreograph what other people can't see, envisage solutions that do not yet exist
2. Observe and interpret needs and behaviors and transform them into possible service futures express and evaluate, in the language of experiences, the quality of design
3. Service Design aims to create services that are Useful, Usable, Desirable, Efficient & Effective
4. Service Design is a human-centered approach that focuses on customer experience and the quality of service encounter as the key value for success.
5. Service Design is a holistic approach, which considers in an integrated way strategic, system, process and touchpoint design decisions.
6. Service Design is a systematic and iterative process that integrates user-oriented, team-based, interdisciplinary approaches and methods, in ever-learning cycles."

Service Design - Design is Not Just for Products .., https://www.interaction-design.org/literature/article/service-design-design-is-n (accessed June 25, 2016).

THE DESIGN LADDER

Companies often start at stage one then progress to higher levels. At the beginning of the 5-year study, 36% of 1,000 companies were at stage 1 by the end of the study only 15% of companies remained at stage 1. Companies that were using design only as styling were growing slower on average than companies not using design at all.

Stage 4 Design as Strategy	Design is a key strategic means of supporting innovation. These companies have VPs of Design. Design connected to all business decisions. The cross-disciplinary approach of service design helps place an organization at this level of the ladder.
Stage 3 Design as Process	Design is integral to the development process. Design is often a sub-department of marketing or engineering. Companies may have cross-disciplinary teams.
Stage 2 Design as Styling	Design focuses on and aesthetics. Traditional design education can deliver designers whose primary goals are creative and artistic self-fulfillment, fame and awards rather than team business goals, technological innovation, and user needs.
Stage 1 No design	Design plays no role in product and service development

Source: Danish Design Center study of 1,000 companies 2003

THE DESIGN LADDER IN RELATION TO SUCCESS IN EXPORT

	EXPORT IN % OF TURNOVER	
	AVERAGE	NUMBER OF COMPANIES
STEP 4 DESIGN AS INNOVATION	26.34%	131
STEP 3 DESIGN AS PROCESS	22.67%	330
STEP 2 DESIGN AS STYLING	16.48%	125
STEP 1 NON-DESIGN	12.21%	342
TOTAL	18.5%	927

"There are marked differences regarding exports according to the step on the design ladder. The export share of turnover is considerably larger in companies on the highest level than for those companies that do not employ design – and the share rises progressively according to the design-ladder level. The largest increase in export share of turnover is achieved where a systematic approach to design has been adopted, namely, companies that employ professional designers and purchase design externally. The increase in exports is twice the size of companies that employ designers and purchase design externally (33.5%) compared to companies that neither employ designers nor purchase design externally (17.6 %). *Source: "The Economic Effects of Design" 2003 Denmark*

AVERAGE GROWTH IN TURNOVER

Based on study of 1000 companies and their position on the Design Ladder Danish. Design Center study 2003

Stage 4. Service design is a strategic approach to design and so is more likely to support faster organizational growth. **9.0%**

Stage 3. Design is integral to the development process. Companies may have cross-disciplinary teams. **8.9%**

Stage 2. Companies seeing design only as aesthetics in the Danish study. Turnover grew slower than companies not using design at all. **6.5%**

Stage 1. Design plays no role in product service development **7.4%**

0 10 20 30 40 50 60 70 80 90 100

STORYTELLING

WHAT

A powerful story can help ensure the success of a new product, service or experience. Storytelling can be an effective method of presenting a point of view. Research can uncover meaningful stories from the end that illustrate needs or desires. These stories can become the basis of new designs or actions and be used to support decisions. Research shows that our attitudes, fears, hopes, and values are strongly influenced by story. Stories can be an effective way of communicating complex ideas and inspiring people to change. Characters are a good way to express human needs and generate empathy from your audience

THE BIG QUESTIONS
1. Who are we presenting to?
2. Why are we presenting to them?
3. How do we want them to respond?

STORY STRUCTURE
A story has a beginning, a middle, and an end. It details events and orders them in a way that creates meaning. Stories speak to accomplishments and inspire action.

NARRATIVE
Relates separate events to a central theme but doesn't seek resolution. In a presentation, the narrative encompasses the past, present, and future. "Where we've come from. Where we are. Where we're headed." The narrative is the overarching emphasis of a presentation. Start with the narrative. Advance the Narrative with Stories. Support stories visually.

Source: Micah Bowers

AN EFFECTIVE STORY
1. Answer in your story: What, why, when, who, where, how?
2. Offer a new vantage point
3. Share emotion
4. Communicate transformations
5. Communicate who you are.
6. Show cause and effect Describe conflicts and resolution.
7. Speak from your experience.
8. Describe how actions created change
9. Omit what is irrelevant.
10. Reveal meaning
11. Share your passion
12. Be honest and real
13. Build trust
14. Show connections
15. Transmits values
16. Share a vision
17. Share knowledge
18. Your story should differentiate you.
19. Meets information needs for your audience
20. Offer a new vantage point
21. Tell real-world stories
22. Evoke the future
23. Share emotion
24. Communicate transformations.
25. Communicate who you are.
26. Describe actions.
27. Show cause and effect
28. Speak from your experience.
29. Describe how actions created change
30. Omit what is irrelevant.
31. Share your passion
32. Be honest and real
33. Build trust
34. Transmit values
35. Share a vision
36. Share knowledge
37. Use humor

38. Engage the audience
39. Craft the story for your audience.
40. Pose a problem and offer a resolution
41. Use striking imagery
42. The audience must be able to act on your story.

PLAN YOUR STORY
Plan what you are going to say and how you are going to say it. Describe the the transformation of your character in one sentence. Start with a dozen bullet points describing what you want to say.

Your story should have
1. Action,
2. Conflict
3. Transformation

What is your character trying to do? What stands in the way? What is the insight of your story? What does your character learn?

A character who sees things the way we'd see them gets to a strange place, observes things that interest him (or her), is transformed by what he sees, and fantastic new product or service that we're designing and realize how it can help make their life just that little bit better."

Chelsea Hostetter

AUDIENCE
Think about the elements – plot, setting, characters, conflict, and resolution in relation to the audience. What is going to resonate with your audience?
include a bit of yourself.

CONTEXT
Think about the context of where your audience are hearing the story and what they are doing there. When you introduce your characters outline the context that surrounds them and what led them to this place.

HOW
How are you going to tell your story? How much backstory will you need to give? Are you going to need any artifacts, such as storyboards?

BE AUTHENTIC
Describe how one of your personas will experience the design.

FOCUS ON WHAT'S IMPORTANT
Focus on what is most important to your audience and how the design will meet their unmet needs.

BE VISUAL
Use photos, video, prototypes, storyboards or sketches to support your story.

Source: Adapted from Chelsea Hostetter, Austin Centre for Design

ASK FOR FEEDBACK FROM YOUR AUDIENCE
Engage your audience. Ask them for feedback.

CHALLENGES
1. A story with too much jargon will lose an audience.
2. Not everyone has the ability to tell vivid stories.
3. Stories are not always generalizable.

EFFECTIVE DESIGN BALANCES PEOPLE'S NEEDS, BUSINESS NEEDS, THE BEST TECHNOLOGY AND CONSIDERATION OF THE ENVIRONMENT

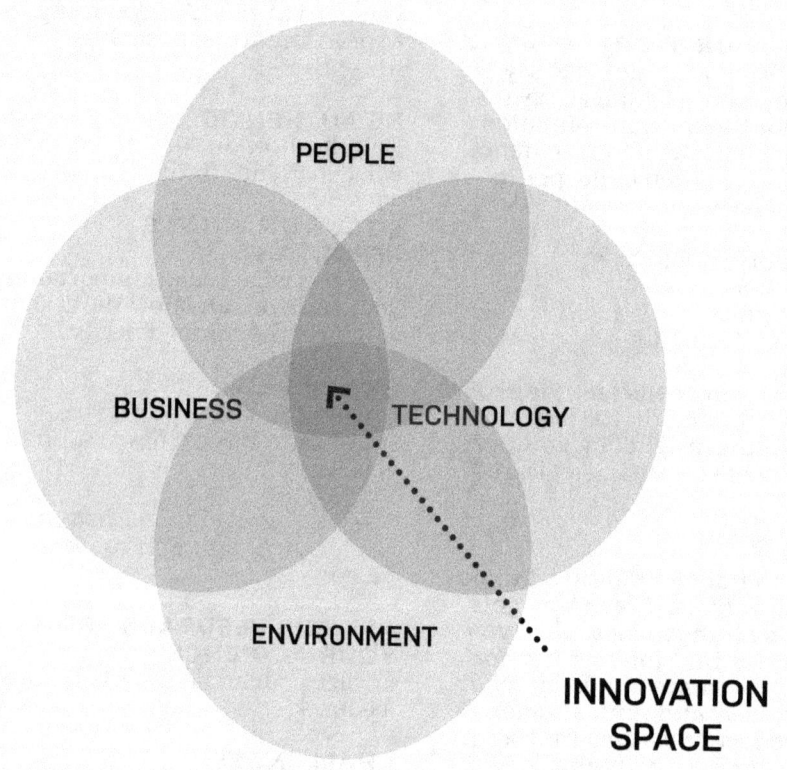

INNOVATION SPACE

Larry Keeley innovation strategist, devised his triangle as a way of expressing how successful businesses are balanced in the concerns about the desirability, technical feasibility and financial viability of their products and services. To the three factors listed by Keeley, this author would like to add the environment to recoginze the role of designers in designing for the environmental challenges we face.

HUMAN NEEDS

	BEING (PERSONAL OR COLLECTIVE ATTRIBUTES)	HAVING (INSTITUTIONS, NORMS, TOOLS)
SUBSISTENCE	Physical health, mental health, equilibrium, sense of humor, adaptability	Food., shelter, work
PROTECTION	Care, adaptability, autonomy, equilibrium, solidarity	Insurance systems, savings, social security, health systems, rights, family, work
AFFECTION	Self-esteem, solidarity, respect, tolerance, generosity, receptiveness, passion, determination, sensuality, sense of humor	Friendships, partners, family, partnerships, relationships with nature
UNDERSTANDING	Critical conscience, receptiveness, curiosity, discipline intuition, rationality	Literature, teachers, method, educational and communication policies
PARTICIPATION	Adaptability, receptiveness, solidarity, willingness, determination, respect, passion, sense of humor	Rights, responsibilities, duties, privileges, work
LEISURE	Curiosity, receptiveness, imagination, recklessness, sense of humor, lack of worry, tranquility, sensuality	Games, spectacles, clubs, parties, peace of mind
CREATION	Passion, determination, intuition, imagination, boldness, rationality, autonomy, inventiveness, curiosity	Abilities, skills, methods, work
IDENTITY	Sense of belonging, consistency, differentiation, self-esteem, assertiveness	Symbols, language, religions, habits, customs, reference groups, roles, groups, sexuality, values, norms, historic memory, work
FREEDOM	Autonomy, self-esteem, determination, passion, assertiveness, open-mindedness, boldness, rebelliousness, tolerance	Equal rights

HUMAN NEEDS

	DOING (PERSONAL OR COLLECTIVE ACTIONS)	INTERACTING (SPACES OR ATMOSPHERES)
SUBSISTENCE	Feed, procreate, rest, work.	Living environment, social setting.
PROTECTION	Co-operate. prevent. plan, take care of, cure. help.	Living space, social environment, dwelling.
AFFECTION	Make love, express emotions. share, .take care of, cultivate, appreciate.	Privacy, intimacy, home, Spaces of togetherness.
UNDERSTANDING	Investigate, study, educate, experiment, meditate, interpret.	Settings of formative interaction, schools, and universities academies groups. communities. family.
PARTICIPATION	Become affiliated, cooperate, propose. share, dissent. obey, interact, agree on, express opinions.	Settings of participative Interaction, parties. associations, communities, neighborhoods, family.
LEASURE	Day-dream, brood, dream recall old times, give way to fantasies, remember. relax, have fun, play.	Privacy, intimacy, spaces of closeness, free time, surroundings, landscapes.
CREATION	Work, invent, build, design, compose, interpret.	Productive and feedback settings, workshops, cultural groups, audiences, spaces for expression, temporal freedom.
IDENTITY	Commit oneself, integrate oneself. confront, decide on, get to know oneself, recognize oneself, actualize oneself, grow.	Social rhythms, every day belongs to. maturation stages
FREEDOM	Dissent, choose to be different from, run risks, develop awareness. commit oneself, disobey, meditate	36/ Temporal/special plasticity

Adapted from Matrix of needs and satisfiers. I. Cruz. A. Stahel . M. Max-Neef 2009

SHOSHIN: THE BEGINNER'S MIND

WHAT

The phrase shoshin means beginner's mind. It refers to having an attitude of full of openness, enthusiasm, and fresh perspectives in learning something new, eagerness, and lack of preconceptions even at an advanced level, like a child.

Shoshin also means "correct truth" and is used to describe a genuine signature on a work of art. It is used to describe something that is perfectly genuine.

WHERE DID IT ORIGINATE?

1. Shoshin is a term from Zen Buddhism and Japanese martial arts.

HOW

1. Withhold judgment. Do not suggest that an idea will not work or that it has negative side-effects. All ideas are potentially good so do not judge them until afterward.
2. Observe and Listen
3. Ask why
4. Be curious
5. Look for new connections

WHY

1. Sometimes expertise can create closed-mindedness.
2. Our assumptions can stand in the way of creating new ideas. A beginner is not aware of biases that can stand in the way of a good new idea.
3. Our experience is an asset but our assumptions may be misconceptions and stereotypes.
4. Innovation often requires looking at a problem in a new way.
5. Beginner's minds can help make breakthroughs
6. Observe and engage users without value judgments.
7. Question your assumptions. Ask why?
8. Be curious and explore.
9. Search for patterns and connections no one else has seen.
10. Be open and listen

Source: http://blog.triode.ca

The older you get as a designer, the more you realize that you just don't know anything. If you can embrace that you don't know, but you know how to go find out, that makes you very effective."

Daniel Burka
Google Ventures

SERVICE DESIGN SPACES

WHAT
An adequate office helps concentrate the energy of the team and build connections between team members.

HOW

PHYSICAL ENVIRONMENT FOR SERVICE DESIGN
1. Space should be flexible.
2. Space should be capable of being personalized.
3. Space should support interaction.
4. Size of working space in a service design office should be adequate in relation to the amount of workers.
5. According to Kelley and Littman (2001) large and empty, as well as, small and cramped offices suppress the creative work
6. All employees have an equal workplace.
7. Each person has an access to an individual, personal working area
8. The space allows project teams to come together for group work within seconds.
9. Space devoted only to the particular team for the whole length of their project.
10. The design team can keep and access all of project related materials
11. Space is customizable.
12. Every employee has to be able to create a personally most suiting and stimulating space (Kelley & Littman 2001, 123–125).
13. Personalization is done through group decisions of furniture setting.
14. Every employee has a say in how the overall office space looks like.
15. Furniture and people are flexible and easily movable to ensure the best setting for each project and team (Brown 2009, 34–35; Kelley & Littman 2001, 123–125).
16. Common areas are designed to increase human interaction.

SPACES FOR CREATIVE WORK HAWORTH RECOMMENDATIONS
1. Lightweight, comfortable, readily movable chairs perhaps on wheels can maximize a relatively small footprint and be arranged in multiple configurations
2. Show your work in progress and let people comment.
3. Surround yourself with the material that your team is working on.
4. Mobile large White-boards 6 ft x 4 ft and pin boards.
5. Mobile boards can have a magnetic White-board on one side and a pin board on

the reverse side.
6. A laptop-sized surface for each attendee
7. Walls can be used for projection, writing, or pinning up information in areas visible to everyone
8. Acoustic privacy should be ensured.
9. Large walls can be used as display spaces.
10. Use work tools that are easily accessible
11. Think of every vertical surface as a potential space for displaying work
12. Use flexible technologies such as wi-fi that allow relocation of services such as Internet and power connections.
13. Have a projector and screen
14. Seating should allow all participants to see one another and read body language
15. Select furniture with wheels that can be easily moved
16. Small tables can be used for breakouts or grouped into a common surface
17. Ample writing and display areas, as well as surfaces for laying things out, support the need for visual cues and reference materials
18. Provide a large area of vertical displays such as walls Whiteboards, pin boards, foam core boards, projection surfaces, that allow users to actively and flexibly interact with the information
19. Build spaces that support different types of collaboration.
20. Consider physical and virtual collaboration.
21. Spaces should be flexible for unplanned collaboration.
22. Provide comfortable group areas for informal interactions and information sharing.
23. The spaces need to be large enough to accommodate all the research materials, visuals, and prototypes in order to keep them visible and accessible all of the time.

Collaborative Spaces - media.haworth.com, http://media.haworth.com/asset/28519/Collaborative%20Spaces Whitepaper_C2..pdf

TACIT KNOWLEDGE

WHAT
Tacit knowledge is the knowledge that is gained through personal experience. Examples of tacit knowledge are the ability to ride a bicycle or recognizing someone's face. Tacit knowledge is difficult to pass on to another person by writing it down or describing it. Tacit knowledge is a form of intellectual property. Tacit knowledge includes best practices, stories, experience, wisdom, and insights.

WHO FIRST USED THE TERM?
Michael Polanyi 1958

WHY
1. Tacit knowledge is valuable to any organization.

CHALLENGES
1. Mapping tacit knowledge needs immersion in context.
2. A researcher can map behavior and perceptions.

HOW
The methods of capturing tacit knowledge include:
1. Interviews
2. Observation

RESOURCES
Camera
Notepad computer
Digital voice recorder

QUALITATIVE RESEARCH

WHAT
Qualitative or ethnographic research is a core part of the approach of service design. It seeks to understand people in the context of their daily experiences. Uses ethnographic methods including observation and interviews. Aims to understand questions like why and how. Obtains insights about attitudes and emotions. Often uses small sample sizes. Seeks to see the world through the eyes of research subjects. Methods are flexible. Used to develop an initial understanding.

WHO INVENTED IT?
The Royal Statistical Society founded in 1834 pioneered the use of quantitative methods. Early examples of ethnographers include Malinowski 1922, Radcliffe Brown, Margaret Mead, Gregory Bateson and Franz Boas, all of whom studied 'native' populations abroad, and Robert Park and the work of the Chicago school where the focus was on the life and culture of local groups in the city.

CHALLENGES
1. Concerned with validity
2. Subjective
3. Hard to recreate results
4. People may behave differently to the way they say they behave
5. Experiences cannot be generalized.
6. Methods are static. Real-world changes.
7. Structured methods
8. Difficult to control the environment
9. Can be expensive if studying a large number of people.

HOW
1. Define research question
2. Select research subjects and context to study.
3. Collect data
4. Interpret data.
5. Study data for insights
6. Collect more data
7. Analyze data

QUESTIONS TO CONSIDER

PEOPLE
1. What user group does this service or experience target?
2. What problems or needs does our product help with for this group?
3. When and how and where is our product, service or experience used?
4. What features are most important to end users?
5. How should our service or experience look and work?
6. Who should we employ?
7. What external partners do we need?
8. What does the customer need?
9. What does the customer want?
10. How does the customer learn to use this product or service?
11. What is the experience when the customer enters this experience?
12. How does the customer purchase or initiate this experience?
13. How does the customer interact with each touchpoint?
14. How are customers retained?
15. What are the barriers to a customer returning?

What is the process if a customer has an unsatisfactory experience?

16. We will know this assumption is true when we see:
- What market feedback?
- What quantitative measure?
- What qualitative insight?

BUSINESS
1. We will make money by:
2. Our customers will find our service or experience valuable because:
3. We will acquire customers through:
4. It will cost how much to establish these products or services. It will cost how much per month/year to offer these services and maintain our business.
5. Establishing these or services will be funded by:
6. My primary competition of brand and products in the market will be:
7. We will eat them because:
8. Our biggest business risk is:
9. We will reduce this risk by:
10. What could cause our business to fail?

TECHNOLOGY
Why do particular technologies/ materials/ processes/ finishes offer a strategic advantage?

THINKING STYLES

ABDUCTIVE THINKING

Abductive reasoning is the core thinking approach in service design. With abductive reasoning, unlike deductive reasoning, the premises do not guarantee the conclusion. Abductive reasoning can be understood as "inference to the best explanation" Abductive reasoning typically begins with an incomplete set of observations and proceeds to the likeliest possible explanation. Its goal is to explore what could possibly be true. Abductive thinking allows designers to find solutions in ambiguous, changing situations. It is the thinking approach necessary for innovation. Abductive thinking finds solutions by creating prototypes and testing and improving the designs. This mode of thinking wasn't taught in management, science and engineering schools. It doesn't start with clearly defined evidence.

> *A person or organization instilled with that discipline is constantly seeking a fruitful balance between reliability and validity, between art and science, between intuition and analytics, and between exploration and exploitation. The design-thinking organization applies the designer's most crucial tool to the problems of business. That tool is abductive reasoning."*
>
> Roger Martin

Charles Sanders Peirce originated the term and argued that no new idea could come from inductive or deductive logic.

1. **Abductive logic**: The logic of what might be.
2. **Deductive logic** reasons from the general to the specific.
3. **Inductive logic** reasons from the specific to the general.

DEDUCTIVE THINKING

The process of reasoning from one or more general statements (premises) to reach a logically certain conclusion. Deductive reasoning is one of the two basic forms of valid reasoning. It begins with a general hypothesis or known fact and creates a specific conclusion from that generalization.

Described by Aristotle 384-322bce, Plato 428-347bce, and Pythagoras 582-500 BCE

INDUCTIVE THINKING
Inductive thinking is a kind of reasoning that constructs or evaluates general propositions that are derived from specific examples. Inductive reasoning contrasts with deductive reasoning, in which specific examples are derived from general propositions. Described by Aristotle 384-322 BCE.

CRITICAL THINKING
"The process of actively and skillfully conceptualizing, applying, analyzing, synthesizing, and evaluating information to reach an answer or conclusion. disciplined thinking that is clear, rational, open-minded, and informed by evidence, willingness to integrate new or revised perspectives into our ways of thinking and acting". Critical thinking is an important element of all professional fields and academic disciplines."

DESIGN THINKING
Design Thinking is not a style of thinking. Design Thinking is a formal method for practical, creative resolution of problems and creation of solutions, with the intent of an improved future result. In this regard it is a form of solution-based, or solution-focused thinking

Source: Deductive, Inductive and Abductive Reasoning - TIP Sheet.

Historically most organizations were managed by divergent or analytical thinkers. Over the last ten years, this has changed.

> *Silicon Valley didn't think a designer could build and run a company. They were straight up about it. We weren't MBAs, we weren't two PhD students from Stanford."*

Brian Chesky
Co-founder of AirBnb
Graduate of the Rhode Island School of Design

> *Coming up with a way to fix mistakes challenges your creativity and your critical thinking skills and your resourcefulness. Often you end up with something better than what you planned on in the first place."*

Mark Frauenfelder

DIVERGENT AND CONVERGENT THINKING

DIVERGENT THINKING
Divergent thinking is a thought process or method used to generate creative ideas by exploring many possible solutions. Divergent thinking occurs in a spontaneous, free-flowing, 'nonlinear' manner.

During the divergent phase of design the designer creates a number of choices. The goal of this approach is to analyze alternative approaches to test for the most stable solution. Divergent thinking is what we do when we do not know the answer when we do not know the next step. Divergent thinking is followed by convergent thinking, in which a designer assesses, judges, and strengthens those options.

A study by J.A. Horne, and a separate study by Ullrich Wagner and his colleagues in Germany have shown that sleep loss can significantly impair creativity.

Left brain people are said to be more rational, analytic, and controlling, while right brain people are said to be more intuitive, creative, emotionally expressive and spontaneous. There is evidence that regions of the right hemisphere have a role in what is called divergent thinking and creative problem-solving.

CONVERGENT THINKING
The psychologist J.P. Guilford first coined the terms convergent thinking and divergent thinking in 1956. The design process is a series of divergent and convergent phases.

This process is systematic and linear. This kind of thinking is particularly appropriate in science, engineering, maths and technology. Convergent thinking is opposite from divergent thinking in which a person generates many unique, design solutions to a design problem.

The design process is a series of divergent and convergent phases. During the divergent phase of design the designer creates a number of choices. The goal of this approach is to analyze alternative approaches to test for the most stable solution. Divergent thinking is what we do when we do not know the answer, when we do not know the next step. Divergent thinking is followed by convergent thinking, in which a designer assesses, judges, and strengthens those options.

On his account, the left brain is specialized for convergent thinking, while the right brain is specialized for divergent thinking.

RESEARCH TRIANGULATION

WHAT

Denzin (1978) defined triangulation as "the combination of methodologies in the study of the same phenomenon".

Triangulation is a powerful technique that facilitates validation of data through cross verification from two or more sources. to see if the different methods give similar findings. The researcher looks for patterns to develop or support an interpretation by comparing the results from two or more different research methods. The researcher looks for patterns of convergence to develop or corroborate an overall interpretation One example of triangulation is to compare observed behavior with the responses of a survey.

The term originates in surveying land where triangulation is used to create a map.

Denzin (1978) and Patton (1999) identify four types of triangulation:
1. Methods triangulation - checking out the consistency of findings generated by different data collection methods.
   - It is common to have qualitative and quantitative data in a study.
   - These elucidate complementary aspects of the same phenomenon.
   - Often the points were these data diverge are of great interest to the qualititive researcher and provide the most insights.
2. Triangulation of sources - examining the consistency of different data sources from within the same method. For example:
   - at different points in time
   - in public vs. private settings
   - comparing people with different viewpoints.
3. Analyst Triangulation - using multiple analysts to review findings or using multiple observers and analysts
   - This can provide a check on selective perception and illuminate blind spots in an interpretive analysis.
   - The goal is not to seek consensus, but to understand multiple ways of seeing the data.
   - Theory/perspective triangulation - using multiple theoretical perspectives to examine and interpret the data. *Source: qualres.org*

PRIMARY RESEARCH

WHAT
Primary research also called as field research involves collecting data first hand created during the time of the study. Primary research methods can include, including questionnaires and interviews and direct observations.

WHO INVENTED IT?
Robert W. Bruere of the Bureau of Industrial Research 1921 may have been the first to use the term.

WHY
You can collect this information yourself. There may be no secondary research available. It may be more reliable than secondary research. It may be more up to date than secondary research.

CHALLENGES
1. May be more expensive than secondary research.
2. Information may become obsolete
3. Large sample can be time-consuming

HOW
Methods such as:
1. Diaries
2. E-mail
3. Interviews
4. News footage
5. Photographs
6. Raw research data
7. Questionnaires
8. Observation

RESOURCES
Camera
Notebook
Pens
Digital Voice recorder
Diaries
E-mail

> *Every problem can be solved as long as you use common sense and apply the right research and techniques.*
>
> Daymond John

SECONDARY RESEARCH

WHAT
Research data that conveys the opinions and experiences of others. Secondary research is the most widely used method of data collection. Secondary research accesses information that is already gathered from primary research.

WHO INVENTED IT?
Robert W. Bruere of the US Bureau of Industrial Research 1921 may have been the first to use the term secondary research.

WHY
1. Ease of access
2. Low cost
3. May be the only resource, for example, historical documents
4. Only way to examine large scale trends

CHALLENGES
1. Possible bias in sources
2. May be out of date
3. May not be aligned with research goals
4. Lack of consistency of perspective
5. Biases and inaccuracies
6. Data affected by context of its collection

HOW
1. Define goals.
2. Define the context of the problem to be researched.
3. Frame research questions.
4. Develop procedure.
5. Select and retrieve appropriate data.
6. Proceed with analysis and interpretation
7. Compare your findings and interpretations with other relevant studies.
8. Draw conclusions.

RESOURCES
Books
Internet
Online search engines
Magazines
E-books
Bibliographies
Biographical works
Commentaries, criticisms
Dictionaries, Encyclopedias
Histories;
Newspaper articles
Website

Steps in the research process - University of Hong Kong, http://www4.caes.hku.hk/acadgrammar/report/resProc/steps.htm (accessed July 03, 2016).

WHY USE MAPPING METHODS?

CRAFT A BETTER USER EXPERIENCE

1. Understand your customer's point of view.
2. Deliver a seamless, useful experience.
3. Bring more humanity to your business.
4. Designing the moments of truth
5. Identify those moments of a user experience that leave a lasting impression both positive or negative.
6. The entire company can focus on the vision of creating an exceptional customer experience.
7. Compare what your customers want with what your competitors are providing.
8. Understanding the ideal experience
9. Reveal the truth through your customer's eyes
10. Understand what customers think about your products and services rather than what you think they think.
11. Identify opportunities
12. When you understand where a customer experience is poor, it is an opportunity to improve your competitiveness and make your business more profitable. Evolve and stay competitive. Adapt to changing customer needs and expectations.
13. Empathize with your customers
14. Lack of understanding your customer's point of view is the number one reason new
15. Products and services fail. More than 50% of new goods and services fail in the market.
16. Get connected to your customers or end users
17. 80% Of service companies believe they offer superior services. Only 8% of their customers agree.
18. Develop more relevant products services and experiences for your customers or end users
19. Balance the needs of stakeholders more efficiently.
20. Diagnose experience problems.

IMPROVE YOUR BUSINESS PERFORMANCE

1. Strategic and tactical innovation.
2. Help all your employees and external stakeholders to contribute to the change process.
3. Improve business systems
4. Ensure systems are efficient,
5. And customer-focused.
6. Take cost & complexity out of the system.
7. Develop a better roadmap. Decide where you should be going with your business, what products and services you can and should be delivering and when it is best to introduce them. Build

strategic advantage against competitors.
8. Identify duplicated touchpoints and position people and other resources where they are most needed.
9. Prioritize competing deliverables
10. Plan how to allocate resources. Decide what should be the top priorities for your business to grow and generate the best returns on investment. Your decisions are guided by real customer data and feedback.
11. Plan for hiring. Plan strategically and select the best employees and skills for long-term expansion of your business.
12. Bring your whole organization together around the common goal of customer experience.
13. Understand the role that each department plays in a customer-focused strategy. Overcome silo thinking. Help different groups identify common ground.
14. Build and share knowledge. Build a common understanding both internally and externally.
15. Understand competitive positioning.
16. Knowledge of customer behaviors and needs across channels. Customers commonly access a number of different channels when engaging an organization. Understand complex processes across channels.
17. Drive ideation and innovation
18. Decide how to allocate resources to improve best current offerings or to build whole new sets of deliverables based on what customers need and want rather than what your employees think that they want, benchmark your current performance against competitors and help you plan future initiatives.
19. Make intangible services tangible
20. Understand where friction exists between the needs of different market segments
21. Various interested parties commonly have conflicting needs and desires.
22. Tailor your experiences more efficiently to different segment's needs
23. Understand the differences in their expectations and experience.
24. Introduce metrics for what matters most for your customers
25. Plan strategically to achieve long-term organizational goals and to measure progress towards those goals
26. Align your offerings to brand promise
27. Understand where your current business supports or conflicts with your brand promise.
28. Eliminate potential failure points
29. See where your customer experience is most likely to fail and to plan to reduce the

risk and cost of failure.
30. Improve efficiency
31. Break down organizational silos
32. Reduce duplication. Prioritize between competing requirements. Identify cheapest 'cost to serve', and set performance indicators that you can measure.
33. Imagine future product and service experiences
34. Plan and implement future product and service offerings.
35. Holistic thinking
36. Balance the competing needs of your customers, your business, and technology.
37. Improve your whole organization's performance
38. Work towards one goal of the best possible customer experience rather than multiple departmental goals
39. A living strategy
40. Improve and evolve your strategy as your business changes and your customer needs and expectations evolve.
41. Make better decisions
42. Ethnographic methods used by design thinking practitioners reduce the risk of design development by validating designs as they are being designed with end users.

" *I believe that all brands will become storytellers, editors and publishers, all stores will become magazines, and all media companies will become stores. There will be too many of all of them. The strongest ones, the ones who offer the best customer experience, will survive.*

Natalie Massenet
Chair of the British Fashion Council

" *Making things people want is better than making people want things."*

" *Customers want high-quality food, good service, and good store experience, and most retailers fail to deliver on those."*

John Mackey

DESIGN ETHNOGRAPHY

WHAT
Design ethnography is a collection of methods that helps create better more compelling and meaningful design. It helps a designer understand the points of view of people who will use the designs. Ethnographers study and interpret culture, through fieldwork.

WHO INVENTED IT?
Bronisław Malinowski 1922

WHY
1. To inform the design and innovation processes rather than basing your designs on intuition.
2. To ensure that your design solutions resonate with the people that you are designing for.
3. Ethnography helps designers see beyond their preconceptions.

CHALLENGES
1. People may behave differently when they are in groups or alone.
2. Researchers need to be aware of the potential impacts of the research on the people and animals they study.

HOW
There are many different ethnographic techniques. Some of the general guidelines are:
3. Listen.
4. Observe.
5. Be empathetic and honest.
6. Do research in context, in the environments that the people you are studying live or work.
7. Influence your subject's behavior as little as possible with your presence.
8. Beware of bias.
9. Take photos and notes.
10. Have clear goals related to understanding and prediction.
11. Study representative people.

RESOURCES
Notepad computer
Pens
Post-it-notes
Video camera
Camera
Voice recorder
White-board
Dry-erase pens.

Source: Publication bias: raising awareness of a potential problem

SERVICE DESIGN

SOME DISRUPTIVE TRENDS THAT NEED NEW DESIGN APPROACHES

The methods described in this book are a more effective approach than traditional applying traditional design skills like sketching when working with design problems that involve these types of complex, ill-defined and sometimes ambiguous global trends.

1. Being human in a digital world.
2. Entrepreneurship.
3. Focus on regional/ local characteristics
4. Growth of Asian markets
5. Information society
6. Internet of things. Connected devices.
7. Less predictable world.
8. Looking at the creative community holistically to tackle larger societal issues.
9. Massive data sets.
10. Move from transaction to experience society.
11. Multidisciplinary collaboration
12. Outsourcing.
13. Storytelling.
14. Tiny moments of value rather than big wow delight.
15. Urgency for innovation
16. Wearables.
17. a never- ending cycle of decisions and choices.
18. Design automation.
19. Service design in the public sector.
20. Data + Design
21. Brands will become less branded.
22. Design as a discipline becomes more accepted in the business world. Elevation of design.
23. Design Research is expanding to use intelligent tools such as machine learning.
24. The death of short-termism.
25. T-shape designers. Designers are specialist in one area, while generalists in related fields.
26. Design metrics.
27. The war for talent. Growing challenges in talent recruitment.
28. Digital experiences have democratized luxury and elevated our standard of living.
29. Digital trust.
30. Continuing education. Education doesn't happen in college only, people get trained all their life.
31. Networking. "Everything is networked now," says Pinterest co-founder Evan Sharp, whom I interviewed for my project on designer founders. "All of culture, all of communications, it all is going through networks."
32. Artificial intelligence.
33. Machine learning.
34. Fortune 500 Design firm acquisitions.
35. Digital design.
36. Advertising and marketing budgets will be diverted to design.
37. Wisdom of crowds. Many individuals provide content

and make decisions rather than a few experts.
38. Mobile technology becomes an integrated part of communication.
39. Health monitoring. Consumers are now routinely using wearable health monitoring devices.
40. Telework. More employees enjoy flexibility in working hours and locations.
41. Design focus moves from styling to human-centered design.
42. Neuroscience and Design Research. Now when we test prototypes, we can measure behavior, cognition, emotional reactions, physiological markers, and brain activity.
43. Transit culture. People live and work in many cultures.
44. Social networking. People share interests and activities in online communities.
45. The personalization of content, products, and services.
46. Digital security.
47. Luxury
48. Service Economy. Service industry now employs 90% of Americans.
49. Smaller organizations. Small organizations and startups have the opportunity to enter the market and compete with large organizations.
50. Wellbeing.
51. The strategic contribution of design is expected.
52. Brands that focus on customer experience.
53. Active Listening.
54. App integration.
55. Micro co-creation
56. Growth of user experience design.
57. User generated content & open sharing People provide information and share their information online.
58. Virtual reality.
59. Privacy by design

Design today is no longer about designing objects, visuals or spaces; it is about designing systems, strategies and experiences."

Gjoko Muratovski
Professor in design and innovation. Tongji University, Shanghai

We need to invent a new and radical form of collaboration that blurs the boundaries between creators and consumers. It's not about "us versus them" or even "us on behalf of them." For the design thinker, it has to be "us with them."

Tim Brown IDEO

SEGMENTATION

WHAT

Market segmentation involves subdividing a market into a number of groups where the people in each group have some commonality, or similarity. Members of a market segment share something in common. Segmentation is done to provide deign solutions that work for a group of people without the expense of developing a different solution for each person. There are many ways to segment a market. The best way to segment customers depends on your goals. For example if you are entering a new global market one way is to segment your customers by where they live.

GEOGRAPHIC SEGMENTATION

This is one of the more common methods of market segmentation. For example, a company selling products in Europe may segment their customers by the country that they live in. In Europe regional differences in customer preferences exist. You may decide to segment you customers by those who live in a city and those who live in a rural location.

DISTRIBUTION SEGMENTATION

Experience maps and Service blueprints help designers understand a market where most people access multiple channels when purchasing or using a product or service

PRICE SEGMENTATION

Another common way of segmenting a market is by income. Different price-points for a product or service may appeal to people with different incomes. Mass market car companies like ford have models that appeal to people with lower incomes and luxury models that appeal to customers with higher incomes.

DEMOGRAPHIC SEGMENTATION

Demographic segmentation is possibly the most commonly used type of segmentation. There are large number of demographic factors such as gender, age, type of employment and education that are often used for segmentation. Some products and brands are targeted mainly at men. Most people over the age of 40 require glasses to read.

TIME SEGMENTATION

Some products are sold at a particular time of day or year. For example surfboards are sold in summer.

PSYCHOGRAPHIC OR LIFESTYLE SEGMENTATION

Psychographic or lifestyle segmentation, is based on, values, behaviors, emotions, perceptions, beliefs, and interests. For example some customers prefer luxury products. Some customers may follow a particular sporting team.

Markets segments should be large enough to justify creating targeted products and services. Four to six market segments is often a manageable number. Targeting too many segments is sometimes unsuccessful. Products usually do not appeal to everyone.

Consider the income potential of each segment carefully when defining segments.
When defining segments consider:
1. Can you measure the segment?.
2. Is the segment big enough to make a profit?
3. Is the segment changing or evolving?
4. Can you reach the segment?
5. Is there one factor that unites everyone in the segment?
6. Do you have enough data to understand the segment?

PERSONAS

WHAT

"A persona is a archetypal character that is meant to represent a group of users in a role who share common goals, attitudes and behaviors when interacting with a particular product or service personas are user models that are presented as specific individual humans. They are not actual people, but are synthesized directly from observations of real people."*(Cooper)*

WHO INVENTED IT?
Alan Cooper 1998

WHY
1. Helps create empathy for users and reduces self reference.
2. Use as tool to analyze and gain insight into users.
3. Help in gaining buy-in from stakeholders.
4. Personas are user models, characters with a purpose who will represent your target users throughout the design process from brainstorming ideas to designing ideal user experience journey.
5. Personas support storytelling, foster user understanding and evolve design. Stories help communicate information in a compelling manner and evoke emotions and action.

HOW

1. Inaccurate personas can lead to a false understandings of the end users. Personas need to be created using data from real users.
2. Collect data through observation, interviews, ethnography.
3. Segment the users or customers
4. Create the Personas
5. Avoid Stereotypes
6. Each persona should be different. Avoid fringe characteristics. Personas should each have three to four life goals which are personal aspirations,
7. Personas are given a name, and photograph.
8. Design personas can be followed by building customer journeys.

RESOURCES

Raw data on users from interviews or other research
Images of people similar to segmented customers.
Computer
Graphics software

ORIGIN OF PERSONAS

The Inmates Are Running the Asylum, written by Alan Cooper published in 1998, introduced the use of personas as a design tool. Alan Cooper describes his first application of the persona technique:

"In 1995 I was working with the three founders of Sagent Technologies, pioneers in the field of what is now called "Business Intelligence" software. It was almost impossible for those brilliant, logical programmers to conceive of a single use of their product when it was obviously capable of so many uses. In frustration I demanded to be introduced to their customers.

The users fell into three distinct groups, clearly differentiated by their goals, tasks, and skill levels. Had I been creating the software myself, I would have role-played those users as I had with Ruby and Super Project, but in this case I had to describe those user models to the Sagent team. So I created Chuck, Cynthia, and Rob. These three were the first true, Goal-Directed, personas. At the next group meeting, I presented my designs from the points of view of Chuck, Cynthia, and Rob instead of from my own. The results were dramatic. While there was still resistance to this unfamiliar method, the programmers could clearly see the sense in my designs because they could identify with these hypothetical archetypes. The product was so successful that it defined a new product segment. The company was a success, too, going public four years later.
Over the next few years, we developed and perfected the technique.

Many of my predecessors have employed ethnographic user research and created persona-like constructs to aid their designing. Product marketing professionals have also been using persona-like entities for many years to define demographic segments. But personas are unique and uniquely effective."

TYPES OF PERSONAS

PRIMARY
The users who are the main focus of the product or service.

SECONDARY
Secondary users may use the product but are not the primary focus.

STAKEHOLDERS
Stakeholders are people who may be affected by the products or services. A patient may be the primary persona but stakeholders may be doctors, nurses, hospital workers, medical insurance company employees, or relatives of the patient.

Usually persona are not created for each stakeholder. There may be conflicts between the needs of different stakeholders that should be considered.

EXCLUSIONARY
Someone we're not designing for. It is useful to consider non users when defining personas.

BIOGRAPHICAL INFORMATION

NAME
Give each persona a name that may be representative of the user group.

PHOTO
Choose a photograph which represents someone like the persona that you have constructed.

COUNTRY/ REGION
Where within the country does the persona live?

CITY/METROPOLITAN SIZE
9. Under 5,000,
10. 5,000-10,000,
11. 10,000 -20.000
12. 20,000-50,000,
13. 50,000- 250,000,
14. 250,000-500,000,
15. 500,000-1 million,
16. 1 million-4 million,
17. More than 4 million

URBAN OR RURAL?
Do they live in the city or in the country?

DEMOGRAPHIC

AGE
Give the persona a precise age. Segments often give age as a range:
1. Under 6
2. 6-11
3. 12-20
4. 20-35
5. 35-50

6. 50-65
7. Over 65

GENDER
Male or female?

FAMILY SIZE
1. 1-2
2. 3-4
3. More than 5

SINGLE OR MARRIED?
Single married or divorced?

LIFE STAGE
1. Child
2. Teenager
3. Young
4. Middle aged
5. Elderly

INCOME
1. Under $10,000;
2. $10,000-20,000,
3. $20,000-30,000,
4. $30,000-50,000,
5. $50,000-100,000,
6. $100,000-150,000
7. Over 150.000

HOUSING
Renter or owner?
Type of dwelling?

OCCUPATION
1. Sales
2. Office worker
3. Nurse
4. Waiter
5. Administration
6. Building
7. Professional
8. Other

EDUCATION
1. Grade school
2. High school
3. College
4. Post Graduate

ETHNICITY
Consider with nationality

NATIONALITY
Many different groups are represented with nationality.

PSYCHOGRAPHIC

SELF-IMAGE
Outgoing, leader, shy

BELIEFS
Focus on those beliefs that may be most relevant to your product or service.

ATTITUDES
Favorable and unfavorable attitudes relevant to the product or service.

TECH STATUS
1. Innovator
2. Early adopter
3. Fast followers
4. Early mainstream
5. Late mainstream
6. Lagger

INTERESTS
1. Music
2. Sport
3. Food
4. Others

MEDIA
1. Websites

2. TV shows
3. Magazines
4. Other

WEB

TENURE
How long has the persona been using the web?

TIME ONLINE
Hours per week or month

TYPE OF USAGE
1. Email
2. Social networking
3. News
4. Other

BANDWIDTH
How fast is their connection?

INTERNET DEVICE
1. Desk
2. Tablet
3. Phone
4. Other

BROWSER
Type of browser

Sources:"Principles of Marketing" 8th Edition, Phillip Kotler and Gary Armstrong, "The People Who Make Organization Go – Or Stop," Rob Cross and Laurence Prusak, Havard Business Review, June Persona Creation and Usage Toolkit, George Olsen 2004

PROBLEM STATEMENT

CREATING A PROBLEM STATEMENT
A problem statement includes three elements:
1. user
2. need
3. insight

User xxxx needs xxxx because xxxx

1. What is the need?
2. Who has the need?
3. Why is there a needs?

1. Create a number of problem statements based on different user groups and different needs.
2. Compare the problem statements.
3. Use the problem statement during the ideation phase. Don't try to solve all problems.

DIVERSITY

> **WHAT**
> Diversity means different genders, different ages, be from different cultures, different socioeconomic backgrounds and have different outlooks to be most successful.

WHY
1. To attract good people
2. It broadens the customer base in a competitive environment.
3. Diversity brings benefits including better decision making and improved problem-solving, creativity and innovation, which leads to enhanced product development, and more successful marketing to different types of customers.
4. Diversity provides organizations with the ability to compete in global markets

HOW
1. Treat everyone fairly.
2. Creating an inclusive culture.
3. View employees as individuals.
4. Ensure equal access to opportunities.
5. Compliance with statutory duties and requirements.
6. everyone staff with the skills to challenge inequality and discrimination in their environment.
7. Ensure policies, procedures and processes promote equality and diversity.
8. Seek the commitment from key participants.
9. Engage with communities.
10. Recognize, and encourage employees to see that their cultures are of value to the organization.
11. Articulate the benefits more diverse organization.
12. Develop a definition of diversity that is linked to organizational mission.
13. Identify models locally and internationally that might serve as models for diversity efforts.
14. Develop a realistic action plan.
15. Develop metrics for success.
16. Create a safe environment for participation.
17. Set goals for bringing about organizational diversity.
18. Articulate goals.
19. Become culturally competent.
20. Commit to continuous improvement.

EMPATHY

WHAT
Empathy is defined as 'standing in someone else's shoes' or 'seeing through someone else's eyes'. It is The ability to identify and understand another's situation, feelings, and motives. In design it may be defined as: identify with others and, adopting his or her perspective. It is different to sympathy. Empathy does not necessarily imply compassion. Empathy is a respectful understanding of other people's point of view.

WHO INVENTED IT?
The English word was coined in 1909 by E.B. Titchener in an attempt to translate the German word "Einfühlungsvermögen". It was later re-translated into the German language as "Empathie".

WHY
1. Empathy is a core skill for designers to design successfully for other people.
2. Empathy is needed for business success and for designs to be accepted and used by those people we are designing for.
3. Empathy builds trust.

CHALLENGES
1. Increasing use of teams.
2. The rapid pace of globalization.
3. Global need to retain talent.

HOW
1. Put yourself in contact and the context of people who you are designing for.
2. Ask questions and listen to the answers.
3. Read between the lines.
4. Observe.
5. Don't interrupt.
6. Listen.
7. Ask clarifying questions.
8. Restating what you think you heard.
9. Recognize that people are individuals.
10. Notice body language. Most communication is non-verbal
11. Withhold judgment when you hear views different to your own.
12. Take a personal interest in people.

EXPERIENCE DESIGN

WHAT
Experience design is the practice of designing products, processes, services, events, and environments with a focus placed on the quality of the user experience. Experience design is concerned with moments of engagement, or touchpoints, between people and brand. Experience design requires a cross-disciplinary approach.

Source: On Point Creative, http://opcatl.com/ (accessed July 03, 2016)

WHO INVENTED IT?
Donald Norman 1990s

WHY
A user experience can be more valuable than an individual product or service.

CHALLENGES
1. Research methods are necessary to understand another person's experiences
2. Observations can be subjective.

HOW
1. Experience evaluation. Methods include:
2. Diary Methods.
3. Experience sampling method.
4. Day reconstruction method.
5. Laddering interviews.

RESOURCES
Cameras
Video cameras
Notepad computer
Digital voice recorder
Cell phones
Tablets

What we know about the destination resort business is clearly established. But it's all about one thing, and one thing only. All of the razzmatazz and jazz we hear about facilities and everything else doesn't amount to a hill of beans. It's customer experience that determines the longevity and endurance of these enterprises.

Steve Wynn

HUMAN NEEDS

The greatest single cause of failure of design projects according to many studies is a lack of understanding of the what is most important to the customer or end user

This really comes down to a lack of identification of what are unmet user needs. Unmet needs represent market opportunities. customers struggle to get a job done.

Identifying and addressing those unmet needs is the key to success.

Many managers do not have a process for identifying what is most important to their customers. Knowing which customer needs to address in priority order is a key requirement of the innovation process.

> *Post-modernism is dead because it didn't address human needs.*

David Guterson

"One of the oldest human needs is having someone to wonder where you are when you don't come home at night."

Margaret Mead

> *Human needs are a powerful source of explanation of human behavior and social interaction. All individuals have needs that they strive to satisfy, either by using the system, 'acting on the fringes.' or acting as a reformist or revolutionary. Given this condition, social systems must be responsive to individual needs, or be subject to instability and forced change."*

Preface," in The Power of Human Needs in World Society, ed. Roger A. Coate and Jerel A. Rosati, ix. Boulder, CO: Lynne Rienner Publishers.

"The work of an advertising agency is warmly and immediately human. It deals with human needs, wants, dreams and hopes. Its 'product' cannot be turned out on an assembly line."

Leo Burnett

SERVICE DESIGN

HUMAN NEEDS

PHYSICAL SUSTENANCE
1. Air
2. Food
3. Health
4. Movement
5. Physical Safety
6. Rest / sleep
7. Shelter
8. Touch
9. Water

SECURITY
1. Consistency
2. Order/Structure
3. Peace
4. Peace of mind
5. Protection
6. Safety
7. Stability
8. Trusting

LEISURE/RELAXATION
1. Humour
2. Joy
3. Play
4. Pleasure

AFFECTION
1. Appreciation
2. Attention
3. Closeness
4. Companionship
5. Harmony
6. Intimacy
7. Love
8. Nurturing
9. Sexual Expression
10. Support
11. Tenderness
12. Warmth

UNDERSTANDING
1. Awareness
2. Clarity
3. Discovery
4. Learning

> *Our real goal, then, is not so much fulfilling manifest needs by creating a speedier printer or a more ergonomic keyboard; that's the job of designers. It is helping people to articulate the latent needs they may not even know they have, and this is the challenge of design thinkers."*

Tim Brown
IDEO

> *The most secure source of new ideas that have true competitive advantage, and hence, higher margins, is customers' unarticulated needs."*

Jeanne Liedtka
Darden School of the University of Virginia

AUTONOMY
1. Choice
2. Ease
3. Independence
4. Power
5. Self-responsibility
6. Space
7. Spontaneity

MEANING
1. Aliveness
2. Challenge
3. Contribution
4. Creativity
5. Effectiveness
6. Exploration
7. Integration
8. Purpose

MATTERING
1. Acceptance
2. Care
3. Compassion
4. Consideration
5. Empathy
6. Kindness
7. Mutual Recognition
8. Respect
9. To be heard, seen
10. To be known, understood
11. To be trusted
12. Understanding others

COMMUNITY
1. Belonging
2. Communication
3. Cooperation
4. Equality
5. Inclusion

1. Mutuality
2. Participation
3. Partnership
4. Self-expression
5. Sharing

SENSE OF SELF
1. Authenticity
2. Competence
3. Creativity
4. Dignity
5. Growth
6. Healing
7. Honesty
8. Integrity
9. Self-acceptance
10. Self-care
11. Self-knowledge
12. Self-realization
13. Mattering to myself

TRANSCENDENCE
1. Beauty
2. Celebration of life
3. Communion
4. Faith
5. Flow
6. Hope
7. Inspiration
8. Mourning
9. Peace (internal)
10. Presence

Sources: Marshall Rosenberg, Manfred Max-Neef, Miki and Arnina Kashtan

Susan Margolis

Demographic

Age
Marital status
Occupation
Location
Income
Archetype

Personality

Introvert/extravert
Driven
Social
Active
Competitive

Technology

IT & internet
Software
Mobile apps
Social networks

Frustrations

Fears

Pain points

Unmet needs

Goals

Motivations

Brands

Bio/ background

Quote:

Download a free pdf copy of this template from our site www.dcc-edu.org

Copyright (c) Design Community College Inc. 2017

PERSONAS

WHAT

"A persona is a archetypal character that is meant to represent a group of users in a role who share common goals, attitudes and behaviors when interacting with a particular product or service personas are user models that are presented as specific individual humans. They are not actual people, but are synthesized directly from observations of real people."*(Cooper)*

WHO INVENTED IT?
Alan Cooper 1998

WHY
1. Helps create empathy for users and reduces self reference.
2. Use as tool to analyze and gain insight into users.
3. Help in gaining buy-in from stakeholders.
4. Personas are user models, characters with a purpose who will represent your target users throughout the design process from brainstorming ideas to designing ideal user experience journey.
5. Personas support storytelling, foster user understanding and evolve design. Stories help communicate information in a compelling manner and evoke emotions and action.

HOW
1. Inaccurate personas can lead to a false understandings of the end users. Personas need to be created using data from real users.
2. Collect data through observation, interviews, ethnography.
3. Segment the users or customers
4. Create the Personas
5. Avoid Stereotypes
6. Each persona should be different. Avoid fringe characteristics. Personas should each have three to four life goals which are personal aspirations,
7. Personas are given a name, and photograph.
8. Design personas can be followed by building customer journeys.

RESOURCES
Raw data on users from interviews or other research
Images of people similar to segmented customers.
Computer
Graphics software

ORIGIN OF PERSONAS

The Inmates Are Running the Asylum, written by Alan Cooper published in 1998, introduced the use of personas as a design tool. Alan Cooper describes his first application of the persona technique:

"In 1995 I was working with

SERVICE DESIGN

PERSONA TEMPLATE

PHOTO OF PERSONA   PERSONA NAME

image of persona

DEMOGRAPHICS

Occupation   Income
Location   Gender
    Education

CHARACTERISTICS

demograhic factors

GOALS

What does this person want to achieve

MOTIVATIONS
Incentives
Fear
Growth

Achievement
Power
Social

FRUSTRATIONS   QUOTE

What experiences does this person wish to avoid?

Characteristic quote

BRANDS

What brands does

CHARACTERISTICS

sliders show relevant factors

······X············ ···········X·········
EXTROVERT

···········X······· ···············X·····
TRAVEL   LUXURY GOODS

····X············· ······X··············
TECHNICAL SAVVY   SPORTS

···············X···· ·················X···
SOCIAL NETWORKING   MOBILE APPS

the three founders of Sagent Technologies, pioneers in the field of what is now called "Business Intelligence" software. It was almost impossible for those brilliant, logical programmers to conceive of a single use of their product when it was obviously capable of so many uses. In frustration I demanded to be introduced to their customers.

The users fell into three distinct groups, clearly differentiated by their goals, tasks, and skill levels. Had I been creating the software myself, I would have role-played those users as I had with Ruby and Super Project, but in this case I had to describe those user models to the Sagent team. So I created Chuck, Cynthia, and Rob. These three were the first true, Goal-Directed, personas.
At the next group meeting, I presented my designs from the points of view of Chuck, Cynthia, and Rob instead of from my own. The results were dramatic. While there was still resistance to this unfamiliar method, the programmers could clearly see the sense in my designs because they could identify with these hypothetical archetypes. The product was so successful that it defined a new product segment. The company was a success, too, going public four years later. Over the next few years, we developed and perfected the technique.
Many of my predecessors have employed ethnographic user research and created persona-like constructs to aid their designing. Product marketing professionals have also been using persona-like entities for many years to define demographic segments. But personas are unique and uniquely effective."

TYPES OF PERSONAS

PRIMARY PERSONAS
The users who are the main focus of the product or service.

SECONDARY PERSONAS
Secondary users may use the product but are not the primary focus.

STAKEHOLDERS
Stakeholders are people who may be affected by the products or services. A patient may be the primary persona but stakeholders may be doctors, nurses, hospital workers, medical insurance company employees, or relatives of the patient.

Usually persona are not created for each stakeholder. There may be conflicts between the needs of different stakeholders that should be considered.

EXCLUSIONARY PERSONAS
Someone we're not designing for. It is useful to consider non users when defining personas.

BIOGRAPHICAL INFORMATION

NAME
Give each persona a name that may be representative of the user group.

PHOTO
Choose a photograph which represents someone like the persona that you have constructed.

COUNTRY/ REGION
Where within the country does the persona live?

CITY/METROPOLITAN SIZE
9. Under 5,000,
10. 5,000-10,000,
11. 10,000 -20.000
12. 20,000-50,000,
13. 50,000- 250,000,
14. 250,000-500,000,
15. 500,000-1 million,
16. 1 million-4 million,
17. More than 4 million

URBAN OR RURAL?
Do they live in the city or in the country?

DEMOGRAPHIC

AGE
Give the persona a precise age. Segments often give age as a range:
1. Under 6
2. 6-11
3. 12-20
4. 20-35
5. 35-50
6. 50-65
7. Over 65

GENDER
Male or female?

FAMILY SIZE
1. 1-2
2. 3-4
3. More than 5

SINGLE OR MARRIED?
Single married or divorced?

LIFE STAGE
1. Child
2. Teenager
3. Young
4. Middle aged
5. Elderly

INCOME
1. Under $10,000;
2. $10,000-20,000,
3. $20,000-30,000,
4. $30,000-50,000,
5. $50,000-100,000,
6. $100,000-150,000
7. Over 150.000

HOUSING
Renter or owner?
Type of dwelling?

OCCUPATION
1. Sales
2. Office worker
3. Nurse
4. Waiter
5. Administration
6. Building
7. Professional
8. Other

EDUCATION
1. Grade school
2. High school
3. College
4. Post Graduate

ETHNICITY
Consider with nationality

NATIONALITY
Many different groups are represented with nationality.

PSYCHOGRAPHIC

SELF-IMAGE
Outgoing, leader, shy

BELIEFS
Focus on those beliefs that may be most relevant to your product or service.

ATTITUDES
Favorable and unfavorable attitudes relevant to the product or service.

TECH STATUS
1. Innovator
2. Early adopter
3. Fast followers
4. Early mainstream
5. Late mainstream
6. Lagger

INTERESTS
1. Music
2. Sport
3. Food
4. Others

MEDIA
1. Websites
2. TV shows
3. Magazines
4. Other

WEB

TENURE
How long has the persona been using the web?

TIME ONLINE
Hours per week or month

TYPE OF USAGE
1. Email
2. Social networking
3. News
4. Other

BANDWIDTH
How fast is their connection?

INTERNET DEVICE
1. Desk
2. Tablet
3. Phone
4. Other

BROWSER
Type of browser

Sources:"Principles of Marketing" 8th Edition, Phillip Kotler and Gary Armstrong, "The People Who Make Organization Go – Or Stop," Rob Cross and Laurence Prusak, Havard Business Review, June Persona Creation and Usage Toolkit, George Olsen 2004

PERSONA EXERCISE

PERSONAS
What are personas?
Personas are archetypal users of a product or service that represent the needs of larger groups of users, in terms of their goals and personal characteristics. They act as place markers for real users and help guide decisions about functionality and design.

TASKS
Create three one-page personas for primary user groups of a service.

PROCESS
1. Identify a service
2. Brainstorm three substantial groups of users for the service.
3. Create three personas.
4. Add personal details but don't go overboard.

DEFINE FOR EACH OF THREE PERSONAS
1. Persona Name
2. Persona image
3. Brief description up to 7 words
4. Age
5. Income
6. Education
7. Where persona lives
8. Where persona works
9. Family description
10. Household income
11. Behaviors
12. Unmet needs
13. Goals
14. Main problems
15. Frustrations
16. 12. Places this persona spends time.
17. Things standing in the way of what they are trying to achieve.

DELIVERABLES
One page pdf persona for each of three personas

A GOOD PERSONA
1. Reflects patterns observed in research.
2. Focuses on the current state, not the future
3. Is realistic, not idealized
4. Describes a challenging but achievable design target.
5. Helps understand users'
- Context
- Behaviors
- Attitudes
- Needs
6. Challenges pain points
7. Identifies goals and motivations.
8. Represents a major user group
9. Expresses and focus on the major needs and expectations of the important user groups
10. Describes realistic people with backgrounds, goals, and values.

02
APPLYING MAPPING METHODS IN YOUR ORGANIZATION

APPLYING MAPPING METHODS IN YOUR ORGANIZATION

Here is some advice to help you introduce mapping methods into your organization.

FIRST LEARN ABOUT MAPPING METHODS
Arrange for several leaders in your organization representing the main cross-functional departments to do a substantial course in mapping methods together. The author presents a number of on-line classes which may be reviewed at www.dcc-edu.org

GIVE EVERYONE A VOICE
Invite everyone to a series of meetings to discuss the introduction of mapping in your organization.

LEAVE YOUR OFFICE AND EXPERIENCE YOUR CUSTOMER'S WORLD
Listen to your customers to understand what their problems are. Don't solve the wrong problem because you are remote from your customers.

COLLABORATE
Define the goals together as a team with everyone's input.

WHEN YOU HAVE A PRELIMINARY DESIGN GET FEEDBACK FROM CUSTOMERS
Share the designs as widely as possible with internal and external stakeholders and invite their feedback.

LEARN BY FAILING AND TRYING AGAIN
It is important to understand that if you are trying new things not every design idea will be successful. Use the methods in this book to minimize the cost of inevitable failures during prototyping and experimentation.

INVITE ALL DEPARTMENTS AND EXTERNAL STAKEHOLDERS TO YOUR WORKSHOPS
You should have one team composed of stakeholders with different perspectives.

CHOOSE THE TEAM MEMBERS IN YOUR GROUPS CAREFULLY
Four to eight people is an optimum groups size. If you have a larger group break it into smaller groups. Consider diversity and personalities when forming groups. Don't put several people with strong personalities into the same group. Create space for discussion where people feel safe.

START WITH A MANAGEABLE DESIGN PROBLEM

Run several small-scale mapping methods exercises before taking on a larger project.

> **"**
> *Because we invested in building innovation skills into our employee base, we are not only a design-thinking company, we're a design-driven company. Meaning, we're going from creating a culture of design thinking to building a practice of design doing, where we relentlessly focus on nailing the end-to-end customer experience. This means that before anything gets built, the whole team engineers, designers, marketers, product managers are interfacing with the customers to ensure they understand the problem well, and together, they design the best solution."*
>
> Suzanne Pellican,
> Vice President Of Experience Design at Intuit

EMPATHY IS NOT THE SAME AS HUMAN FACTORS
Mapping tools consider not just usability issues but also people's emotions, attitudes, and values.

THINK HOLISTICALLY
Analytical thinkers can sometimes focus on the small details rather than the bigger issues. The process of mapping will allow you to consider both. Think about design problems systematically, products, services, and experiences. How are these things connected?

LOOK FOR UNMET NEEDS
Consider and involve the customer at every stage.

BUILD UP YOUR SOLUTIONS
Prototype early and learn and build up the solution by asking questions.

CONSIDER THE CUSTOMER JOURNEY NOT JUST THE DESTINATION
The customer journey consists of a series of micro-experiences. Mapping tools allow you to consider and optimize each of these moments to build a better overall experience.

BUILD A WAR ROOM
Place all your research and all your ideas on a wall where everyone in tour team can see it and think about and discuss what may be relevant and connected. Keep one space dedicated to your project for the entire project. Pick a large space with natural light.

GIVE PEOPLE DEFINED TIMES FOR EACH ACTIVITY
Don't give them too much time. 30-minutes to generate

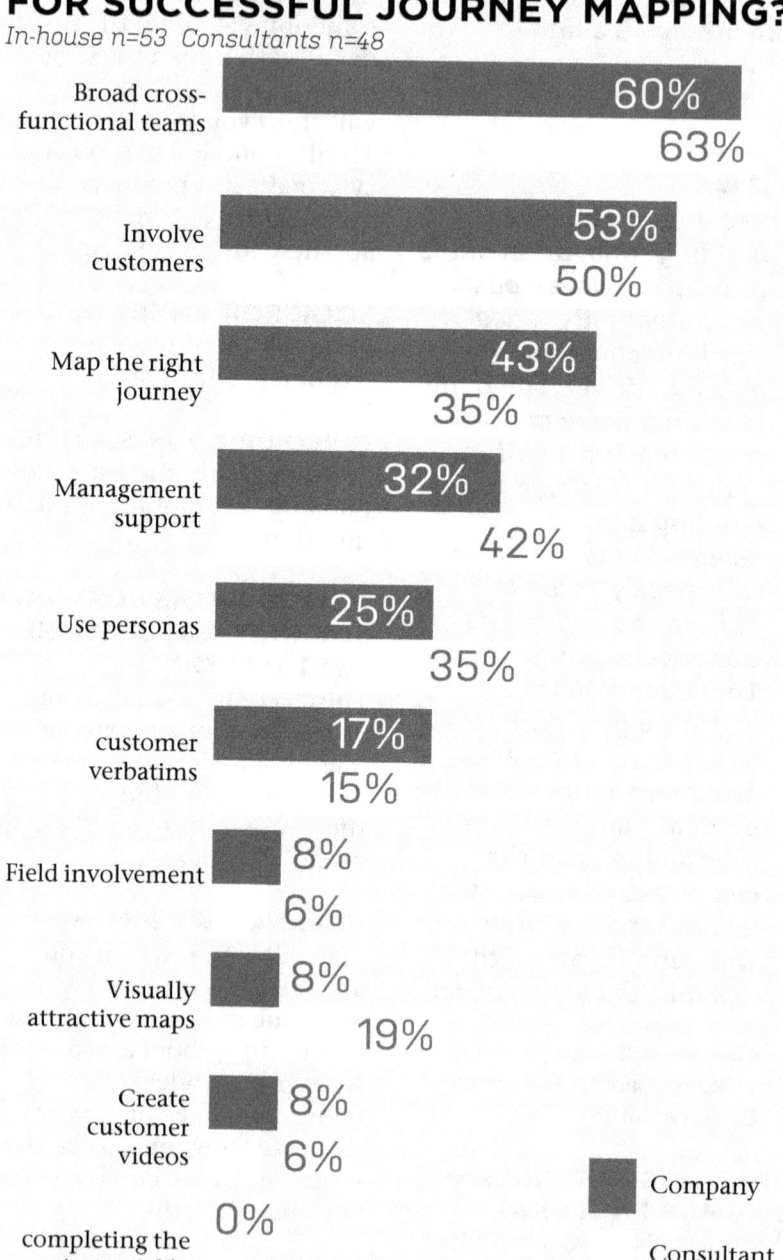

ideas, 15 minutes for discussion, 20-minutes to make a fast prototype. Keep the activities focused and moving. Have clear goals with each team activity.

MODERATING GROUPS

If you have the resources have two people moderate. The moderator can facilitate the group discussion while the assistant moderator takes notes and looks after the video camera. Moderating a team activity successfully is a skill which is partly a talent and partly developed through experience.

ROLES

1. **Facilitator.** The person who moderates the group.
2. **Recorder.** The person who captures the discussion
3. **Data Analyst.** The person who analyses the notes or recordings of the group discussion
4. **Report Writer.** The person who writes executive summary of the discussions.
5. **Scheduler.** The person who schedules the meetings.
6. **Manager of Logistics.** The person who manages the room and other logistics.

ASSISTANT MODERATOR

1. Manages the equipment and refreshments
2. Arranges the room
3. Manages video camera and other recording equipment
4. Welcome participants as they arrive
5. Has good listening skills
6. Has good observation skills
7. Has good writing skills
8. Acts as an observer, not as a participant
9. Can remain impartial
10. Take notes throughout the discussion
11. Notes should include observation of non-verbal behavior
12. Notes should include themes, follow-up questions, body language, confusion, nonverbal communication, facial expressions, gestures, signs of agreement, disagreement, frustration, and participant concerns, head nods, physical excitement, eye contact between participants, or other clues that would indicate level of support, or interest.
13. Notes follow-up questions that could be asked
14. The assistant moderator does not get involved in the group discussion.
15. Assistant should be a "fly on the wall" and only observe the discussion.
16. Should not influence the discussion by their presence.
17. Provides participant seating arrangement
18. Operate recording equipment
19. Do not participate in the discussion
20. Ask questions when invited

WHICH METHODS DID YOU USE TO RESEARCH YOUR CUSTOMERS?

In-house n=34

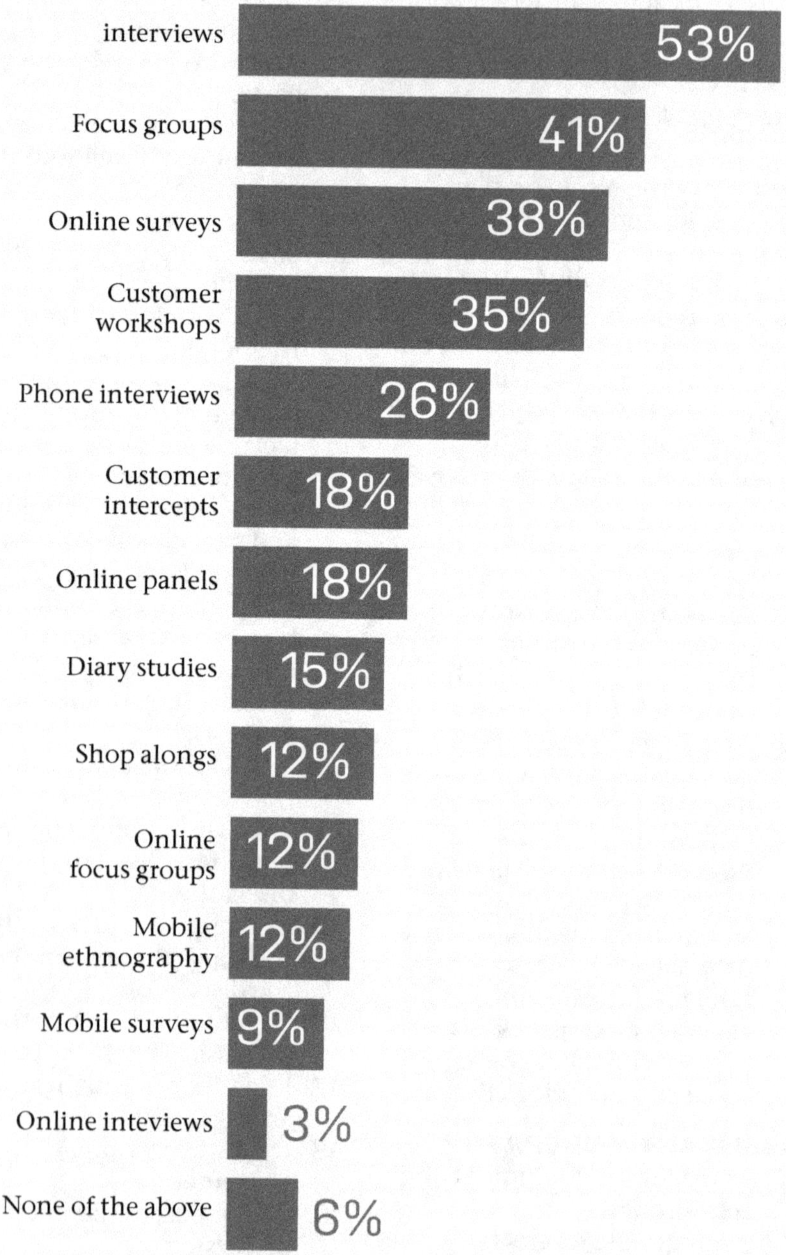

- interviews — 53%
- Focus groups — 41%
- Online surveys — 38%
- Customer workshops — 35%
- Phone interviews — 26%
- Customer intercepts — 18%
- Online panels — 18%
- Diary studies — 15%
- Shop alongs — 12%
- Online focus groups — 12%
- Mobile ethnography — 12%
- Mobile surveys — 9%
- Online inteviews — 3%
- None of the above — 6%

Source of data: 2016 Survey of 134 CX professionals by The Customer Experience Professionals Association and Heart of the Customer

21. Give an oral summary
22. Debrief with moderator
23. Give feedback on analysis and reports
24. Can Handle logistics & refreshments
25. Collects signed informed consent (if required)
26. Takes careful notes
27. Does not participate in discussion
28. Can recap major themes at end of discussion (used before wrap-up question)
29. Monitors recording equipment
30. Liaison between moderator and observers/clients
31. Debriefs with moderator after session
32. Assist with analysis and reports
33. Not required, but can be useful in some situations
34. Balance out strengths/weaknesses in moderator
35. Use to match moderator (without being obvious)
36. Switch leading discussion (good for long or intense discussions)
37. Support leader by keeping on track, recapping major themes, etc.

MODERATOR
Select the moderator carefully.
1. Someone who is culturally like the people participating.
2. Manages the process of the discussion rather than the content.
3. The moderator should have empathy with the group but also have authority.
4. Does not need to be an expert on the discussion topic but needs to show skill in managing discussion.
5. Should not share views,
6. Probes the discussion points to reveal the underlying reasons.
7. Should 'Warm up' the group to help participants feel at ease,
8. Should develop rapport with the participants.
9. Needs to stay focused.
10. Should ensure that all participants are involved in the discussion.
11. Spends the minimum time necessary speaking.
12. Should not show bias.
13. Directs the discussion in real time
14. Follows the question guide.
15. Have an assistant to take notes and manage equipment and time.
16. The moderator should have good listening skills.
17. Use an experienced moderator.
18. A person able to create and manage a friendly and participatory environment.
19. Use pauses and probes
20. Probes:
    - "Can you explain further?"
    - "Could you give an example?"
21. Manage participants
    - Verbal and nonverbal communication
    - Short responses
    - Experts
    - Dominant talkers

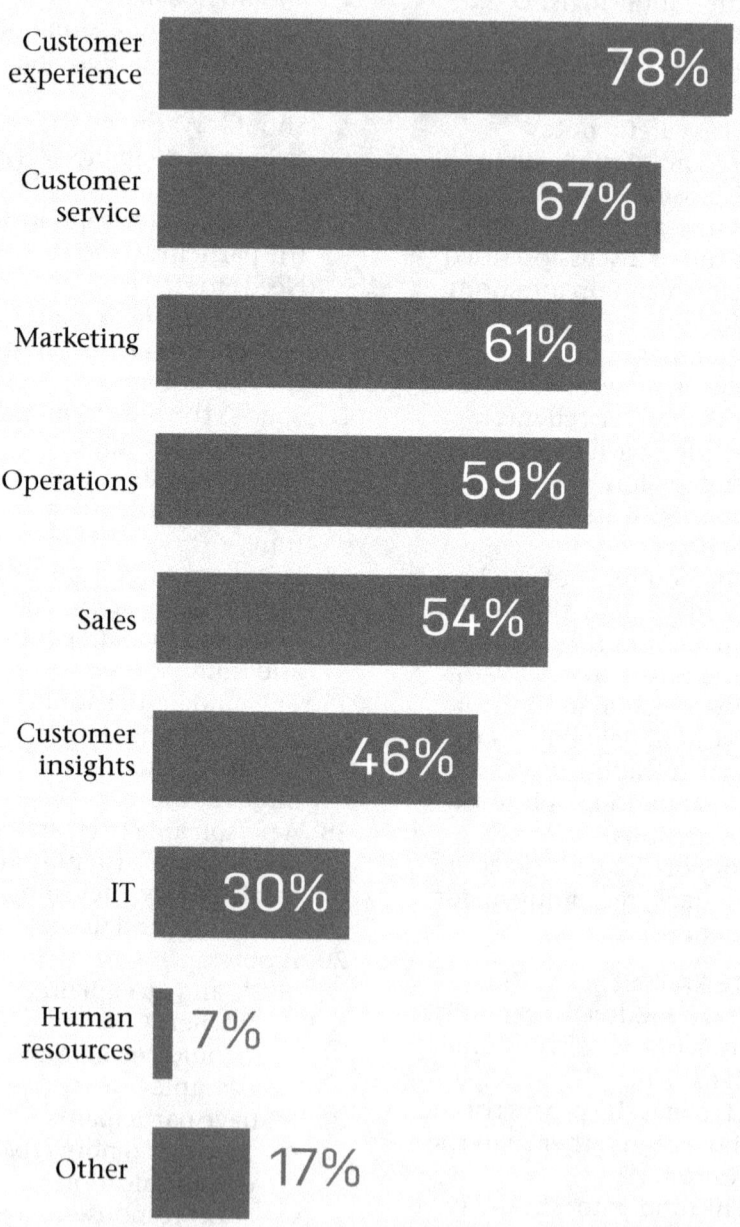

- Shy participants
- Ramblers
22. The moderator should remain neutral and not show extremes of emotion such as surprise or anger during the conversation.
23. The moderator should be diplomatic.
24. The moderator prevents some participants from dominating the conversation.
25. Can clearly summarize and articulate the views expressed.
26. Do not let the discussion stray into areas that are emotionally charged.

GROUP BEHAVIOR

CONSTRUCTIVE GROUP BEHAVIORS

1. Collaboration. The members of the group are interested and listen to the views of other participants.
2. Clarifies points. Asks questions in order to understand ambiguous ideas.
3. Inspires the group with relevant examples.
4. Harmony. Works to build group cohesion
5. Takes risks. Sticks their neck out to achieve the goals.
6. Reviews the process so they properly understand the goals, agenda, schedule and other points.

DESTRUCTIVE GROUP BEHAVIORS

1. Dominates the conversation with one opinion.
2. Wants to move on before the discussion is complete.
3. Does not participate in the discussion.
4. Discounts or ridicules other opinions.
5. Loses focus on the topic or goals.
6. Blocks unfamiliar ideas.
7. Self-Appointed Experts. Thank them for their knowledge and redirect question to the rest of the group
8. If one participant tries to dominate the session, the moderator should invite each person to speak in turn.
9. Shy Participants. Respect someone's right to be quiet, but do give them a chance to share their ideas
10. Ramblers. Intervene, politely summarize and refocus. Use nonverbal cues; redirect.
11. Side Talking/Side Conversation. Remind the group or individuals about the ground rules

INTERVENTION

A good moderator will intervene in the discussion when necessary Establish the ground rules in the introduction. This gives common expectations so that the team members can help manage people who exhibit destructive behavior. Listen to each person's ideas. Ask questions to clarify points or reveal bias.

1. Break a large group into

WHAT TYPE OF JOURNEY DID YOU LAST MAP?

In-house n=57

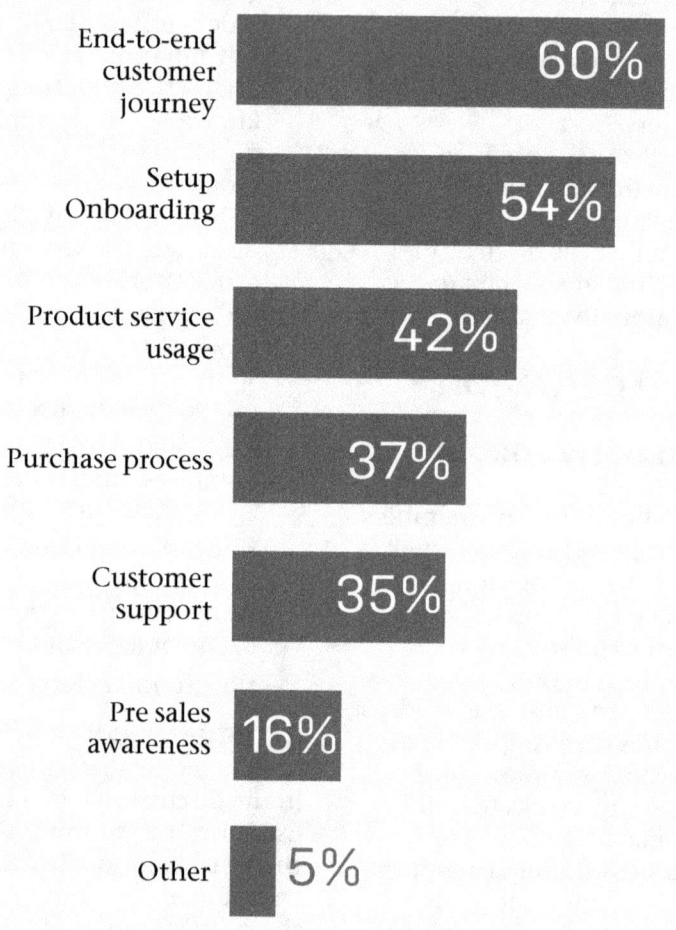

- End-to-end customer journey: 60%
- Setup Onboarding: 54%
- Product service usage: 42%
- Purchase process: 37%
- Customer support: 35%
- Pre sales awareness: 16%
- Other: 5%

Source of data: 2016 Survey of 134 CX professionals by The Customer Experience Professionals Association and Heart of the Customer

smaller groups of 4 people.
2. Remind the group of the task.
3. Take a break and speak to a disruptive participant about the goals.
4. Break the problem into smaller parts.
5. Define a way to make decisions.
6. List the areas of agreement.

TIME MANAGEMENT
It is important that time is planned and managed well so that all the topics can be covered.

KEEPING THE SESSION ON TRACK
One of the important skills for a moderator is to steer the conversation back to the topic if it strays and to move on from question to question.

USE THE INTERVIEW GUIDE
Write in prompts to remind you to check the time at several points during the discussion.

DO NOT RUSH THE DISCUSSION
Interrupt as little as possible and not rush them.
1. Have good listening skills
2. Have good observation skills
3. Have good speaking skills
4. Can foster open and honest dialogue among diverse groups and individuals
5. Can remain impartial.
6. this can influence what people say)
7. Can encourage participation when someone is reluctant to speak up
8. Can manage participants who dominate the conversation
9. Are sensitive to gender and cultural issues
10. Are sensitive to differences in power among and within groups.

MODERATOR SKILLS
BUILDING RAPPORT
1. Building rapport is important.
2. Show the participants that you are a person who is prepared and willing to listen to them with interest.
3. Let the participants know that you are there to learn from them.
4. It is important to present yourself as someone facilitating rather than as a friend. Balance rapport and professionalism.

LISTENING TO DISCUSSION PARTICIPANTS
The guidelines for conducting discussions are closely connected to building rapport. These guidelines include communicating to the participants that you are listening to them as well as these strategies: neutrality, silence, and guidance.
1. Show participants that you are listening.
2. Stay neutral.
3. You want to gather information that is as honest as possible.
4. Silence is acceptable. Asking clarifying questions.

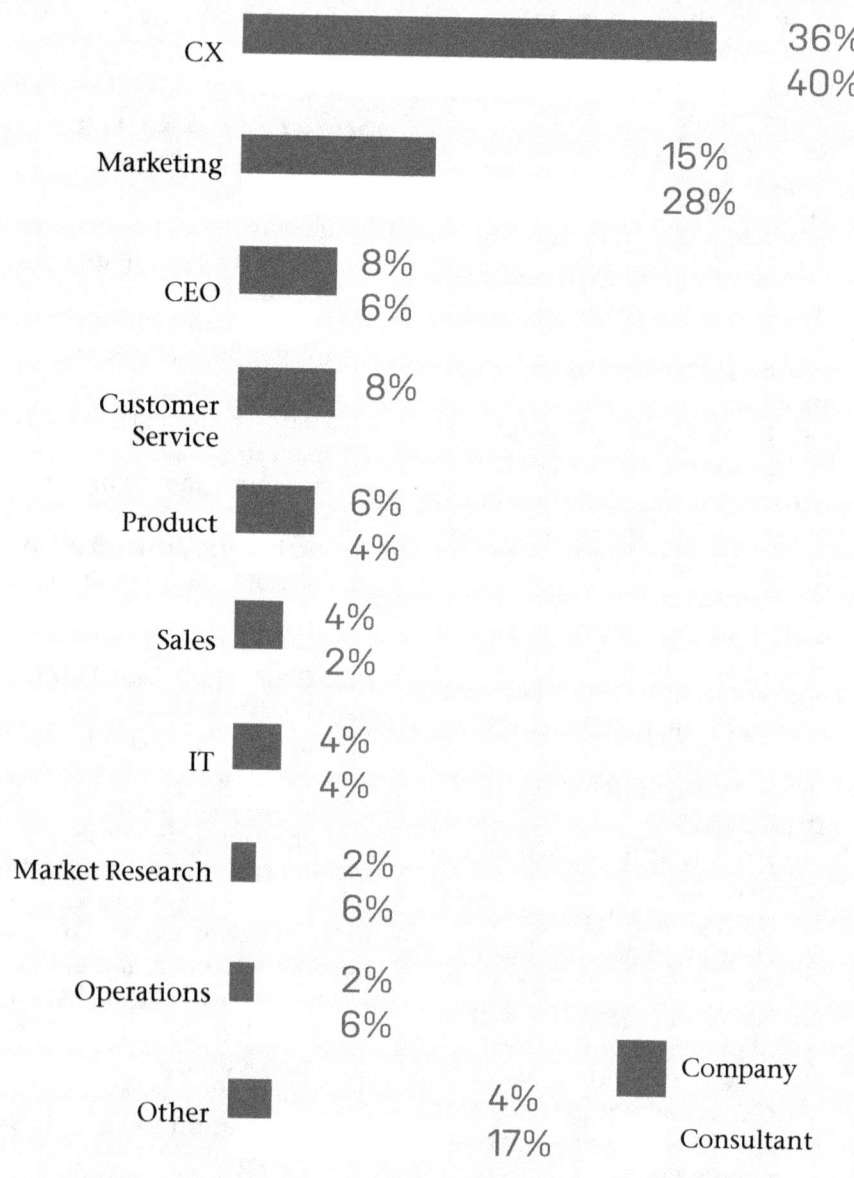

TEAMS

History demonstrates that great projects and products are often the result of great teams.

Start with a goal and a deadline. The most successful designers were team players. In six years, Thomas Edison generated four hundred patents for the telegraph. telephone phonograph, and light bulb- with the help of a fourteen-man team. As Francis Jehl, Edison's longtime assistant, explained, "Edison is in reality a collective noun and means the work of many men."

The right kinds of specializations are important, but specialization is not the only quality required. To make a design project successful, we need T-shaped people. T-shaped people have a depth of knowledge and experience in their own fields but they can also reach out and connect with others horizontally and create meaningful collaborations.

DIVERSITY

Each team member brings their unique perspective and expertise to the team, widening the range of possible outcomes. If you want a breakthrough idea, you're more likely to get it with a diverse team.

Diverse teams see the same problem from many angles. They have a better understanding of any given situation and generate more ideas, making them more effective problem solvers. While it takes effort to harness and align such different perspectives, it's at the intersection of our differences that our most meaningful breakthroughs emerge. Cross-disciplinary teams will provide you with the best results. Teams may consist of people unfamiliar with each other, with external members brought on board either as specialists or facilitators depending on the availability of skills.

Identity
1. Age and ability
2. Gender identity
3. Race and ethnicity

Experience
1. Cultural upbringing
2. Geography
3. Language

Expertise
1. Education
2. Organization
3. Discipline

Source: IBM

The right kinds of specializations are important, but specialization is not the only quality required. To make a Design Thinking project successful, we need T-shaped people. T-shaped people have a depth of knowledge and experience in their own fields but they can also reach out and connect with others horizontally and create meaningful collaborations.

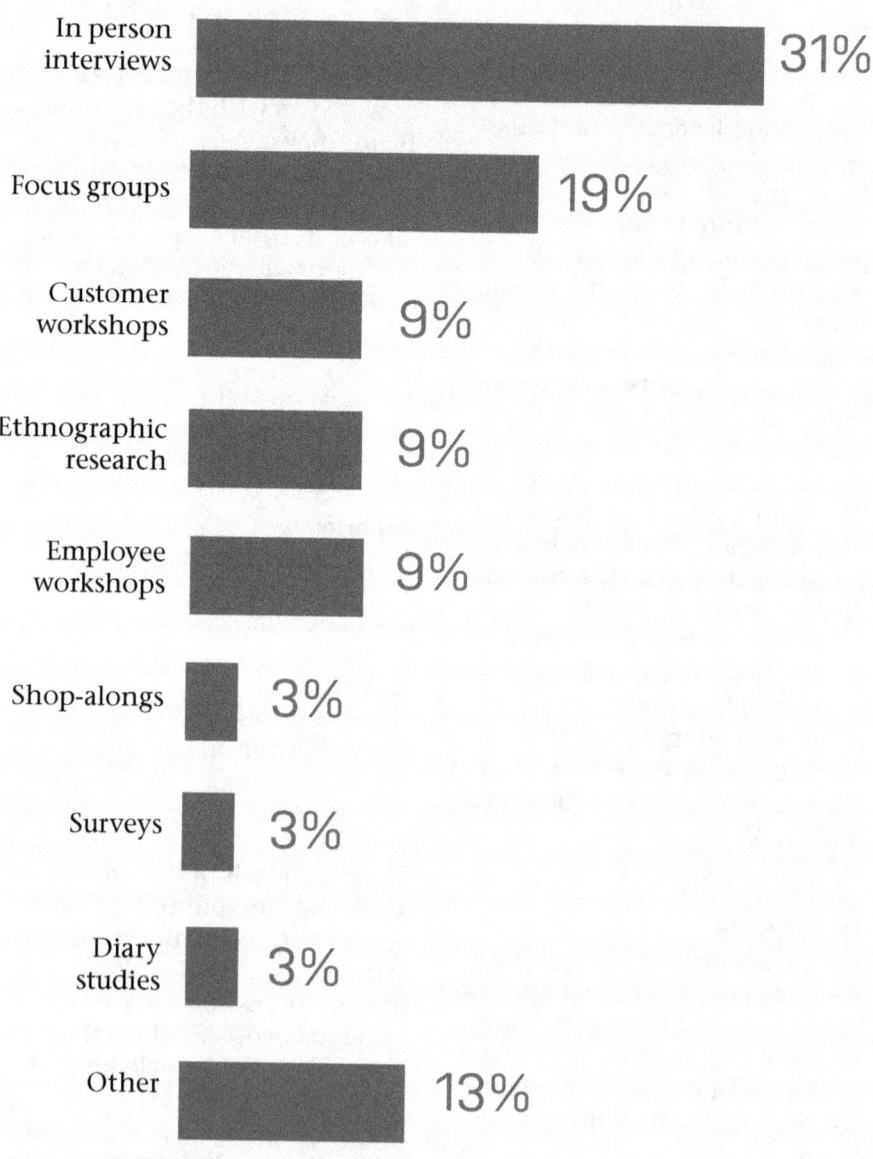

A Design Thinking team should ideally be a cross/multi-disciplinary team consisting of a mix of specializations, including specialists associated with problem areas contributing but not dominating the journey. While specialists may have vast knowledge on a technical level, they are working towards solutions targeted towards non-specialists in many cases and require outside perspectives in addition to what they already know.

EMPOWERMENT

Teams should be equipped with the expertise and independence to deliver outcomes without relying on others for decisions or technical support.

Grant them the authority to handle day-to-day activities on the team and hold them accountable for achieving their assigned outcome.

FACILITATION

1. Start with a clear goal and a serious deadline
2. Explain the five stages of the Design Thinking Process.
3. Provide your team members with printed out models of the Design Thinking process and modes to help them understand and recognize the benefits of the Design Thinking work process.
4. Explain how Design Thinking builds a third way – combining the analytical and information-driven approach of science with the holistic, empathic and creative ways of thinking in ethnography and design.
5. Explain that there are lots of proven methods
6. Knowing the background and underlying structure will help your team members to feel safer as they know that there's a solid background
7. Bring together a diverse team with different thinking styles and specializations.
8. Develop an innovative team culture, which embraces inclusiveness, collaboration, and co-creation.
9. Level the playing field to allow for a diverse set of perspectives to influence the process.
10. Ensure the right person is in charge.
11. Break the ice with some creative exercises to loosen things up.

> *One must still have chaos in oneself to be able to give birth to a dancing star."*
> Friedrich Nietzsche

CONFLICT

> *Diversity invites conflict—and conflict is a wellspring of creativity. Harnessing this creativity requires us to listen to*

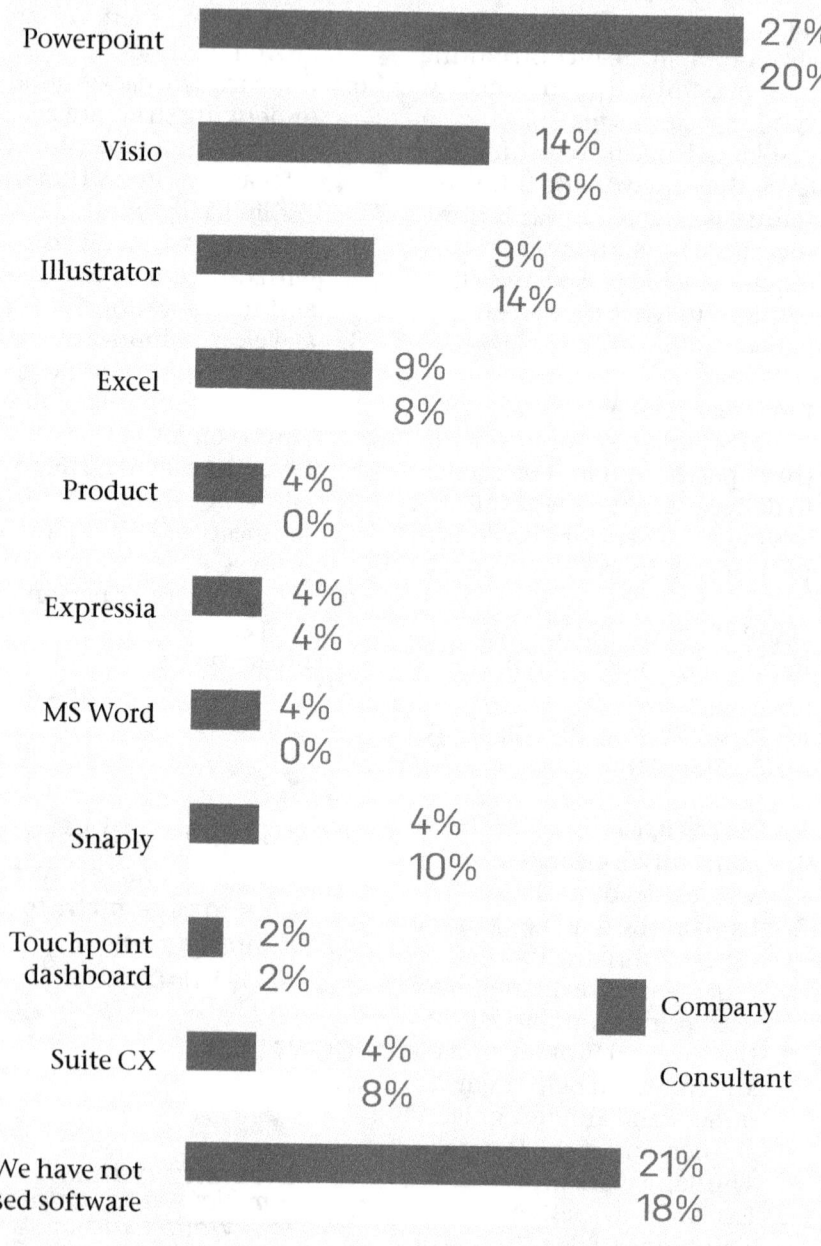

Source of data: 2016 Survey of 134 CX professionals by The Customer Experience Professionals Association and Heart of the Customer

understand, not just argue, with those who may disagree. When you listening to understand, you uncover brand new ideas together and contribute to a more open and collaborative culture."

"Empathy: first with each other. Then with our users."

IBM

1. Instinct often leads us to avoid conflict and seek out those who think alike.
2. At minimum, critical team conversations should include representatives from every discipline affected. It would be unwise for engineering to make timeline decision without engaging offering management in a conversation, or for product designers to make brand decisions without consulting the marketing team.
3. This kind of radical collaboration requires a foundation of trust, respect, and shared ownership across the team.

"
Edison is, in reality, a collective noun and means the work of many men."

Francis Jehl
Edison's assistant

"
Which skills and mindsets do team players need for a design project?

1. Openness: smell, touch, taste, observe, listen, ask, hear, feel...
2. Able to find the right questions.
3. Able to suspend your judgment and look beyond the obvious.
4. Able to understand different points of view,
5. See the big picture and create common grounds.
6. Able to imagine and build solutions haven't seen before.
7. Able to create cheap experiments in order to learn faster."

D Osterwalder,
Anna Ploskonos

COLLECTIVE INTELLIGENCE
Collective intelligence is a type of shared intelligence that emerges from the collaboration of many people and is expressed in consensus decision-making.

Collective intelligence requires

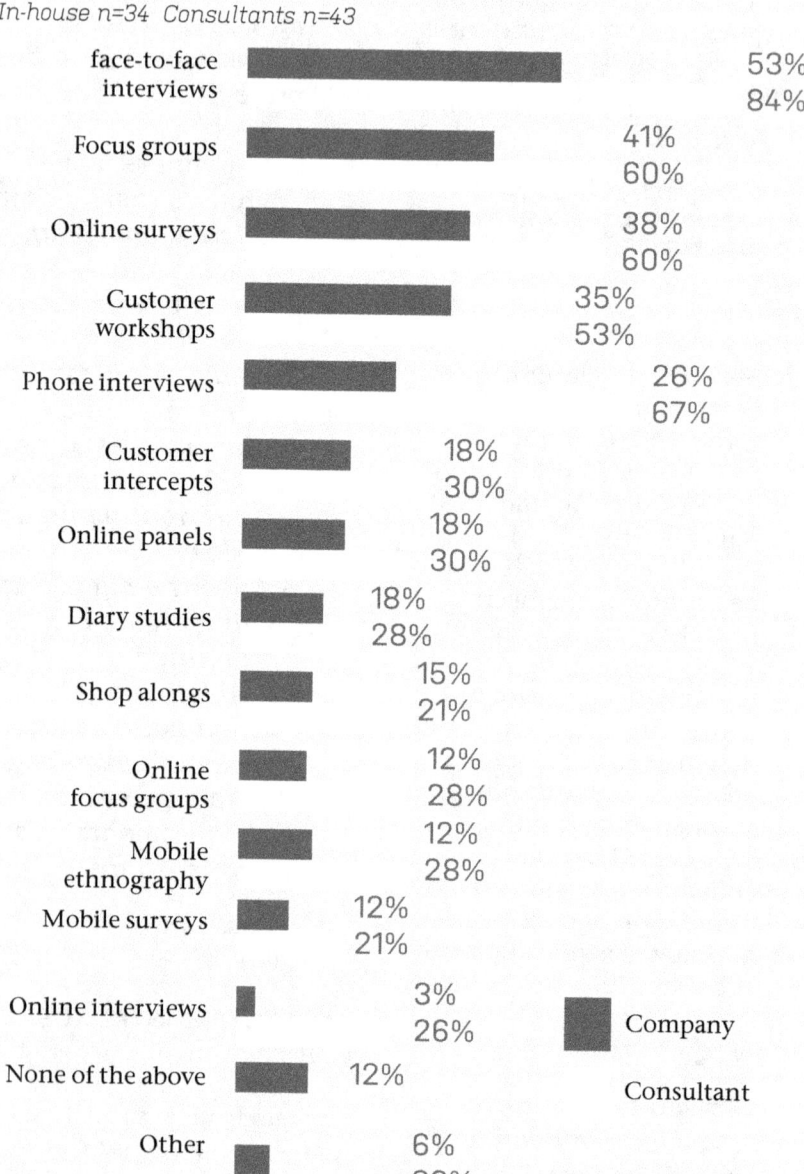

four conditions to exist.
1. Openness Sharing ideas, experiences and perspectives
2. Peering people are free to share and build on each other's ideas freely.
3. Sharing knowledge, experiences ideas.
4. Acting globally

CROSS POLLINATION
Use cross-disciplinary teams. Share ideas and observations with people outside your organization. Travel can help your design team get exposed to new ways of looking at a problem. Talk to people in different industries.

CROSS-DISCIPLINARY COLLABORATION
Depending on the design challenge, design teams can engage anthropologists, engineers, educators, doctors, lawyers, scientists, etc. in the innovative problem-solving process.

Design Thinking draws on the creative and analytical talents of the design team to reframe the design problem as needed. Design Thinking combines the wisdom and skills of many disciplines working in close and flexible collaboration. Each team member requires disciplinary empathy allowing them to work collaboratively with other discipline members.

EVERYONE CONTRIBUTES
The Design Thinking process involves many stakeholders in working together to find a balanced design solution. The designer is a member of the orchestra. The customer is involved throughout the design process and works with the design team to communicate their needs and desires and to help generate design solutions that are relevant to them.

The process is one of co-creation and the designer is a listener and a facilitator. Everyone adds value to the design. Design thinking is not just for professional designers. Everyone can contribute. Many schools are now teaching Design Thinking to children as an approach that can be applied to life.

Organizations that focus on journey optimization perform dramatically better than those that do not
- *10 to 15% Greater revenue growth*
- *15 to 20% Lower cost to serve*
- *20% Greater customer satisfaction*
- *20 to 30% More engaged employees"*
-

Source: McKinsey

03
DESIGN SPRINTS

GOOGLE SPRINT

THE COMPANY
Industry
- Internet
- Software
- Computer hardware

Founded
September 4, 1998
Menlo Park, California, U.S.

Founders
Larry Page
Sergey Brin

Headquarters
Googleplex, Mountain View, California, U.S.

Key people
Sundar Pichai (CEO)
Ruth Porat (CFO)

Revenue
89.46 billion USD
December 31, 2016

Number of employees
73,992 (2017)

Parent
Alphabet Inc. (2015–present)

Source: Wikipedia

WHAT IS A GOOGLE SPRINT?

A design sprint is a five-phase framework based on design thinking that helps answer critical business questions through rapid prototyping and user testing. Sprints let your team reach clearly defined goals and deliverables and gain key learnings, quickly. The process helps spark innovation, encourage user-centered thinking, align your team under a shared vision, and get you to product launch faster.

Source: Adapted from Google design sprint kit

WHO INVENTED THE GOOGLE SPRINT?

> *The Google design sprint framework was created in 2010. Over the years, working alongside Google Ventures, we've studied and tested 300 different business strategy, design thinking, and user research methods from places like IDEO and Stanford d.school. We*

DESIGN SPRINTS 95

took the most effective ones and evolved them, arranging them into a framework that supports both divergent thinking (creative brainstorming that results in multiple possible solutions) and convergent thinking (using defined, logical steps to arrive at one solution). The methodology has evolved over time and continues to be refined and tested."

THE PROCESS

UNDERSTAND
1. Who are the users?
2. What are their needs?
3. What is the context?
4. Competitor review.
5. Formulate strategy.
6. invite stakeholders to share: business goals, technology capability, and user need. The goal of this stage is to expand the understanding of the product/project.

DIVERGE
1. Envision
2. Develop lots of solutions.
3. Ideate
4. Anything is possible. Participants in the Design Sprint should explore all possible solutions to their user's problems.

DECIDE
1. Choose the best idea.
2. Storyboard the idea.
3. Review all ideas and vote for the best options

PROTOTYPE
1. Build something quick and dirty to show the users.
2. Focus on usability not making it beautiful.
3. Prototype and test without investing a lot of time, money, or resources.

VALIDATE
1. Show the prototype to real users outside the organization.
2. Learn what doesn't work.

WHEN TO USE IT
1. You can use it at the beginning of a project to define what your product is offering, or to create a shared vision;
2. When you are stuck and not making progress.
3. To speed up the design development process.

BENEFITS OF RUNNING A DESIGN SPRINT
1. It is fast.
2. User validation.
3. It is agile.
4. Collaboration tool.

1. WRITE A SPRINT BRIEF
What are the
1. Deliverables
2. Resources
3. Logistics
4. Timeline?

THE SPRINT CHALLENGE:
Validate the challenge with managers. Common challenges are to redesign something, to explore something to improve something.

2. DO RESEARCH
Audit existing research. Review the gaps. Fill the gaps with new research.
Types of Research:
1. Participant Observation
2. User Interviews
3. Surveys
4. Diary Study

3. ASSEMBLE YOUR TEAM
A cross-functional team. The ideal working size is 5-7 people per team. If you have a larger group you can break up into smaller sub-groups.

The team usually include a UX designer, a User Researcher, a Product Manager, an Engineer and or a UX writer. Ideally you would also have any key leadership who have the ability to reject the outcomes of the sprint.

Roles
Sprinters Knowledge Experts
User Research Participants Sprint Master Stakeholder

4. LIGHTNING TALKS
Invite team members and external stakeholders and experts to be speakers. Having key team members hold lightning talks Include the users.

5. CREATE A DECK

6. FIND THE SPACE

7. GET SUPPLIES
1. Sharpies
2. Post-it-notes
3. Paper
4. Tape
5. Scissors
6. 2 Large whiteboards
7. White-board markers

8. CHOOSE AN ICE BREAKER

9. SET THE STAGE
Lay out the ground rules and schedule.

GROUND RULES:
1. Ask for people's full attention
2. Laptops closed until they are needed
3. Mobile phones away

SPRINT BRIEF
1. What is the sprint challenge?
2. Something real
3. Something that there is a defined need for
4. Something inspiring.
5. Something clear and concise
6. Includes a time frame.

DELIVERABLES:
1. List the deliverables

LOGISTICS
1. Who?
2. When?
3. Where?
4. Who is the Sprint Master?

GOOGLE SPRINT SCHEDULE-3 DAYS

DAY 1
9:00　　Arrival and registration
9:30　　Introductions
- Overview of Sprint and rules (5 min)
- Ice Breaker/Meet the team (15 min)
- Introduce the Challenge (3 min)
- Directions for HMW's (2 min)

10:00　　Understand: Lightning Talks
Business Perspective - Voice of the User -
User Journeys and Pain Points
Design Evolution/Product
Audit Competitive Landscape
Technological Opportunities
11:30　　HMW's and Affinity Mapping
12:30　　Lunch
13:30　　Review existing User Journey Map out an improved journey Success Metrics
14:30　　Comparable Problem in Parallel Space
15:00　　Boot up
Crazy 8's Sketching
16:00　　Solution Sketch
17:00　　End of day Team check-in

DAY 2
9:30　　Open with a Daily Inspiration & Recap of Day 1
Present Solution Sketches
Assumptions & Sprint Questions
Vote and decide on what to Prototype
11:00　　Begin Storyboarding
12:30　　Lunch
13:30　　Finish Storyboard
14:00　　Assign tasks & Start Prototyping
17:00　　End of day check-in

DAY 3
9:30　　Opening with Recap of Day 2
Finish Prototype
Prepare script for user sessions
12:15　　Lunch
13:00　　User testing session 1/2
13:45　　Debrief
14:00　　User testing session 3/4
14:45　　Debrief
15:00　　User testing session 4/5
16:00　　Debrief & Share back with the team
17:00　　End of Sprint

Source: Adapted from Google design sprint kit. https://designsprintkit. INithgcogle.com'planning/

DESIGN AND ARCHITECTURAL CHARRETTES

WHAT
A design charrette is a collaborative design workshop usually held over one day or several days. Charrettes are a fast way of generating ideas while involving diverse stakeholders in your decision process. Charrettes have many different structures and often involve multiple sessions. The group divides into smaller groups. The smaller groups present to the larger group worked together to complete or improve these projects. The meaning of the word has evolved to imply a collection of ideas or a session of intense brainstorming. An intensely focused activity intended to build consensus among participants, develop specific design goals and solutions for a project, and motivate participants and stakeholders to be committed to reaching those goals. Participants represent all those who can influence the project design decisions."

Source: A Handbook for Planning And Conducting Charrettes for High-Performance Projects August 2003 • NREL/BK-710-33425 Gail Lindsey, FAIA Design Harmony, Inc. Joel Ann Todd Environmental Consultant Sheila J. Hayter National Renewable Energy Laboratory.

WHO INVENTED IT?
The French word, "charrette" spelled with two r's means "cart" This use of the term is said to originate from the Ecole des Beaux Arts in Paris during the 19th century, where a cart, collected final drawings while students finished their work.

> *During the 19th century, students of l'Ecole des Beaux Arts in Paris would ride in the cart sent to retrieve their final art and architecture projects. While en route to the school in the cart, students frantically*

WHY
1. Fast and inexpensive.
2. Increased probability of implementation.
3. Stakeholders can share information.
4. Promotes trust.
5. Charrettes can save time and

DESIGN SPRINTS

money and improve project performance.
6. Provide a voice for diverse stakeholders.
7. Begin planning the project.
8. Motivate participants.
9. identify key short-, mid-, and long-term priority goals.
10. Save time and money by soliciting ideas, issues, and concerns for the project design to help avoid later iterative redesign activities.
11. Establish a multidisciplinary team that ca set and agree on common project goals.
12. Develop early consensus on project design priorities.
13. Provide early understanding of the potential impact of various design strategies.
14. Identify project strategies to explore with their associated costs, time considerations, and needed expertise to eliminate costly "surprises" later in the design and construction processes.
15. Identify partners that can provide expertise.
16. Set a project schedule and budget that all team members feel comfortable following.

Source: A Handbook for Planning And Conducting Charrettes for High-Performance Projects August 2003 • NREL/ BK-710-33425 Gail Lindsey, FAIA Design Harmony, Inc. Joel Ann Todd Environmental Consultant Sheila J. Hayter National Renewable Energy Laboratory.

HOW
1. Definition of the problems.
2. Analysis of the problem
3. Alternative possible solutions.
4. Small groups to clarify issues.
5. Research
6. Concepts for alternative solutions.
7. Presentation and analysis of final proposal.
8. Discussion and consensus.

CHALLENGES
1. Managing workflow can be challenging.
2. Stakeholders may have conflicting visions.

WHEN
1. Define intent
2. Know context and user
3. Frame insights
4. Explore concepts
5. Make Plans

RESOURCES
Large space
Tables
Chairs
White-boards
Dry-erase markers
Camera
Post-it-notes

1.5 DAY MINI-CHARRETTE
HOW DAY 1
1. Evening mixer night before event.
2. Breakfast 30-minutes.
3. Moderator introduces participants expectations and goals.
4. Overview of project 30 mins
5. Break 15 minutes
6. Individual presenters present

information about aspects of project 1 hour
7. Lunch 1 hour
8. Further presentations related to aspects of project 1 hour
9. Question and answer session 15 minutes
10. Multidisciplinary breakout groups 2.5 hours
11. Group size preferred 4 to 8 participants.
12. Groups explore strategies and issues.
13. Groups present strategies and goals to larger group 30-minutes. Larger group brainstorms goals.
14. Site tour 1 hour - for urban or architectural projects.

DAY 2
1. Breakfast 30-minutes
2. Review of Day 1, 30-minutes.
3. Breakout groups explore concept solutions as sketches 2.5 hours.
4. Groups present to larger group 30-minutes.
5. Larger group brainstorms next steps 30-minutes
6. Lunch 1 hour

2.0 DAY DESIGN CHARRETTE

HOW
DAY 1
1. Evening mixer night before event.
2. Breakfast 30-minutes.
3. Moderator introduces participants expectations and goals.
4. Overview of project 30 mins
5. Break 15 minutes

6. Individual presenters present information about aspects of project 1 hour
7. Lunch 1 hour
8. Further presentations related to aspects of project 1 hour
9. Question and answer session 15 minutes
10. Multidisciplinary breakout groups 2.5 hours
11. Group size preferred 4 to 8 participants.
12. Groups explore strategies and issues.
13. Groups present strategies and goals to larger group 30-minutes. Larger group brainstorms goals.
14. Site tour 1 hour - for urban or architectural projects.

DAY 2
1. Breakfast 30-minutes
2. Review of Day 1, 30-minutes.
3. Breakout groups explore concept solutions as sketches 2.5 hours.
4. Groups present to larger group 30-minutes.
5. Lunch 1 hour
6. Breakout groups refine concept solutions as sketches 2.5 hours.
7. Groups present to larger group 30-minutes.
8. Wrap up and next steps 30-minutes

4.0 DAY ARCHITECTURAL CHARRETTE

HOW
1. Define problem
2. Public meeting Vision
3. Brief group

4. Alternative concepts generated
5. Small groups work
6. Small groups present.
7. Whole group discussion
8. Public meeting input
9. Preferred concepts developed
10. Small groups work
11. Small groups present.
12. Whole group discussion
13. Open house review
14. Small groups work
15. Small groups present.
16. Whole group discussion
17. Further plan development.
18. Public meeting confirmation of final design.

0.5 DAY PRODUCT CHARRETTE
HOW
1. Choose a problem to focus on.
2. Select moderator.
3. Select and invite participants.
4. Team size of 4 to 20 participants preferred representing users, managers, design and diverse group of stakeholders.
5. Break down teams over 8 into smaller groups of 4 or 5 participants.
6. Brief participants in advance by e-mail.
7. Allow one hour per problem
8. Use creative space such as a room with a large table and whiteboard.
9. Brief participants allow 15 minutes to one hour for individual concept exploration.
10. Give participants a goal such as 5 concepts.
11. Output can be sketches or simple models using materials such as cardboard or toy construction kits.
12. Each individual presents their concepts to the group.
13. In larger groups each group of 4 can select 3 favored ideas in smaller group to present to larger group. Each smaller group selects a presenter.
14. Moderator and group can evaluate the concepts using a list of heuristics.
15. Put all the sketches or post-it-notes on a wall.
16. Group concepts into categories of related ideas.
17. Dot vote each category to determine best ideas to carry forward.
18. Do another round of sketching focusing of 3 best ideas.
19. Iterate this process as many times as necessary.
20. Record session with digital images.
21. Smaller group can take preferred ideas and develop them after the session.

0.5 DAY UX CHARRETTE
HOW
1. Choose a problem to focus on.
2. Select moderator.
3. Select and invite participants.
4. Team size of 4 to 20 participants preferred representing users,

managers, design and diverse group of stakeholders.
5. Break down teams over 8 into smaller groups of 4 or 5 participants.
6. Brief participants in advance by email.
7. Allow one hour per problem
8. Use creative space such as a room with a large table and whiteboard.
9. Brief participants allow 15 minutes to one hour for individual concept exploration.
10. Give participants a goal such as 5 concepts.
11. Output can be wireframes or storyboards.
12. Each individual presents their concepts to the group.
13. Moderator and group can evaluate the concepts using a list of heuristics.
14. Put all the sketches or post-it notes on a wall.
15. Group concepts into categories of related ideas.
16. Dot vote each category to determine best ideas to carry forward.
17. Do another round of sketching focusing of 3 best ideas.
18. Iterate this process as many times as necessary.
19. Record session with digital images.
20. Smaller group can take preferred ideas and develop them after the session.

> *As you navigate through the rest of your life, be open to collaboration. Other people and other people's ideas are often better than your own. Find a group of people who challenge and inspire you, spend a lot of time with them, and it will change your life."*

Amy Poehler

> *Good design begins with honesty, asks tough questions, comes from collaboration and from trusting your intuition."*

Freeman Thomas

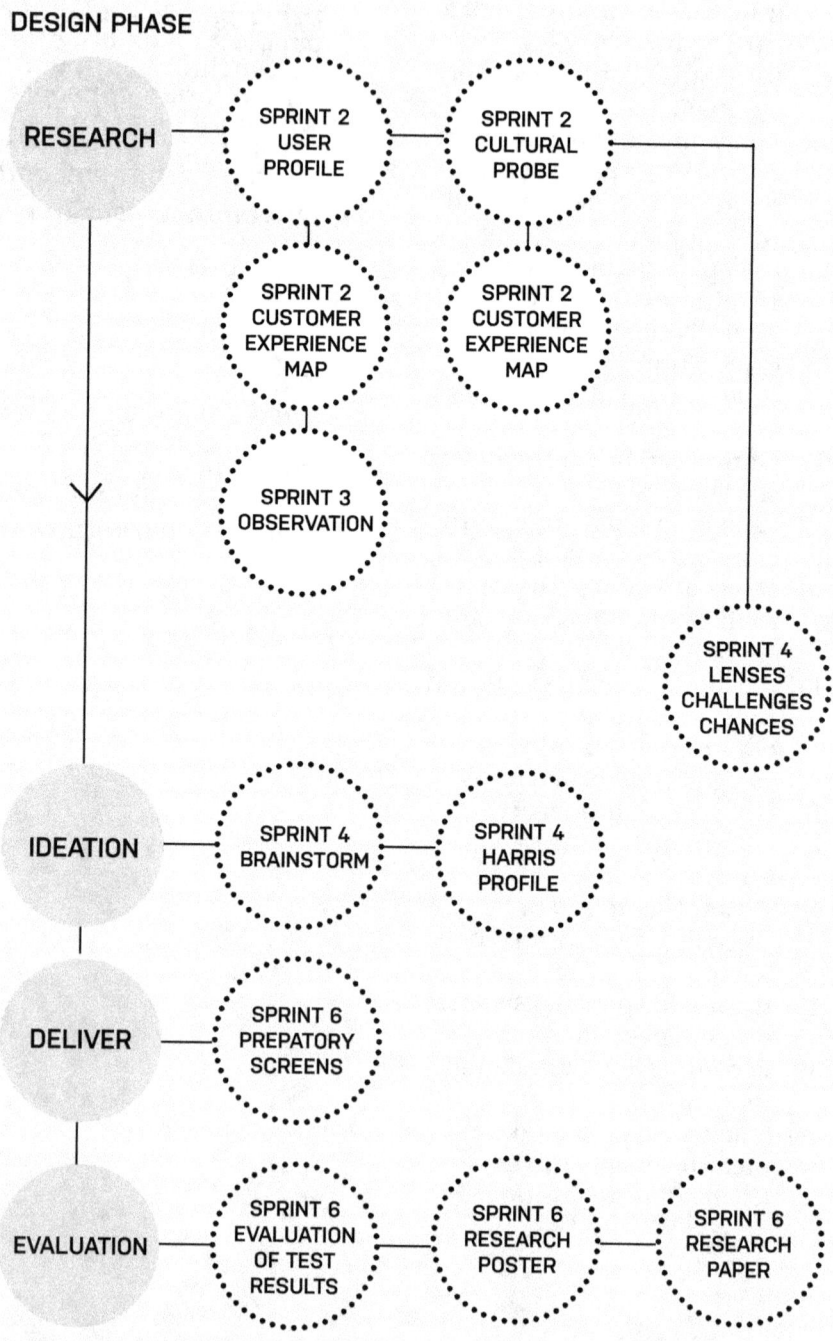

DESIGN SPRINTS

04
THE DESIGN PROCESS

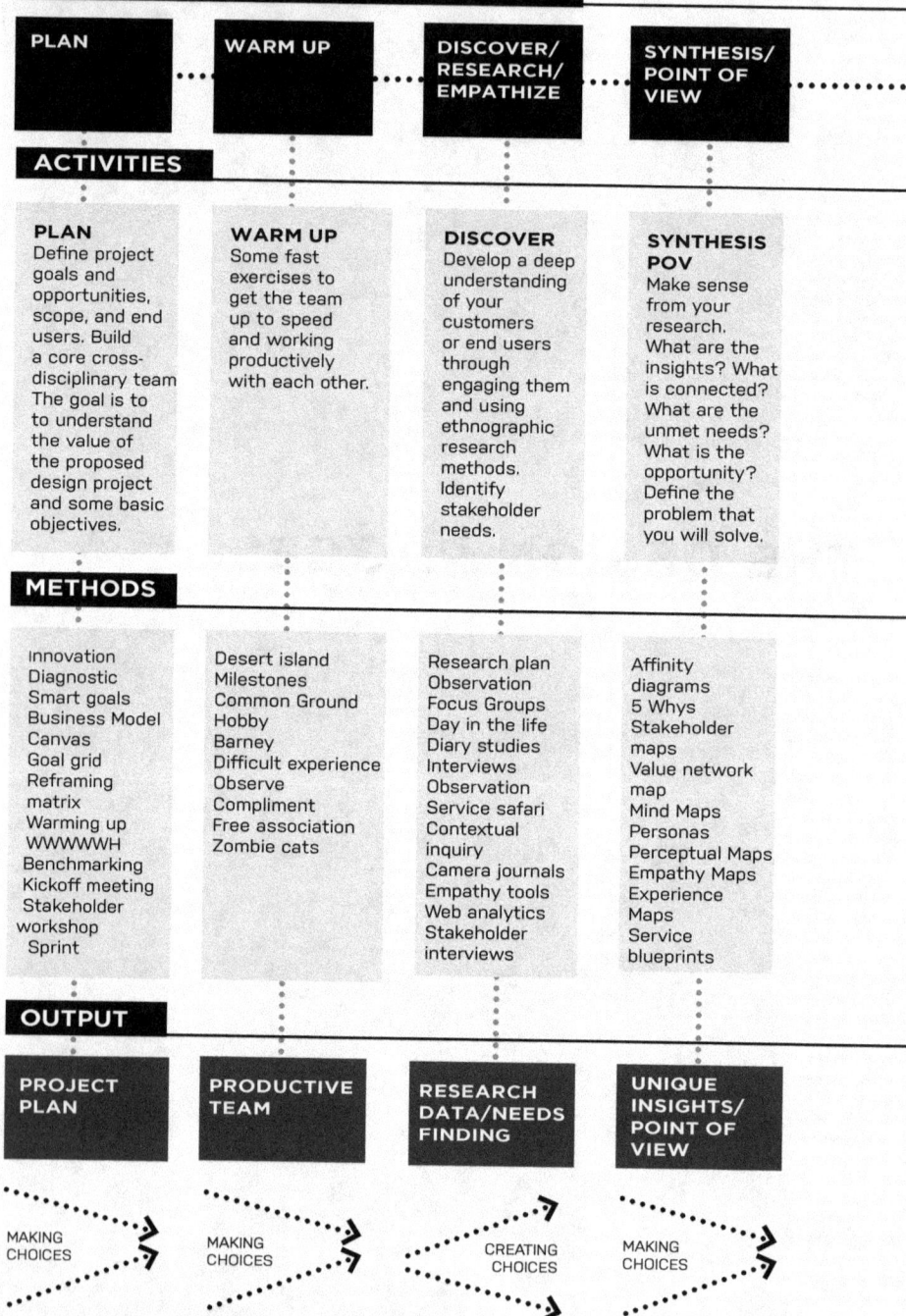

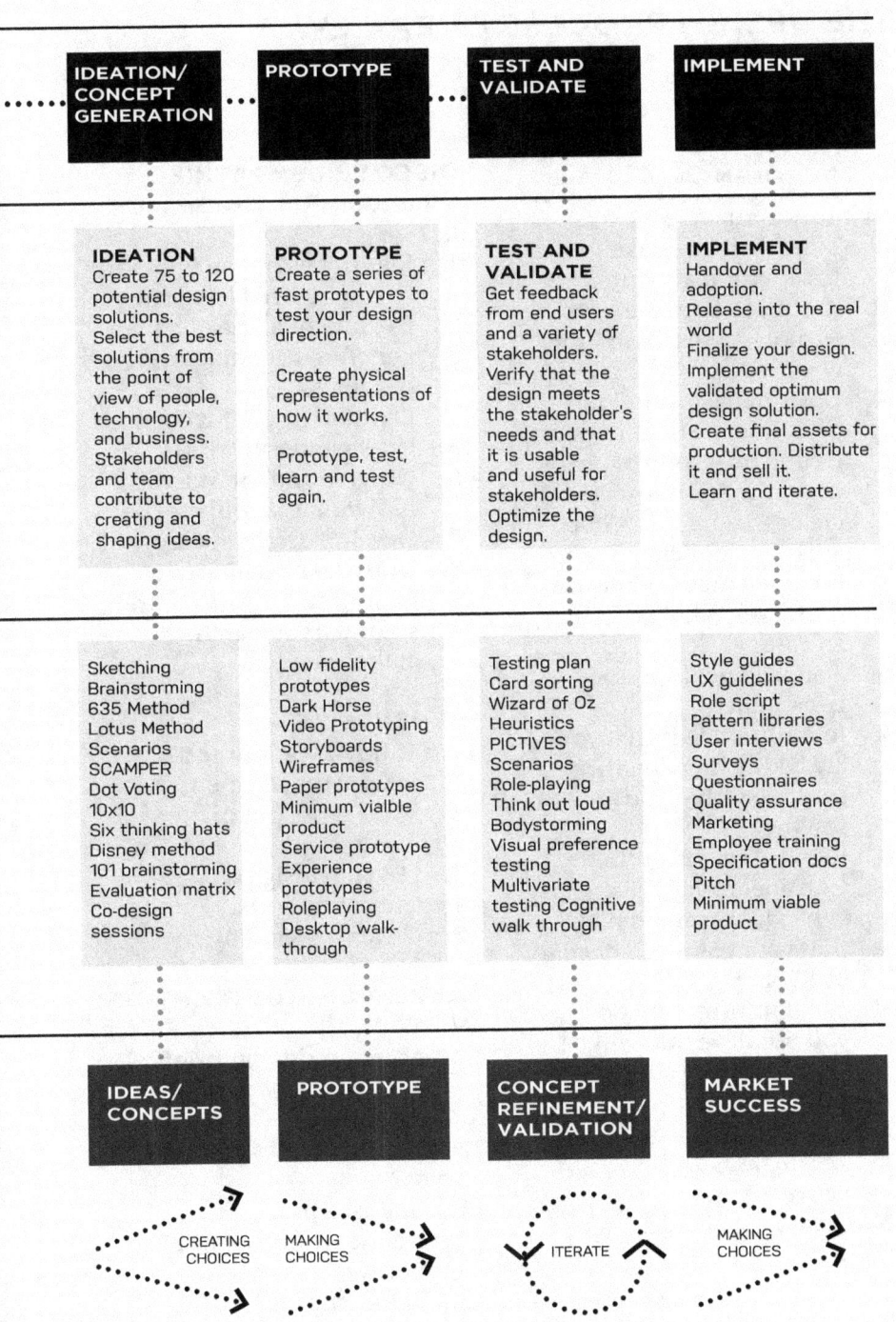

THE DESIGN PROCESS OVERVIEW

PLANNING
What are our goals?
1. Meet with key stakeholders to set vision and intent.
2. Assemble a diverse team
3. Explore scenarios of user experience.
4. Document stakeholders performance requirements
5. Define the group of people or user segment that you are designing for. What are their gender, age, and income range? Where do they live? What is their culture?
6. Define your scope and constraints
7. Identify a needs that you are addressing. Identify a problem that you are solving.
8. Identify opportunities.
9. Consider project risks
10. What are the main hurdles that your team will need to overcome?
11. What information do you not have that will be necessary for a successful design?
12. Create a budget and plan.
13. Create tasks and deliverables.
14. Create a schedule.

DISCOVER EMPATHIZE
What does the research tell us?
1. Identify what you know and what you need to know.
2. Document a research plan
3. Benchmark competitive products.
4. Explore the context of use
5. Understand the risks.
6. Observe and interview individuals, groups, experts.
7. Develop design strategy.
8. Undertake qualitative, quantitative, primary and secondary research.
9. Talk to vendors.

SYNTHESIZE
What have we learned?
1. Review the research.
2. Make sense out of the research.
3. Develop insights.
4. Cluster insights.
5. Create a hierarchy.

HAVE A UNIQUE POINT OF VIEW
What is the design brief?

IDEATE
How is this for as a starting point?
1. Brainstorm
2. Define the most promising ideas.
3. Refine the ideas.
4. Establish key differentiation of your ideas.

5. Investigate existing intellectual property.

PROTOTYPE TEST ITERATE
How could we make it better?
1. Make your favored ideas tangible.
2. Create low-fidelity prototypes from inexpensive available materials.
3. Develop question guides.
4. Develop test plan.

Test prototypes with stakeholders.

5. Get feedback from people.
6. Refine the prototypes.
7. Test again.
8. Build in the feedback.
9. Refine again.
10. Continue iteration until design works.
11. When you are confident that your idea works make a prototype that looks and works like a production product.

IMPLEMENT AND DELIVER
Let's make it. Let's sell it.
1. Create your proposed production design.
2. Test and evaluate.
3. Review objectives.
4. Manufacture your first samples.
5. Review first production samples and refine.
6. Launch.
7. Obtain user feedback.
8. Conduct field studies.
9. Define the vision for the next product or service.

> *We struggle with the right words to describe the design process at Apple. But it is very much about designing and prototyping and making."*

> *"Deep in the culture of Apple is this sense and understanding of design, developing, and making. Form and the material and process - they are beautifully intertwined - completely connected."*

> *"A small change at the beginning of the design process defines an entirely different product at the end."*

> *"We shouldn't be afraid to fail- if we are not failing we are not pushing. 80% of the stuff in the studio is not going to work. If something is not good enough, stop doing it."*

> *"There are 9 rejected ideas for every idea that works."*

Quotes from
Jonathan Ive
Apple

THE DESIGN PROCESS IN DETAIL

THE PLANNING PHASE

WHAT

One of the most critical factors for project's success is having a good project plan. The plan is a roadmap for the project. The project plan is created by the project manager and team through a process of discussion with stakeholders. Good planning is most important when the task is complex.

HOW TO PLAN A DESIGN PROJECT

1. Study the project assignment carefully.
2. Think about what your final result will look like. Will it be a physical product or a digital one? Will it involve a service?
3. Select your team.
4. Define a project space.
5. Define team roles and responsibilities.
6. Develop project vision and strategy
7. Determine the activities
8. How team makes decisions
9. Develop team communication plan.
10. Develop a scope statement.
11. Plan the activities in time.
12. Identify important milestones
13. Determine and identify interdependencies between your activities
14. Develop the schedule and cost estimates.
15. Create management plan.
16. Analyze project risks.
17. Develop reporting plan.
18. Plan how project information will be stored and how different stakeholders can access it.

SMART GOALS

1. **SPECIFIC.** The desired results should be explicitly formulated and not too general.

2. **MEASURABLE.** The results should be formulated in a way that it is possible to measure whether they have been completed. 'I will produce minimal 5 ideas' instead of 'I will produce several ideas'

3. **ACCEPTABLE.** Be sure that there is a consensus (among the members of your team or with your tutor) on what the results entail or try to accomplish.

4. **REALISTIC.** Results should be feasible; they can be completed in the scope of the project.

5. **TIME.** When will the results be completed?

SERVICE PLANNING & STRATEGY

HOW CUSTOMERS SELECT A SERVICE PROVIDER
1. Price
2. Availability
3. Speed
4. Convenience
5. Dependability
6. Personalization
7. Quality
8. Reputation
9. Safety

GUIDELINES FOR SUCCESSFUL SERVICE DESIGN
1. Define the service package in detail
2. Focus on customer's perspective (expectation and perception)
3. Recognize that designer's perspective is different from the customer's perspective
4. Define quality for tangible and intangible elements.
5. Make sure that recruitment, training, and rewards are consistent with service expectations
6. Establish procedures to handle exceptions
7. Establish systems to monitor service.

SERVICE STRATEGY DIFFERENTIATION
Differentiation in service means being unique in brand image, technology use, features, or reputation for customer service.
1. Making the intangible tangible.
2. Customizing the standard product.
3. Reducing perceived risk
4. Giving attention to personnel training.
5. Controlling quality.

SERVICE STRATEGY FOCUS
Cost and differentiation for a particular target market, not the entire market.
1. Buyer Group
2. Service Offered
3. Geographic Region

SERVICE PACKAGE
1. Spaces
2. Physical evidence
3. Websites
4. Channels
5. Touchpoints
6. Backstage interactions
7. Frontstage interactions
8. Support processes
9. Information
10. Training

Source: NKFUST

WARMING UP

WHAT

A warming up exercise is a short exercise at the beginning of a design project that helps the design team work productively together as quickly as possible. The duration of an icebreaker is usually less than 30-minutes.

They are an important component of collaborative or team-based design. The service design approach recognizes the value of designers working productively as members of a diverse cross-disciplinary team with managers, engineers, marketers and other professionals.

There are many types of warming up exercises. On following pages are some exercises that have been used for design teams. Select an exercise that suits the culture of your group.

RESOURCES
White-board
Dry erase markers
Large table
Chairs
Post-it-notes
A comfortable space
Digital camera

TIME ESTIMATE 10-15 MINUTES

POINTS TO CONSIDER
1. Be aware of time constraints.
2. Should limit the time to 15 to 30-minutes
3. Make it simple
4. It should be fun
5. You should be creative
6. Be enthusiastic
7. If something isn't working, move on.
8. Consider your audience
9. Chairs can be arranged in a circle to help participants read body language.
10. Select exercises appropriate for your group.

WHY DO WARMING UP EXERCISES?
When a designer works with others in a new team it is important that the group works as quickly as possible in a creative constructive dialogue. An icebreaker is a way for team members to quickly start working effectively together. Icebreakers help start people thinking creatively, exchanging ideas and help make a team work effectively.

WHEN TO DO WARMING UP EXERCISES
1. When team members do not know each other
2. When team members come from different cultures
3. When team needs to bond quickly
4. When team needs to work to a common goal quickly
5. When the discussion is new or unfamiliar
6. When the moderator needs to know the participants

DISCOVERY PHASE

WHAT

Before you start designing you need to understand whether various stakeholders feelings, thoughts, and attitudes and whether other similar designs already exist.

Studies show that greatest single reason for the failure of new services is a lack of empathy within the design team of the perspectives of the stakeholders. Over 75% of new product initiatives fail in the market and lack of empathy is the number one reason that they fail so this stage will significantly improve the return on investment of your project if done diligently.

During this phase we investigate our users unmet needs and develop a deep understanding understand the way they think, what they feel, the behaviors they engage in and the values they hold through engaging them observing and listening to them explain their point of view, their problems, and their underlying needs.

In order to create a design effectively, we need to understand the context that surrounds the end users. We use a variety of research techniques to investigate the user needs and the design context.

By the end of this phase, we will have an overview of user needs, existing services, and their effectiveness and have a foundation to explore many possible design directions. We will investigate the business requirements of the design. We explore user unmet needs through.

1. Workshops
2. Interviews
3. Observation
4. Focus groups
5. Affinity diagrams
6. Discovery methods

DISCOVER

1. Who your users are.
2. Your users' needs and how you're not meeting them.
3. The people you need on your team.
4. What the stakeholder journey or experience looks like.

> **"**
> *When you talk, you are only repeating what you know, but when you listen then you learn something new."*
>
> Dalai Lama

HOW?
1. Develop empathy for your stakeholders.
2. Develop and implement a research plan.
3. Assume a beginner's mindset.
4. Carry out user research
5. Imagine yourself in that person's situation.
6. Adopt a beginner's way of thinking. Withhold judgment and preconceived bias.
7. Identify gaps in knowledge.
8. Set aside your beliefs, concerns and personal agenda and try to see things from the stakeholders' points point of view.
9. Question everything. Be curious.
10. Listen.
11. Talk to users to uncover underlying needs.
12. Immerse yourself in your customer's reality.
13. Walk in your user's shoes.
14. Look for your end user's workarounds for their problems.
15. Learn what the stakeholder would do.
16. Immerse yourself in the problem. Walk in your user's shoes, observe what's not being said.
17. Capture your learnings.

OUTPUTS
Outputs of this phase could include:
1. A list of user needs
2. A list of user unmet needs
3. A hierarchy of user needs
4. A plan for the resources required to complete the project.
5. the ability to scope and plan an alpha
6. a decision to progress to next phase
7. Perhaps a low fidelity prototype or several low fidelity prototypes.
8. Four to six personas is an optimum number to cover an organization's customer segments.
9. A list of the most important stakeholders both internally in your organization and externally.
10. A benchmarking of existing or competitive services and a SWOT analysis of these services.
11. A definition of the target audience.

Adapted from Discovery phase Government Service Design Manual, https://www.govuk/service-manual/phases/discovery (accessed July 06, 2016).

THE DISCOVERY PROCESS

ASSEMBLE YOUR TEAM
You will need different skills and the team roles and team size may evolve during the different development phases.

Select a diverse cross-disciplinary group of people. Have different disciplines, different genders, ages, cultures, represented for the most successful results. Have some T shaped people. These are people who have more than one area of experience or training such as design and management. They will help your team collaborate productively.

MULTIDISCIPLINARY TEAM
A multidisciplinary team helps you to:
1. Build your service
2. Keep improving it based on user needs
3. Make decisions quickly

SOME TEAM SKILLS
1. Analyze user needs, including accessibility and assisted digital needs, and turn these into user stories
2. Create user stories and prioritize them
3. Manage and report to stakeholders and manage dependencies on other teams
4. Procure services from third parties, if needed
5. Test with real users
6. Find ways of accrediting and handling data

DEFINE YOUR TARGET AUDIENCE
Creating a projected user models will keep the development team rooted to realistic user requirements and minimizes user frustration with the real product. Having a deep understanding of users can help development team better understand the wants & needs of the targeted customers. This will help the development team relate better to the target user. Understanding user tasks helps in developing design solutions that will ensure that the user expectations are met & avoid design errors and customer frustration. Use research methods such as interviewing, observation, empathy maps and user experience maps to better understand your audience. Market segmentation is basically the division of market into smaller segments. It helps identify potential customers and target them.

TYPES OF SEGMENTATION
1. Behavior segmentation.
2. Benefit segmentation.
3. Psychographic segmentation.
4. Geographic segmentation.
5. Demographic segmentation.

SEGMENTATION QUESTIONS
1. What is your target group's goals emotions, experiences, needs and desires?
2. Information collected from just a few people is unlikely to be representative of the whole range of users.
3. What are the user tasks and activities?
4. How will the user use the product or service to perform a task?
5. What is the context of the user?
6. Where are they? What surrounds them physically and virtually or culturally?
7. How large is your user group?

When defining your target audience consider:
1. Age

2. Gender
3. Occupation
4. Industry
5. Travel
6. Citizenship status
7. Marital state
8. Income
9. Culture
10. Language
11. Religion
12. Location
13. Education
14. Nationality
15. Mobility
16. Migration
17. Mental state
18. Abilities
19. Disabilities
20. Health

SHARE WHAT YOU KNOW
1. In the project kick-off meeting ask every team member to introduce themselves and to describe in 3 minutes what experience they have that may be relevant to the project.
2. The moderator can list areas of knowledge on a whiteboard.

IDENTIFY WHAT YOU NEED TO KNOW
Arrange a project kick-off meeting. Invite your team and important stakeholders. On a whiteboard or flip chart create two lists. Ask each person to introduce themselves and describe what they know or have experienced that may be useful for implementing the project. Brainstorm with your group the areas that are unknown and how that information may be obtained. Formulate a research plan and assign responsibilities, tasks, and deliverables with dates.

UNCOVER NEEDS
1. "What causes the problem?"
2. "What are the impacts of the problem?"
3. "What are possible solutions?"
4. Probe about workarounds How do people adapt their environment to solve problems that they have?
5. Ask what their single biggest obstacle is to achieve what they are trying to achieve How can you help them?
6. Ask what's changing in their world What are the trends?
7. Observe people
8. Can you see problems they have that they perhaps do not even recognize are problems?
9. Ask other stakeholders

DEFINE YOUR GOALS
A goal is the intent or intents of the design process.

1. Write a detailed description of the design problem.
2. Define a list of needs that are connected to the design problem.
3. Make a list of obstacles that need to be overcome to solve the design problem.
4. Make a list of constraints that apply to the problem.
5. Rewrite the problem statement to articulate the above requirements.

SYNTHESIS PHASE

WHAT

Synthesis is the convergent part of the design process. In this stage, we review the research, make connections, uncover insights, distill the data. We make sense of the information. What are the insights? What is connected? What are the unmet needs and desires of your audience? How can your design be unique, and better than what is already out there?

ACTIONABLE INSIGHTS

Service design provides insights that are based on unrecognized or unmet needs. An insight is a fresh point of view based on a deep understanding of the way of thinking and behavior. An insight occurs by mentally connecting two or more things that have not been connected before. These things may be things that many people have seen or experienced but not connected before. A goal of service design is to build actionable insights

USER NEED OR POV STATEMENT

The user need statement or question is a statement of the desires or needs of end users expressed in their own words.

User Need Statement:
I am a doctor who has a hard time keeping babies warm because I do not have electricity.

POINT OF VIEW STATEMENT

A point-of-view (POV) is reframing of a design challenge into an actionable problem statement. The term Point of View Statement is often used in service design to describe a user need statement. The POV is used as the basis for design ideation. The POV defines the design intent. The POV helps reframe he design problem into an actionable focus for the generation of ideas.

Information Architecture and Design Strategy: The Importance of Synthesis during the Process of Design Jon Kolko, Savannah College of Art and Design.

> **The true Renaissance person is endowed with panoramic attention.... The habit of noticing the ensemble of everything and its constituent parts is a matter of will, not of innate aptitude. It involves the conscious noticing of things and the gaps that separate and connect them."**

Christy Wampole

WHAT IS AN INSIGHT?

WHAT

1. An unrecognized fundamental human truth.
2. A new way of viewing the world that causes us to reexamine existing conventions and challenge the status quo.
3. A penetrating observation about human behavior that results in seeing consumers from a fresh perspective.
4. The act or result of understanding the inner nature of things or of seeing intuitively (called noesis in Greek)
5. A discovery about the underlying motivations that drive people's actions.
6. An understanding of cause and effect based on identification of relationships and behaviors within a model, context, or scenario.
7. The power of acute observation and deduction, discernment, and perception.

YOU HAVE A SIGNIFICANT INSIGHT WHEN

1. It reexamines existing conventions.
2. It solves a real problem.
3. It inspires action.
4. Grounded in real data
5. Simple in language and concept
6. Meaningful and memorable
7. Speaks to your audience
8. Inspires clear, direct action
9. Reinforces ownership and commitment
10.

Source: Michael Morgan Senior User Experience Researcher at ADP Innovation Labs New York

Groups typically perform better on insight problems than individuals. Insights that occur in the field are typically reported to be associated with a sudden "change in understanding" and with "seeing connections and contradictions" in the problem.

Source: Smith, C. M.; Bushouse, E.; Lord, J. "Individual and group performance on insight problems:

ACTIONABLE INSIGHTS

In order to be actionable, as the expression of a consumer truth, an insight should be stated as a sentence, containing:
1. An observation or a wish, e.g. "I would like to ...."
2. A motivation explaining the wish, e.g. " because ..."
3. A barrier preventing the consumer from being satisfied with the fulfillment of his/her motivation, e.g. " but..."

INSIGHTS RECOGNIZE RELATIONSHIPS

1. Connections
2. Tensions
3. Contrasts.
4. Events

5. Failures
6. Cause & Effect
7. Gaps
8. Mismatches
9. Misaligned
10. Frustrations
11. Pain Points
12. Timeliness
13. Outcomes planned and unintended.

ASK THOUGHTFUL QUESTIONS
1. Put oneself in user situations, keep asking "why".
2. Capture the insights on post-its.

LOOK FOR EMERGING PATTERNS
1. Recurring Points or themes; similar situations
2. Experiences
3. Intensity of the experience

UNDERSTAND THE ACTION AND BEHAVIOR
1. Perceive the social context.
2. Sense the motivations.
3. Feel the Emotions.
4. Recognize the relationships.

INSIGHT TOOL SAM/ THINK FEEL DO FRAMEWORK

1. **Social context**
   - Who they do the 'action or activity' with?
   - What is their relationship, social interaction?
   - Why they behave the way they do?
2. **Action or behavior**
   - What is the behavior?
   - What actions or activities they are involved?
   - Why?
3. **Motivations**
   - What do they think?
   - How do they feel?
   - What are the reason(s) for actions and/or behavior?
   - What are the beliefs?
   - What are the values?
   - What is the underlying thinking?
   - What are the aspirations?
   - What are the Emotions or Feelings?

Source: Adapted from Design Thinking Guidebook for Public Sector innovation in Bhutan

THE POINT OF VIEW STATEMENT

WHAT
A Point of View (POV) is an opportunity statement. It condenses the need you have uncovered, description of the user who has this need, the underlying reason for the need and the angle from which you are looking at the problem.

What is a Point of View?
[USER] needs to [USER'S NEED] because [SUPRISING INSIGHT]

WHY
A strong POV will help you in many ways:

1. Stay focused on the problem.
2. Inspire your team.
3. Keep your user in mind
4. Communicate to and get buy-in from others.
5. Keeps the team grounded.
6. Captures the hearts and minds of the stakeholders
7. Fuels brainstorming.
8. Allows team members to determine the relevance of competing ideas.
9. Saves teams from the impossible task of developing concepts trying to be all things to all people.
10. helps to ensure that you are working on something that was actionable, largely applicable, and resonates with potential user base.

HOW
To write a helpful POV, you need a solid description of the user, a clear need, and an insight (something remarkable you have uncovered about why the need is there.

1. Define your audience
2. Define the problem that you will solve
3. Define the need that you will address.
4. Keep in mind that POVs often evolve over time…
5. It is important to keep in mind the perspectives of all key stakeholders.

THE POV SHOULD:
1. Provide focus
2. Frame the problem
3. Provide a reference for evaluating competing ideas
4. Empower and inspire team members
5. Fuel brainstorms and "how might we" statements
6. Be captivating
7. Allow you to revisit and reformulate the POV as you learn by doing.
8. Support innovation

MAKE YOUR OWN POV STATEMENT

END USER [OR STAKEHOLDER]:

....

NEEDS TO:

....

BECAUSE [YOUR INSIGHT]:

....

REFRAMING THE PROBLEM

WHAT
Reframing is to look at, present, or think of (beliefs, ideas, relationships, etc) in a new or different way or from this new perspective. Innovative solutions often involve reframing a problem.

WHO INVENTED IT?
Tudor Rickards 1974 Manchester Business School

WHY
1. To create different perspectives and new ideas.

RESOURCES
1. Pen
2. Paper
3. Whiteboard
4. Dry Erase markers

HOW
Define the problem that you would like to address.

Complete these sentences while considering your problem.
1. There is more than one way of looking at a problem. You could also define this problem in another way as."
2. "The underlying reason for the problem is."
3. "I think that the best solution is."
4. "If I could break all laws of reality I would try to solve it by."
5. "You could compare this problem to the problem of."
6. "Another, different way of thinking about it is"

REFRAMING MATRIX

WHAT
The reframing matrix is a method of approaching a problem by imagining the perspectives of a number of different people and exploring the possible solutions that they might suggest.

WHO INVENTED IT?
Michael Morgan 1993

WHY
This is a method for assisting in empathy which is an important factor in gaining acceptance and creating successful design.

CHALLENGES
The reframing is not done with stakeholders present or in context so may be subjective

HOW
1. Define a problem.
2. On a whiteboard or paper draw a large square and divide it into four quadrants.
3. Select 4 different perspectives to approach the problem. They could be four professions or four people or four other perspectives

REFRAMING MATRIX

PRODUCT	**PLANNING**
1. Is there something wrong with the product or service? 2. Is it priced correctly? 3. How well does it serve the market? 4. Is it reliable?	1. Are our business plans, marketing plans, or strategy at fault? 2. Could we improve these?
POTENTIAL	**PEOPLE**
1. How would we increase sales? 2. If we were to seriously increase our targets or our production volumes, what would happen with this problem?	1. What are the people impacts and people implications of the problem? 2. What do people involved with the problem think? 3. Why are customers not buying the product?

DESIGN PROBLEM ....

....

....

....

....

....

....

....

....

that are important for your problem.
4. With your team brainstorm a number of questions that you believe are important from the perspectives that you have selected.
5. The moderator writes the questions in the relevant quadrants of the matrix.
6. The group discusses each of these questions.
7. The answers are recorded and the perspectives are incorporated into the considerations for design solutions.

"WHAT IF" AND "HOW MIGHT WE" QUESTIONS

WHAT
When you've defined your design challenge in a problem statement or Point Of View, you can ask some "How Might We". questions. The "How Might We" question maintains a level of ambiguity and opens up the exploration space to a range of possibilities.

"How Might We" questions are the best way to open up Brainstorm sessions.

HOW
1. Define your point of view statement before asking how might we questions.
2. Your Point Of View should neither be too narrow so as to make it overly restrictive nor too broad so as to leave you wandering forever in infinite possibilities.
3. Break that larger POV challenge up into smaller actionable questions.
4. Six to twelve "How Might We" questions for one POV is good.
5. Brainstorm the "How might we" questions before the ideation brainstorm.
6. Do your " How Might We" questions allow for a variety of solutions? If not, then broaden them.
7. Aim for a narrow enough frame to let you know where to start your ideation Brainstorm

POINT OF VIEW EXERCISE

BACKGROUND
Developing a Point of View requires you and your team to extract relevant insights from the research that you have collected. You should start by reframing your insights in different ways. The POV should be a meaningful and actionable problem statement. A point-of-view (POV) is your reframing of a design challenge into an actionable problem statement that will launch you into generative ideation. It defines the right challenge to address based on your new empathy with your target audience.

The POV statement is created by making sense of who the users are, what their needs are, and the insights that come from the observations made. 'Needs' should be verbs, and the insight should reflect your clear synthesis of the research material.

A good Point of view is one that:
1. Provides focus and frames the problem.
2. Inspires your team.
3. Takes you somewhere that you haven't been before
4. Helps you see things from the end user's perspective.
5. Focuses on implicit needs rather than explicit problems.
6. Offers criteria for evaluating competing ideas.
7. Empowers your team to make decisions independently, in parallel.
8. Captures the hearts and minds of the people you meet
9. Keeps you awake at night.
10. Saves you from the impossible task of developing concepts that are all things to all people.
11. Is actionable with your available team, time and resources.

STRUCTURE OF A POINT OF VIEW STATEMENT
[End user] needs to [user need] because [insight]

TASK
Create a point of view statement for an end user.

DELIVERABLES
One Point Of View Statement.

GOAL FORMING EXERCISE

INSTRUCTIONS

What are your goals?
Answer the following questions

Specific
What will you design?

Measurable
How will you know when you have the best solution.
How will you measure progress toward your goal?

Attainable
Is your goal a possible to achieve with your time and resources?

Realistic
Is your goal realistic and within your reach? Are you willing to commit to your goal?

Relevant
Is your goal relevant to your long-term needs?

Time
What is your target time-frame to reach the goals?

THE IDEATION PHASE

WHAT

Populate the solution space. Use the diverse perspectives of the team members to create 75 to 120 good design solutions that effectively balance the needs of people, appropriate use of technology and business goals. Keep an open mind until the ideas have been tested and compared. Once you have identified your target audience unmet needs, the starting point of ideation phase is the problem statement.

[CUSTOMER] XXXX [NEEDS] XXXX Because XXXX[INSIGHT]

> *To have a great idea, you have to have lots of ideas."*
>
> Davis Kelley IDEO

Now you can start generating ideas. Find a good space with natural lighting a large table and some whiteboards.

Your most productive creative team is a diverse group of people. Have different genders, cultures, ages, and professions represented. Between four and eight people is the ideal team size for ideation. A larger team becomes harder to manage. Before you start, review the insights and themes from the previous synthesis stage.

Try to generate as many ideas as possible. At first, it is good to explore wild blue sky directions. You can always pull the ideas back to reality and budgets as they are refined. We like to generate around 100 to 120 ideas as a starting point. Then narrow them down to around seven preferred directions by combining and developing the ideas through several stages of iteration.

Physical prototypes and acting out activities will allow you to make intangible ideas tangible so that you can get feedback and discuss alternative concept directions.

Designers use a range of techniques which include sketches, scenarios, video, bodystorming, paper prototypes, wireframes and PICTIVES to explore and create low fidelity prototypes of ideas. In this chapter, we will look at some of the commonly used techniques.

Make sure that you have ample display space. Sheets of foam core board make low-cost pinboards. Put a box of post its and markers in the center of a large table to be shared by the group.

WHY

In this phase, your team moves from identifying unmet needs to exploring possible solutions. You to harness the collective perspectives and strengths of your team to go bravely where no one else has gone before you. This is innovation.

WHY IS INNOVATION NECESSARY?

Innovation is the key element in providing growth, and for increasing bottom-line results.

> *Innovation is: production or adoption, assimilation, and exploitation of a value-added novelty in economic and social spheres; renewal and enlargement of products, services, and markets; development of new methods of production; and establishment of new management systems. It is both a process and an outcome.*
>
> Crossan and Apaydin

HOW

1. Generate ten "what are ways of " questions base on your POV statement. For example "what are ways of giving each train traveler a personal experience?"
2. Defer judgment
3. Encourage wild ideas
4. Build on ideas of others (and not but)
5. Stay focused
6. Be visual
7. One conversation
8. Go for quantity!
9. We need fluency-lots of ideas and flexibility-lots of different ideas.

Use different techniques to generate ideas, not just one. Go through iterative cycles of generating ideas and then voting with your team on the best of the ideas. Then develop more ideas based on the selected ideas. The goal is to select a small set of possible solutions to take into prototyping.

> *Inspiration is for amateurs. The rest just show up and get to work."*
>
> Chuck Close, artist

WHAT IS GOOD DESIGN?

WHAT IS UNIVERSAL DESIGN?

Universal design (UD) is a set of guidelines that aims to produce environments that work well for everyone. The Center for Universal Design at North Carolina State University identified seven principles of universal design

UNIVERSAL DESIGN GUIDELINES

1. The design is equitable in use to people with diverse abilities.
2. The design is flexible enough to allow a wide range of individual preferences and abilities.
3. The use of the design is simple and intuitive, easy to understand regardless of previous experience or skill.
4. The design is perceptible, such that it communicates information effectively to the user.
5. The design is tolerant of error, such that it minimizes adverse consequences
6. if used incorrectly. The design requires low physical effort, allowing use with minimal effort.
7. The design accommodates the size, space, and approach necessary for use.

Source: www.ncsu.edu/ncsu/design/cud/about_ud/udprinciplestext.htm

DIETER RAMS TEN PRINCIPLES OF "GOOD DESIGN"

1. Good design is innovative
2. Good design is useful
3. Good design is aesthetic
4. Good design is understandable
5. Good design is unobtrusive
6. Good design is honest
7. Good design is long-lasting
8. Good design is thorough down to the last detail
9. Good design is environmentally friendly
10. Good design is as little design as possible

Source: http://www.archdaily.com/198583/dieter-rams-10-principles-of-good-design

50 PHRASES THAT WILL PREVENT YOU FROM BEATING YOUR COMPETITORS

1. Our place is different.
2. We tried that before.
3. It costs too much.
4. That is not my job.
5. They're too busy to do that.
6. We don't have the time.
7. Not enough help.
8. It is too radical a change.
9. The staff will never buy it.
10. It is against the company policy.
11. The union will scream.
12. That will run up our overhead.
13. We don't have the authority.

14. Let's get back to reality.
15. That's not our problem.
16. I don't like the idea.
17. I am not saying you are wrong but..
18. You're two years ahead of your time.
19. Now is not the right time.
20. It isn't in the budget.
21. Can't teach an old dog new tricks.
22. Good thought but impractical.
23. Let's give it more thought.
24. We'll be the laughing stock of the industry.
25. Not that again.
26. Where did you dig that one up?
27. We did alright without it before.
28. It's never been tried.
29. Let's put that one on the back burner for now.
30. Let's form a committee.
31. It won't work in our place.
32. The executive committee will never go for it.
33. I don't see the connection.
34. Let's all sleep on it.
35. It can't be done.
36. It's too much trouble to change.
37. It won't pay for itself.
38. It's impossible.
39. I know a person who tried it and got fired.
40. We've always done it this way.
41. We'd lose money in the long run.
42. Don't rock the boat.
43. That's what we can expect from the staff.
44. Has anyone else tried it?
45. Let's look into it further.
46. We'll have to answer to the stockholders.
47. Quit dreaming.
48. If it ain't broke don't fix it.
49. That's too much ivory tower.
50. It's too much work.

Source: Daniel DuFour

BRAINSTORMING

WHAT
Process for generating creative ideas and solutions through intensive group discussion. each participant suggests as many ideas as possible. Criticism of the ideas is allowed only when the brainstorming session is evaluation begins after the session.

WHO INVENTED BRAINSTORMING?
Brainstorming was taught at UCLA in the 1920s. Advertising executive Alex F. Osborn is credited with popularizing brainstorming in the United States. He began developing methods for creative problem-solving in 1939. He was frustrated by employees' inability to develop creative ideas individually for ad campaigns. In response, he began hosting group-thinking sessions and discovered a significant improvement in the quality and quantity of ideas produced by employees. Osborn

outlined his method in the 1948 book "Your Creative Power" in chapter 33, "How to organize a squad to create ideas."

Source: Adapted from Wikipedia.

PREPARING FOR BRAINSTORMING

Come to the brainstorm session prepared.
1. Bring a lot of paper and markers.
2. Pens
3. Post-it-notes
4. Index cards
5. A flip chart
6. White-board or wall
7. Video camera
8. Camera
9. One clear goal per brainstorming session.
10. Determine who will write things down and document the proceedings?
11. Allow one to two hours for a brainstorming session.
12. Recruit good people.
13. 8 to 12 people is a good number
14. Prepare brainstorm questions that you think will help guide the group.

CREATE A STRATEGY
1. What do you want to achieve?
2. What problem do you want to be solved?
3. Define the goal
4. How will you define the problem to the participants?
5. How long will the session be?
6. How many people will be involved?
7. What will be the mix of people?
8. Will there be a follow-up session?
9. Will you send out information before the session?
10. Do the participants have the information that they need?
11. Who should you invite?
12. Assemble a diverse team.
13. Do the participants have the right skills and knowledge for the task?
14. Where will the brainstorm be held?
15. Who owns the intellectual property?
16. Will the session be free of interruptions?
17. How will you record the ideas?
18. What will you do with the information?
19. What brainstorming technique will be used and is it best for your purpose?
20. Be mindful of the scope brainstorm questions. Neither too broad nor too narrow.
21. 45-60-minutes for brainstorm time. Warm up 15-30-minutes.
22. Wrap up 15-30-minutes.

CHOOSING A TECHNIQUE
1. There are many different brainstorming methods.
2. Choose a method that suits your task and participants
3. Try different methods over time to find which ones work best for you.

REFRESHMENTS
1. An army marches on it's stomach
2. Offer tea, coffee water, soda.

FACILITATING
1. The basic brainstorming procedure seems simple enough that anyone could facilitate a

session, but the social dynamics of product groups are both complex and subtle
2. Motivate participants.
3. Understand the issues that affect small group interaction.
4. Keep the focus on the topic.
5. Encourage everyone to contribute.
6. A facilitator also needs to understand how to organize and analyze the data from brainstorming sessions.
7. Review the rules and ask the group to enforce them.
8. Encourage an attitude of shoshin.
9. Ask participants to turn phones off or onto vibrate mode.
10. A facilitator isn't a leader.
11. Do not steer the discussion.
12. Do not let particular people dominate the conversation.
13. Keep the conversations on the topic.
14. Set realistic time limits for each stage and be sure that you keep on time.
15. 5. Have a brainstorm plan and stick to it.
16. The facilitator should create an environment where it is safe to suggest wild ideas.
17. Provide clear directions at the beginning of the meeting.
18. Clearly define the problem to be discussed.
19. Write the problem on the White-board where everyone can see it.
20. Provide next steps at the end of the meeting.
21. Select final ideas by voting.
22. Use your camera or phone to take digital pictures of the idea output at the end of your meeting.
23. Facilitators should avoid inviting someone that is generally feared by the group since this is likely to reduce the quantity of ideas.
24. Facilitators must not let participants belabor their points or start telling long stories. This can reduce the quantity of items and act as an inhibitor since the stories often include some subtle guidance or implied criticism.
25. Good facilitation requires good listening skills.
26. The facilitator should run the White-board, writing down ideas as people come up with them,
27. Prevent people from interrupting others.
28. Invite quieter people to contribute.
29. Hire a facilitator if necessary.
30. Start on time.
31. End on time.
32. Keep things moving .
33. You can filter the best ideas after the session or get the team to vote on their preferred ideas during the session.
34. Listen.
35. Write fast & be visual.
36. Use humor and be playful
37. Thank the group after the session.
38. Provide next steps to the group after the meeting.
39. Keep participants engaged.
40. Encourage interactivity.
41. 100 ideas per hour.
42. Avoid social hierarchy
43. Organize small break-out sessions that cut across traditional office boundaries to establish teams.
44. Encourage passion.
45. Use questioning words such as

"What, What if, Where, Why, When, and How", to develop quality questions.

RULES FOR BRAINSTORMING
1. "Defer judgment Separating idea generation from idea selection strengthens both activities. For now, suspend critique. Know that you'll have plenty of time to evaluate the ideas after the brainstorm.
2. Encourage wild ideas.
3. One conversation at a time Maintain momentum as a group. Save the side conversations for later.
4. Headline Capture the essence quickly ".
5. Focus on quantity, not on quality."

POST-IT VOTING
1. Give every participant 4 stickers and have everyone put stickers next to their favorite ideas.
2. Each person tags 3 favorite ideas.
3. Cluster favorite ideas.
4. Clustering of stickers indicates possible strong design directions.

GROUP REVIEW
Ask everyone to review the boards of ideas, and discuss the specific ideas or directions they like and why.

Source adapted from Hasso Plattner Institute of Design

THE SPACE
1. Select a space not usually used by your team.
2. Refreshments
3. Find a comfortable, quiet room.
4. Comfortable chairs.
5. No interruptions.
6. Turn phones off.
7. Go off-site. A new environment might spur creativity and innovation by providing new stimuli. Helps participants mentally distance themselves from ordinary perceptions and ways of thinking.
8. Location matters.
9. Use big visible materials for writing on.
10. Keep the temperature comfortable Adequate lighting
11. Suitable external noise levels
12. A circular arrangement of seats allows participants to read body language and with no "head of the table."
13. Seats should be not too far apart
14. Select a room with a lot of vertical writing space.

METHODS OF ARRANGING IDEAS
1. 2X2 matrix
2. Clustering
3. Continuum
4. Concentric circles
5. Timeline
6. Pyramid
7. Prioritization
8. Adoption curve

TYPES OF BRAINSTORMING
1. Warm up with wild ideas brainstorm
2. Ideal brainstorm. Imagine your ideal solution if you had the resources.
3. Analogous brainstorm. How do other industries or situations solve this problem? Where else

do we see this problem or need?
4. Hurdles brainstorm. What is standing in the way of solving this problem?
5. Bodystorm. Go to the place your stakeholders are in and act out your users journey with your team members and stakeholders giving feedback to generate ideas.

FOCUS YOUR IDEAS
1. Look for ways to combine ideas.
2. Dot voting. Each team member selects their three favorite ideas.
3. Category voting. choose two ideas from the following.
- The most rational solutions
- The most innovative ideas
- The idea that the stakeholder would prefer.
4. Decision Matrix. Choose criteria to decide what is important.
5. Ask your stakeholders and end users which ideas they prefer.

SOME USEFUL MATERIALS FOR BRAINSTORMING

POST-IT NOTES
I allow at least one block per participant per session.

SHARPIES
A range of different sizes

WHITE-BOARD
A White-board is a good tool as it allows connections to be drawn between groups of post-it notes

DRY ERASE MARKERS
3 or 4 colors

TAPE
One inch masking tape.

CAMERA
A camera with still and video capability. This can be used to record the groups of post-it notes or to create a video of the session for sharing.

FOAM CORE BOARDS
These can be used as an alternative display surface to White-boards and are portable if you are working with a number of groups.

LARGE TABLE
Large enough to seat all the participants.

CHAIRS
For all the participants.

COFFEE AND REFRESHMENTS
People work better with coffee and snacks.

SKETCH	PROTOTYPE
Evocative	Didactic
Suggest	Explore
Question	Answer
Propose	Test
Provoke	Resolve
Tentative	Specific
Noncommittal	Depiction

> *The sketch to prototype continuum. The difference between the two lies in the intent, or purpose they serve. The arrows represent the continuum of sketches developing into prototypes.*

Bill Buxton

INNOVATION IS A NUMBERS GAME

True innovators follow a type of Darwinian process in which they try out many possibilities. Trial and error is essential for innovation.

To develop one successful idea professional designers often ideate more than one hundred and sometimes thousands of concepts.

> *Good ideas come from bad ideas but only if there are enough of them."*

Seth Godin
American author and business executive.

Like everyone else creative geniuses don't really know what they're doing when they embark on a new project. They immerse themselves in many diverse ideas and projects. They are extraordinarily productive.

The quality of creative ideas is a function of quantity: The more ideas creators generate the greater the chance of a successful outcome.

Innovators fail early and often. Indeed, the creative act is often. Creative people learn to see failure as a steppingstone to success.

Source: Adapted from Why Creativity Is a Numbers Game - Scientific American

> *I have not failed; I have just found 10,000 ways that will not work."*
>
> *"Genius is one percent inspiration and ninety percent perspiration."*
>
> *"Opportunity is missed by most people because it is dressed in overalls and looks like work."*
>
> *"The most certain way to succeed is always to try just one more time."*

Thomas A Edison
Developing the light bulb and the electricity service system

> *Out of a hundred ideas, the first sixty ideas produced five that were actually new or different, the next twenty produced nothing but laughter, and ideas eighty to a hundred produced another ten that were amazing. Thankfully, we didn't give up when the well ran dry around idea number sixty."*

Dev Patnaik
The Ebb and Flow of Ideas

EVALUATING AN IDEA
PHYSICAL PRODUCT

GENERAL CRITERIA
1. Is your idea legal
2. What is its environmental impact?
3. Is it safe?
4. Is it high quality?
5. Will it have wide social acceptance?
6. Will it have any negative impact?

INDUSTRY CRITERIA
1. Who is your competition?
2. Does your product require the assistance of existing products?
3. Is there just one product or a line of products?
4. Will pricing be competitive?

MARKETING CRITERIA
1. Does your idea fit into a trend?
2. Is there a need for it?
3. Is it seasonal?
4. Is it a fad, or does it have long-term value?
5. Who will buy it?
6. Does it need instructions?

PRODUCT CRITERIA
1. How much will it cost to get your idea to market?
2. Does it require service or maintenance?
3. Is there a warranty?
4. Does it need packaging?
5. Is it the simplest and most attractive it can be?

Source: https://www.entrepreneur.com/article/81922 Small Business - 21-Point Invention Evaluation Checklist

CHECKLIST FOR
ENVIRONMENTALLY RESPONSIBLE DESIGN

1. Use environmentally responsible strategies appropriate to the product;
2. Reduce overall material content and increase the percentage of recycled material in products;
3. Reduce energy consumption of products that use energy;
4. Specify sustainability grown materials when using wood or agricultural materials;
5. Design disposable products or products that wear out to be more durable and precious;

6. Eliminate unused or unnecessary product features;
7. Design continuously transported products for minimal weight;
8. Design for fast, economical disassembly of major components prior to recycling;
9. Design products so that toxic components are easily removed prior to recycling;
10. Perform comprehensive environmental assessment;
11. Consider all of the ecological impacts from all of the components in the products over its entire life cycle, including extraction of materials from nature, conversion of materials into products, product use, disposal or recycling and transport between these phases;
12. Consider all ecological impacts including global warming, acid rain, smog, habitat damage, human toxicity, water pollution, cancer causing potential, ozone layer depletion and resource depletion;
13. Strive to reduce the largest ecological impacts,
14. Conduct life cycle impact assessment to comprehensively identify opportunities for improving ecological performance
15. Encourage new business models and effective communication
16. Support product 'take back' systems that enable product up-grading and material recycling;
17. Lease the product or sell the service of the product to improve long-term performance and end-of-life product collection;
18. Communicate the sound business value of being ecologically responsible to clients and commissioners
19. Discuss market opportunities for meeting basic needs and reducing consumption.

Source: adapted from design-sustainability.com

"

After all, sustainability means running the global environment Earth Inc. like a corporation: with depreciation, amortization and maintenance accounts. In other words, keeping the asset whole, rather than undermining your natural capital.
Maurice Strong

"

In the 21st century, I think the heroes will be the people who will improve the quality of life, fight poverty and introduce more sustainability.
Bertrand Piccard

PROTOTYPING

WHAT

"The service prototype is a tool for testing the service by observing the interaction of the user with a prototype of the service put in the place, situation and condition where the service will actually exist. The aim is verifying what happens when some external factors interfere during the service delivery, factors that it's not possible to verify during the preceding tests in the laboratory but that have a great impact on the user perception and experience."

Dan Saffer, Designing for Interaction 2007.

The word "prototype" comes from the Greek prototypos, a compound of protos "first" and typos "mold," "pattern," "impression".

Service design involves the development of fast low fidelity prototypes and testing them iteratively with stakeholders. Low-fidelity prototypes are rough representations of concepts that help us to validate those concepts early on in the design process. Low- fidelity prototyping. Unlike high-fidelity prototyping, requires less time, specialized skills and resources. Its purpose is to learn not to sell ideas. Ask diverse stakeholders to give you feedback and use their feedback to improve the designs.

Every prototype should answer a question. What do you want to learn about?

Build prototypes that encourage dialogue about improvements. Give your prototype an unfinished appearance. Prototypes can also be an effective tool if you are rethinking or creating new, complex solutions. A storyboard or a video can help you convey the basic aspects of more complex and intangible experiences. During this phase, we will start to make our ideas real so we can get feedback from stakeholders.

WHAT

1. Detect and fix problems early.
2. Build fast and cheap.
3. Build, observe, and learn quickly.
4. Enhance collaboration within your team.
5. Get feedback from users.
6. Iterate easily.

WHEN TO PROTOTYPE

SERVICE LABORATORY
1. The location doesn't exist
2. The location is not available
3. The location may be inconvenient for users
4. Use of space is under exploration

ON-SITE WHEN
1. The real context is important
2. You can modify the space

NOT REAL END USERS
1. A novel service
2. Everyone is a potential user
3. Cannot recruit real users
4. The hypothesis is unclear.

REAL END USERS WHEN
1. A novel service
2. The value proposition is clear.
3. The target audience has specific needs.
4. Real users are available
5. Failure will not affect the user's trust.

USE MOCK-UPS WHEN
1. The object doesn't yet exist.
2. The real thing is too expensive
3. You need to produce something quickly.
4. The object is not a crucial touchpoint.

REAL PROPS WHEN
1. Props exist
2. Props are available
3. They can be changed or modified
4. The service experience should be tested with real props.
5. The look and feel of the service will have a strong effect on users.

REAL EMPLOYEES WHEN
1. Their expertise is needed
2. Their skills cannot be imitated
3. The staff are co-creators
4. The goal is to communicate to the employees.

ARTIFICIAL EMPLOYEES WHEN
1. The employees do not exist
2. The prototyping process will hinder the employees
3. The role of the employees is unclear.

LOW-FIDELITY PROTOTYPING

WHAT
Low-fidelity prototyping is a quick and cheap way of gaining insight and informing decision-making without the need for costly investment. Simulates function but not aesthetics of proposed design. Prototypes help compare alternatives and help answer questions about interactions or experiences.

WHY
1. May provide the proof of concept
2. It is physical and visible

3. Inexpensive and fast.
4. Useful for refining functional and perceptual interactions.
5. Assists to identify any problems with the design.
6. Helps to reduce the risks
7. Helps members of team to be in alignment with an idea.
8. Helps make abstract ideas concrete.
9. Feedback can be gained from the user

CHALLENGES
A beautiful prototype completed too early can stand in the way of finding the best design solution.

HOW
1. Construct models, not illustrations
2. Select the important tasks, interactions or experiences to be prototyped.
3. Build to understand problems.
4. If it is beautiful you have invested too much.
5. Make it simple
6. Assemble a kit of inexpensive materials
7. Preparing for a test
8. Select users
9. Conduct test
10. Record notes on the 8x5 cards.
11. Evaluate the results
12. Iterate

> *You can use the prototype to engage the most important actors in co-creating a new solution, developing, modifying and refining it iteratively in close cooperation."*

IDEO

LOW FIDELITY PROTOTYPING RESOURCES

WHAT
Here are some suggestions for a kit of materials to help you construct low fidelity prototypes.

1. Copy paper
2. Magnets
3. Masking tape
4. Duct tape
5. Tape
6. Post-it notes
7. Glue sticks
8. Paper clips, (asst colors ideal)
9. Hole punch
10. Scissors
11. Stapler (with staples)
12. Hot glue
13. Glue guns
14. Rulers
15. Pipe Cleaners
16. Colored card
17. Zip ties
18. Foam core sheets
19. Velcro
20. Rubber bands, multicolored
21. Assorted foam shapes
22. Markers
23. Scissors
24. Glue sticks
25. Tape
26. Glue guns
27. Straws
28. Paper Clips
29. Construction Paper
30. ABS sheets
31. Felt
32. Foam sheets
33. String
34. Foil

35. Butcher paper
36. Stickers
37. Pipe cleaners
38. Popsicle sticks
39. Multicolored card

> "Prototype. Build to think. A simple, cheap and fast way to shape ideas so you can experience and interact with them. Start building: Create an artifact in low resolution. This can be a physical object or a digital clickable sketch. Do it quick and dirty. Storyboard: create a scenario you can roleplay in a physical environment and let people experience your solution."

Pieter Baert
Strategic Consultant

> "This human-centered methodology, coupled with a 'fail fast' attitude, allows us to quickly identify, build, and test our way to success. We spend less time planning, more time doing, and, above all else, challenge ourselves to see the world through the eyes of our customers every step of the way."

Evelyn Huang. Director of Design Thinking at Capital One Labs

HIGH FIDELITY APPEARANCE PROTOTYPES

WHAT
Appearance prototypes look like but do not work like the final product. They are often fabricated using a variety of rapid prototyping techniques from digital 3d models or by hand in materials such as hard foam, wood or plastics. Usually, appearance prototypes are "for show" and short-term use and are not designed to be handled.

CHALLENGES
1. Designers can become too attached to their prototypes and allow them to become jewelry that stands in the way of further refinement.
2. Clients may believe that the design is finalized when more refinement is required.
3. They are expensive to produce,

WHY
May be used getting approval for a final design from a client or to create images for literature or a website prior to the availability of manufactured products.

DESIGN PROCESS 141

HOW
Prototypes give non-designers a good idea of what the production object will look like and feel like.

PROTOTYPING SERVICES

WHAT

Make your ideas tangible with a series of fast, inexpensive prototypes. Ask people to give you feedback and use it to improve the design of the service. In this stage we validate an improve our designs through prototyping, testing and feedback.

There are many different service prototyping tools from acting out scenarios to creating a fully operating beta prototype of the service. A service prototype simulates a service experience over time. Service prototypes are best tested in the real-world operating environment or context of the service.

SERVICE STAGING & ROLEPLAY
This technique involve acting out the service in the real-life surroundings. Stakeholders review possible scenarios for the service. Each scenario represents a possible service solution. The stakeholders and design team review and discuss the alternative

SERVICE BLUEPRINTS & EXPERIENCE MAPS
These tools are detailed two dimensional representations of the components that make up a working service. They also describe the emotional response of a user of a service.

These tools are also often used in the synthesis stage. Read a detailed description of mapping methods in that chapter.

STORYBOARDS
This is a technique which has been adopted from cinema by service designers. It is a four-dimensional techniques that can effectively describe a customer experience from their point of view.

OTHER TECHNIQUES
There are many specialized service design prototyping techniques. In this chapter, we describe some techniques that are widely used across different service industries as well as some specialized methods used in particular industries such as web service design.

> *A prototype is worth a thousand meetings"*
>
> IDEO

WHAT

VALIDATION

> Usability testing helps improve a design to make it more usable. Real users undertake particular tasks. Researchers and other stakeholders observe and collect data.

GOALS
Meet with stakeholders, to define your goals.
1. Who uses the product or service?
2. What are their needs and goals?
3. What tasks does the user need to perform?
4. Where are the problems?

VALIDATION PROCESS
1. Develop a test plan
2. Choose a testing space
3. Recruit participants
4. Prepare test materials
5. Conduct the tests
6. Debrief participants
7. Analyze data
8. Conclusions and recommendations

WHAT TO TEST
1. Low-fidelity prototype or paper prototype
2. Wireframes
3. High-fidelity prototype and experience system.
4. Alpha and Beta prototypes.
5. Test competitor's designs
6. Test in the real context of use.
7. Test iteratively
8. Use heuristics and usability guidelines.
9. Test the final design

HOW MANY TO TEST
Test at least four people from each user group.

DIAGNOSTIC EVALUATION
1. Test 4-6 users
2. Find and fix problems
3. When? During design development
4. Test iteratively

SUMMATIVE TESTING
1. How many? 6-12 users
2. Metrics based on usability goals
3. Test to measure the success of a design.
4. When? At end of process
5. Test once

Source: Ginny Redish

DESIGN THE TEST
Document your test plan checklist Test participants tasks under controlled conditions.

WHERE
Usability tests can take place in a lab, conference room, quiet office space, or a quiet public space.

SCENARIOS AND TASKS
Tasks are the activities that your participants undertake. Scenarios frame tasks and provide motivation.

TIPS FOR WRITING

SCENARIOS
Start with a scenario. Scenarios should be a story that provides motivation to your participants. The scenario is a narrative that explains the background of the task in a real-world situation. Create believable scenarios. Keep them simple.

WRITING TASKS
Categories:
1. Prescribed tasks. You determine what the participant will do.
2. Participant defined Have them do the task they describe.
3. Open-ended Participants organically explore the activity based on a scenario you provide.

The order of tasks should follow a natural flow of product use. Don't use jargon. Provide information as needed. Avoid leading the participant.

SELECT DATA TO CAPTURE
Log:
1. Task start and end points
2. Milestones
3. Errors
4. Failures
5. Problems
6. Requests for help

QUALITATIVE DATA
Record behavior, reactions, cody language.

SUCCESS PATHS
Is there only one or several success paths?

RECRUIT PARTICIPANTS
Select participants who represent typical novice average and experienced users.

RECRUITMENT IDEAS
1. Contact databases
2. Recruitment agencies
3. Craig's List
4. Your website
5. Media ads
6. Identify the target criteria for your participants.

SCREENER
Filter the participants with a screener.

COMPENSATION
Motivate participants with cash, a gift certificate or products.

VALIDATION SPACE
Pick a large room with good natural lighting and low background noise.

SCHEDULE PARTICIPANTS
Allow time for contingencies between sessions.

STAKEHOLDERS
Brief stakeholders that their task is to observe. The facilitator may interact with participants or not interact.

Enlist one person to log observations. Create a list of stakeholders. Observing testing helps make the team make improvements to the design. Do not change the design until you understand the meaning of your observations.

SCRIPT
Create a facilitator script.

QUESTIONNAIRES AND SURVEYS
A typical usability study usually has at least two surveys (questionnaires), one administered before the participant starts tasks and one administered at the end of the test,

PRE-TEST SURVEY
Collects demographic and product usage data about participants s

POST-TASK SURVEY
Questions about the usability and satisfaction related to testing tasks. Collect only data that you can legally collect. Use age ranges rather than specific ages when asking participants for their age. Include comment fields

TRIAL RUN-THROUGH
Run through your test yourself to make sure the tasks make sense Conduct a pilot test with a participant. Allow time before the test session to make changes.

THE TEST SESSION
1. Welcome participant
2. Use the script
3. Ask participants to fill out the consent form with a non-disclosure agreement.
4. Allow enough time

FACILITATION
Keep the participant focused. Participants may be asked to keep a running commentary or "think-aloud" protocol. Ask open-ended questions. What are you thinking? What are you trying to do? What did you expect to happen? Keep neutral and do not show emotion, approval or disapproval.

TASK FAILURES
If a participant fails a task ask them to do the task again.

AFTER THE SESSION
Debrief with observers. Clean the space. The impartial observers examine the general methodology and feedback is provided to enhance credibility and to ensure the collection of valid information.

ANALYSIS
1. Review observations
2. Identify problems
3. Identify solutions.

RECOMMENDATIONS
Make sure your recommendations should address the underlying cause of the problem. Keep recommendations short and concise. Use video, wireframes and other visual means to illustrate your conclusions. Recommendations should be objective and evidence-based.

RECRUITMENT SCRIPT
Hello, may I speak with X We are looking for participants to take part in a research study evaluating the usability of the

X Product. There will be $xx payment for the hour-long session, which will take the X Building located downtown. The session would involve one-on-one meeting with a researcher where you would sit down in front of a computer and try to use a product while being observed and answering
questions about the product. Would you be interested in participating? If not: Thank you for taking the time to speak with me. If you know of anyone else who might be interested in participating please have them call me, at xxx-xxx-xxxx

SCREENING SCRIPT

I need to ask you a couple of questions to determine whether you meet the eligibility criteria— Do you have a couple of minutes? If not: When is a good time to call back? Keep in mind that your answers to these questions to not automatically allow or disallow you take part in the study—we just need accurate information about your background, so please answer as well as you can.
Have you ever used X product?
If yes:
How long have you used it for? [criteria: at least 1 yr.]
And how often do you use it? [criteria: at least 3 times a month]
If no:
Have you ever used any data processing products, such as [list competitor or similar products]? [criteria: Yes]
If yes: How long have you used it for? [criteria: at least 1 yr.]
And how often do you use it? [criteria: at least 3 times a month]
Self-identify participant gender via voice and name and other cues.

SCHEDULING

If participant meets criteria: Will you be able to come to the X Building located downtown for one hour between May 15 and 19? Free parking is available next to the building. How is [name available times and dates]? You will be participating in a one-on-one usability test session on [date and time]. Do you require any special accommodations?
I need to have an e-mail address to send specific directions and confirmation information to. Thanks again! If participant does not meet criteria: Unfortunately, you do not fit the criteria for this particular evaluation and
will not be able to participate. Thank you for taking the time to speak with me.

PARTICIPANT RECRUITMENT SCREENER

The usability test of the X Product requires 12 participants from 2 user groups.

User type experienced
Product users
Number 6
Characteristics current product users/customers who have used x product
For at least 1 year and use it at least 3 times a month
3 males, 3 females

User type New product users
Number 6
Characteristics People who have no prior experience with X Product, but do have at least 1 year's experience using similar products
(e.g. data processing tools).
3 males, 3 females

THINK OUT LOAD SCRIPT
When you are doing the testing there may be times that you become frustrated or confused, but you do not say anything, We want you to say it out loud so we can see the problem and improve the design. We only can recognize what you tell us is a problem. Let us know what you are thinking. There here are no wrong answers. We're looking for your genuine impressions. Your comments will help us improve the design.

Source: Usability Testing Basics.

People don't buy what you do, but why you do it."

Simon Sinek

ALPHA TESTING

WHAT

The alpha is a low fidelity prototype with enough resolution to give your intended audience an understanding of how the service will work. An alpha prototype has some of the required features integrated into the prototype for testing.

An alpha prototype allows us to:
1. Explore the major risks
2. Discover whether the project is viable
3. Cost of the project
4. Identify risks

This document covers how to go about executing an alpha project. With an alpha prototype we begin the testing process. The alpha prototype gives you the opportunity to test your proposed design with your intended audience. The alpha is used to resolve important technical challenges.

The alpha prototype will give you a clear idea of what is required for the beta prototype.

Some questions:
1. Is the concept the best solution?
2. Will the concept work?
3. Do you have a clear understanding of your customer's needs?
4. Do you need a second

DESIGN PROCESS 147

prototype to refine the direction?

DURATION
The duration will vary but for software development testing may require a 6 to 8 week period.

TEAM REQUIREMENTS
Keep the team small and multidisciplinary so the development is agile including a variety of stakeholders.

OUTPUT
The outputs for the alpha phase are:
1. Story cards
2. Functioning system that provides that can be shown to a number of stakeholders
3. Decision whether a beta prototype is necessary.
4. Analysis of user needs

GOALS
Define your goals clearly before testing.

IDENTIFYING RISKS
One of the purposes of the alpha prototype is to define the greatest risks and to explore those risks.

RISKS MAY INCLUDE
1. Risks associated with usability
2. Business risks
3. Technical risks

It may take several iterations to solve the user problems.

1. Is it easy to use and understand?
2. What are the user errors?
3. What is the meaning of the user research?
4. How can I build a prototype most efficiently?

THE TEAM
The well-rounded team will need to have skills, including:
1. Design
2. User research
3. User journey
4. Prototyping skills
5. Service integration
6. Implementation management
7. Business skills

Try to complete testing and iterations in one week cycles.

The team must have the core skills to:

PROCESS
Alphas consist of:
1. Inception
2. Iterations design, development and test
3. Alpha termination or
4. Alpha to Beta transition
5. Execution

During the inception the team shares information about hopes and hurdles.
The inception phase should take no longer than 7 days and should look at a variety of business, technical and user aspects of the project.

1. Shared understanding of the service
2. Personas
3. a clarified current business process (where applicable)
4. Goals
5. Understanding of technology

ITERATIONS

Alphas are help clarify alternative design directions Expect to produce several prototypes
If the prototype is uncovering faults in your design then it is doing its job. To iterate faster create lower fidelity prototypes such as paper prototypes.
Rework the experience map at the end of each user testing cycle.

ENDING THE ALPHA

The alpha process helps identify the risks to the Beta program. At the end of the alpha testing the team should be able to show what the alpha has achieved and the feasibility of the beta program.

BETA TESTING

WHAT
The Beta prototype is the prototype that you will test in public and prepare to go live.

WHY CREATE A BETA?
A beta prototype has most of the required features integrated into the prototype.

1. Do people want the design solution?
2. Is the investment warranted?
3. Does it meet the user's expectations?
4. What are the risks?
5. Does the design respond correctly in situations unforeseen during the development?

Involve a wide range of stakeholders both internally and externally. Present workshops with stakeholders to get feedback and refine your design. Sometimes an alpha prototype may lead you to reject your design direction but more commonly it will help you refine the design through a second or beta prototype.

OBJECTIVE

The objective of this phase is to build a fully working service which you test with real customers.

You should be rapidly releasing updates and improvements and testing the impact of your changes.

A beta should involve testing a full, end-to-end version of the service.

PRIVATE BETA

This is a beta testing by invitation only. You might want to do private testing if:

1. gives more control over the audience demographic that

gets to use the beta
2. allows you to restrict the volume of transactions
3. lets you start small and faster

PUBLIC BETA
A public beta is available to everyone.

You may make further refinements before going live.

TEAM
Include designers, developers, web operations specialists and performance analysts as appropriate.

OUTPUT
At the end of the beta phase, you'll have:
1. Delivered an end-to-end service
2. A user testing plan
3. Metrics
4. A working system that can be used, by real end users

> **"**
> *Testing leads to failure, and failure leads to understanding.*
>
> Burt Rutan

DATA ANALYSIS

WHAT
Data analysis is the process of making meaning from the data.

CODING
1. Read through the text data. Divide the text into segments of information.
2. Label the segments with codes

CLUSTERING
1. After open coding an entire text, make a list of all code words.
2. Assign a code word or phrase that accurately describes the meaning of the text segment (30 to 40 codes)
3. Objective: reduce the long list of codes to a smaller, more manageable number (25 or 30)
4. Reduce the overlap and redundancy of codes(reduce to 20 codes) Cluster together similar codes and look for redundant codes

THEMES
Themes are similar codes aggregated together to form a major idea. Themes can also be referred to as categories.
The process of looking for categories that cut across all data sets. You can't classify something as a theme unless it cuts across the preponderance of the data.(5 to 7 themes)

NAME THE THEMES

The names can come from:
The researcher
The participants
Themes should reflect the purpose of the research. Be exhaustive--you must place all data in a category

TYPES OF THEMES
1. Ordinary: themes a researcher expects
2. Unexpected: themes that are surprises and not expected to surface
3. Hard-to-classify: themes that contain ideas that do not easily fit into one theme or that overlap with several themes
4. Major & minor themes: Themes that represent the major ideas, or minor, secondary ideas in a database.
5. Codes such as "seating arrangements," "teaching approach," or "physical layout of the room," might all be used to describe a classroom where instruction takes place

DISPLAY THE DATA VISUALLY
1. Comparison table or matrix
2. Hierarchical tree diagram that represents themes and their connections
3. Boxes that show connections between themes
4. Physical layout of the setting
5. Personal or demographic information for each person or site

VALIDATE YOUR FINDINGS

1. Prolonged engagement & persistent observation in the field
2. Triangulation
3. Peer Review
4. Clarifying researcher bias
5. Member Checking
6. Rich, thick description
7. External Audit

"In qualitative research, a single case or small nonrandom sample is selected precisely because the researcher wishes to understand the particular in depth, not to find out what is generally true of the many" (Merriam, 1998, p. 208).

TRIANGULATION
Use of two or more independent sources of data or data collection methods to corroborate research findings within a study. The researcher looks for patterns of convergence to develop or corroborate an overall interpretation

REPORT
Write a qualitative report providing detailed information about a few themes rather than general information about many themes. Written account should include sufficient data to allow the reader to judge whether the interpretation offered is adequately supported by the data.

TEST PLAN

WHAT

A usability test plan is a type of research plan that explains what testing will be done, the reasons for the testing, who will be tested, the timeline and other factors. It helps ensure that team, client and stakeholders are in alignment on what needs to be tested and why.

SCOPE
Indicate what you are testing Specify how much of the service the test will cover.

PURPOSE
Identify the concerns, questions, and goals for this test. These can be quite broad or specific Identify your focus. Base your test scenarios on your goals and focus.

SCHEDULE & LOCATION
Indicate when and where you will do the test. How many sessions and when will they be held?

TIME
Sessions are often 60 to 90-minutes. Allow 30-minutes contingency between sessions.

EQUIPMENT
Computer, phone,. Are you planning on recording the session?

PARTICIPANTS
1. Number and types of participants to be tested you will be recruiting.
2. How will they be recruited?
3. Screener.

SCENARIOS
Number and types of tasks included in testing.
For a 60 min. test, you should have 10 (+/-2) scenarios for desktop or laptop testing and 8 (+/- 2) scenarios for a mobile/smart phone test. Include more in the test plan so the team can choose the appropriate tasks.

METRICS
Subjective metrics Include the questions you are going to ask the participants prior to the sessions

QUANTITATIVE METRICS
Successful completion rates, error rates, time on task.

ROLES
A list of the staff involved in the usability testing and what role each will play.

Few ideas work on the first try. Iteration is key to innovation."

Sebastian Thrun
Director of the Artificial Intelligence Laboratory at Stanford University

IMPLEMENTATION

WHAT
During implementation phase small scale, iteratively tested, working solutions are brought to market. The design is prepared for low quantity manufacturing or minimum viable product distribution and market testing.. Gather feedback from stakeholders, and determine if your solutions are meeting their needs and fine tune the design. Launch of a new product or process is communicated to stakeholders. Manufacturers, distributors, and retailers or service providers are educated about new product or service, and trained.

WHY
Service design has value only when combined with design doing. The implementation stage is where you take your idea into people's homes, workplaces and lives.

HOW

FINALIZE YOUR DESIGN
The details of this phase will depend on the type of design area that you are working in.

PITCH & COMMIT
Create a short, compelling case for your project. Include:
1. User unmet need
2. Insights
3. Design solution
4. Summary of work
5. Challenges
6. Investment
7. Value to stakeholders.

THIS PITCH WILL HELP
1. Secure support,
2. Partnerships,
3. Funding
4. Organizational commitment

The pitch should be short. Identify the possible "deal breakers". Prototype and test these. Run the solution by as many stakeholders as possible.

BUILD EXTERNAL PARTNERSHIPS
Collaboration with other organizations and individuals is an integral part of the design process. Organizations benefit from their partners' insights and expertise.

SIGN OFF FROM STAKEHOLDERS
When you believe that you have a design that can be successfully distributed and sold, show it to all your stakeholders one last time before documenting the design for final distribution.

AUTHORIZE VENDORS
Review design with vendors.

DELIVER
Do final testing obtain sign off from stakeholders and launch. The design should successfully address the problem identified

LAUNCH ACTIVITIES

WHAT
Here is a list of activities that are undertaken before a service launch. Not every launch will require all of these activities. This information goes beyond what is usually covered in three-day design thinking camps but it is a necessary to part of the implementation of any product or service.

SERVICE

LEGAL
1. Customer contracts are in place.
2. Commercial and legal risks signed off.
3. Agreements in place with suppliers

PRODUCT PROPOSITION
1. Proposition defined.
2. Target customer profile defined.
3. Product name finalized.
4. Product positioning defined against current product portfolio.
5. Product proposition and values are validated with the target audience.

PRODUCT DEVELOPMENT
1. New components are in place.
2. Embedded in existing processes.
3. Customer support is ready.
4. Trial tests are complete and signed off with testers.
5. Packaging, documentation, user guides, website information are updated.

CUSTOMER EXPERIENCE
1. Customers can find the product.
2. Customers can buy the product. Customers can receive the product.
3. Customers can get support for the product.
4. Customers can cancel or return the product.

MARKETING

PRESS
1. PR agency commissioned.
2. Press release is complete.
3. List of journalists, bloggers, and thought leaders compiled and contacted.
4. Product photography complete.

MARKETING COMMUNICATIONS
1. Customer launch planned.
2. Advertising planned.
3. Website updates complete.
4. Online promotions, blogs, and articles planned.
5. Roadshows and promotion planned.

6. Tools in place to measure KPIs.
7. Success metrics defined.
8. White pares and print materials prepared and available for customer segments.

LEAD GENERATION
1. Tools in place to capture new leads.
2. Promotions established for new and existing customers.
3. Events planned for lead generation and sales.

INTERNAL COMMUNICATIONS
1. Internal launch communications prepared.
2. Internal testing complete.

DEMO
1. Demo is available for internal use and testing.
2. Demo available for user testing and promotions.

PRICING

CHANNELS PRICING
1. Channel pricing strategy complete.
2. Pricing for all channels defined.
3. Commission structure defined.

PRICING STRUCTURE
1. Pricing structure defined.
2. Pricing tested.
3. Introductory pricing defined.
4. Campaign pricing and discounts defined.
5. Discount vouchers defined and available.

PRICING TOOLS
1. Pricing documentation complete.
2. Website pricing updated.
3. Tools for pricing for CS and sales complete.

PRICING ANALYSIS
1. Pricing positioning against competitors complete.
2. Pricing across channels analyzed.
3. Pricing validated with customers and suppliers.

CHANNELS

CHANNEL STRATEGY
1. Sales channels strategy defined.
2. Preferred roll-out channels defined.

CHANNEL PLANS
1. Refinements to channel process in place.
2. Channel communication plans defined.
3. Agreements signed for all channels.
4. Channel sales guides, training materials and other collateral complete.

CHANNEL STOCK
1. Sufficient stock is available for launch and post-launch.
2. Stock monitoring and replenishment are in place.

THE PITCH

WHAT
A simple statement of what change you and your product are making in the world. A memorable explanation of what you do for customers. The purpose of the pitch is to stimulate interest for a second meeting.

HOW
PAIN (+ GAIN)
1. What problem is out there in the world?
2. What are you solving for your customers?
3. What opportunities do you provide for people to be faster, more cost-effective, more efficient, happier, safer,..?

PRODUCT
1. As simple as possible: what does your product do for customers?
2. How does it work?
3. How have you tested it with customers?
4. (Be sure not to let the product dominate the pitch.)

PRODUCT DEMO
1. Live demo? (always risky, but powerful if it works...)
2. Or screens-shots? Physical product?
3. Can you show a real customer using it?
4. And do you really need to do a demo?

WHAT'S UNIQUE
1. Technology/Relationships/Partnerships
2. How do you help your customers get
3. results differently to your competition, or
4. alternatives?

CUSTOMER TRACTION
1. Success so far?
2. Pilot customers? Major brands?
3. Customer reference quotes/movies?
4. PR coverage?
5. Use data and facts to strengthen.

BUSINESS MODEL
1. How do you get paid?
2. What's the opportunity for growth?
3. How can you scale beyond your current scope:
4. new industries, territories, applications of
5. partnerships and technology?

INVESTMENT
1. Amount of investment?
2. In how many rounds? How many investors?
3. What type of investor are you looking for?
4. What expectations do you have of your
5. investors; network, expertise?

TEAM
1. What relevant experience does your team have that supports your story?
2. Brands worked for?
3. Achievements? Sales success?

End statement with call to action

TIPS

INTRIGUE/SURPRISE
1. Don't give the whole game away.
2. leave them wanting to know more.
3. Surprising facts or insights about the industry and its trends?
4. New information about a known subject?

WHY YOU?
1. Why do you care about solving this problem for your customers?
2. How has your life been affected by this industry and business?
3. Why should your audience get involved with you.

> *If you want to be a millionaire, start with a billion dollars and launch a new airline."*
>
> Richard Branson

> *You don't learn to walk by following rules. You learn by doing, and by falling over."*
>
> Richard Branson

A SIMPLER PITCHING STATEMENT

FOR	Target Customers/Users
WHO	Pain, Need, Opportunity or Problem
WHAT	Product/Service Name
IS A	Product/service Category
THAT	Key User Benefits & business opportunity
UNLIKE	Competitors & Their Competing Product/Service
WE (OUR SOLUTION)	Solution and Primary Differentiation

LAUNCH PROCESS

LAUNCH PLAN
1. Launch date is set.
2. Communication plans are defined. Launch plan is approved.
3. Customer communication plan defined.

KEY ACTIVITIES
1. Final testing, approval and launch
2. Targets, evaluation and feedback loops.

PRE-LAUNCH
3-4 Weeks before launch:
1. Create the campaign.
2. Evoke emotion.
3. Create desire.
4. Prepare marketing materials.
5. Be original.
6. Review what's working.
7. Create urgency.

MID-LAUNCH
1. Post on blogs, social media and other various communication channels.
2. Listen and adapt.

GO LIVE
Now you are ready to go live.

LAUNCH
Liaise with internal teams in areas such as marketing, communications, and brand.

1. How can you reduce the risk of failure?
2. Have you met your goals?
3. Is it compelling?
4. Set a launch date.

POST-LAUNCH PLAN
1. Sales target is defined.
2. A marketing plan is defined.
3. Performance analysis plan is defined.
4. Budget and resources are secured.
5. Post-launch road-maps are defined.
6. User feedback process is defined.
7. Performance metrics tools defined.
8. Success and failure metrics are defined.

POST-LAUNCH STAGES
The design should now be improved continuously, based on user feedback, analysis, and further research.

POST-LAUNCH
1. Ask for feedback from first buyers
2. Make it memorable.
3. Review and improve.
4. Plan ahead.

DID YOU MEET YOUR GOALS?
Ideas that have emerged during the design process or in post-launch feedback may be put to one side but developed later, and will then go through the design process again on its own.

MEASURE SUCCESS
1. Determine metrics to measure level of success.
2. 2 To 3 months after release measure the success
3. Measure the success and objectively evaluate.
4. Implement metrics and measurements

SOME SUCCESS METRICS

1. Customer satisfaction
2. ROI is A common business measure of project profitability, over the market life of the design expressed as a percentage of initial investment.
3. Increased usage
4. Increased revenue from existing customers
5. Did your design solve the user problem?
6. How many new customers have you gained?
7. What is your real product margin?
8. Cash flow
9. Is your design team satisfied?
10. Improved customer retention rate
11. Increased market share

WHAT COULD BE IMPROVED?

Invite customers to co-create, and integrate feedback.

DEFINE THE NEXT VISION

Time to start planning the next design so that you can stay ahead of the many competitors.

Source: Adapted from Jonathan Mead "The 40 Step Checklist for a Highly Successful Launch"

> *The only purpose of starting is to finish, and while the projects we do are never really finished, they must ship."*

Seth Godin

> *People are in such a hurry to launch their product or business that they seldom look at marketing from a bird's eye view and they don't create a systematic plan*

Dave Ramsey

> *There's no such thing as a creative type. As if creativity is a verb, a very time-consuming verb. It's about taking an idea in your head, and transforming that idea into something real. And that's always going to be a long and difficult process. If you're doing it right, it's going to feel like work."*

Milton Glaser
American graphic designer

05
BUSINESS MODEL CANVAS

BUSINESS MODEL CANVAS

WHAT

The Business Model Canvas is a strategic tool for developing new or documenting existing business models. The headings can be drawn on a whiteboard so groups of people can jointly discuss business model elements with post-it notes or board markers. It is a hands-on tool that fosters understanding, discussion, creativity, and analysis.

WHO INVENTED IT?

The Business Model Canvas was initially proposed by Alexander Osterwalder in 2008.

WHY

1. It is a hands-on tool that fosters understanding, discussion, creativity, and analysis.
2. It assists firms in aligning their activities by illustrating potential trade-offs.

HOW

1. Start by creating a set of personas, humanized portraits of the customers, be the buyer and/or user of the company's product.
2. Personas are average customers in each segment not extreme or fringe end users. Which customers are you creating value for? Who is your most important customer?
3. What is the value proposition for each persona?
4. What are the customer's current alternatives?
5. Your value proposition has to be better than those alternatives for you to get traction so your customer will buy your product or service.
6. What core value do you deliver to the customer?
7. Which customer needs are you satisfying?
8. Once you get a list of value propositions, sort them in order of most to least compelling and record them on the Canvas.
9. What channels will you use to reach your customers? For example online, in-store.
10. Storyboard the customer journey to think through customer relationships and segments.
11. Revenue streams. For what value are your customers willing to pay? What and how do they recently pay? How would they prefer to pay? For example in one payment or by subscription. How much does each revenue stream contribute to the overall revenues?
12. Activities. What key activities does your value proposition require? What activities are most important in distribution channels, customer relationships, and

revenue stream?
13. Resources. What resources does your value proposition require? What resources are most important in distribution channels, customer relationships, and revenue stream?
14. Partners. Who are your key partners? What are the motivations for the partnerships?
15. Costs. What are the greatest costs in running your business
16. Which resources or activities are most expensive?

GOOGLE TRENDS SHOWS THE GROWING POPULARITY OF THE BUSINESS MODEL CANVAS

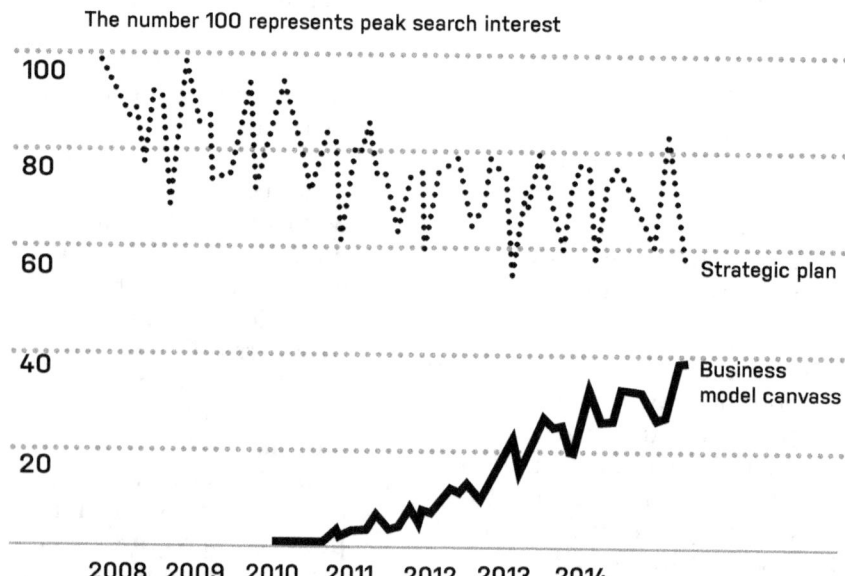

Source: Adapted from http://blog.strategyzer.com

BUSINESS MODEL CANVAS

Key partners	Key activities	Value proposition	Customer relationships	Customer segments
	Key Resources		Channels	

Cost structure	Revenue Streams

Created by : Osterwalder A., Pigneur Y (2010) Business Model Generation.

BUSINESS MODEL CANVAS EXERCISE

BACKGROUND
Are you trying to find innovative ways of creating new services to replace old, outdated ones? The Business Model Canvas is a strategic template for developing new or documenting existing business and service models. It is a visual template with elements describing a firm's or product's value proposition, infrastructure, customers, and finances. A business model describes the rationale of how an organization creates, delivers, and captures value.

GOALS
To become more aware of critical aspects that supports a successful service business.

TASKS
Choose a service which you have consumed recently and set out the underlying business model. What value is created, for whom, by whom and how? Using the BM Canvas framework, map out how this value is created and 'revenue stream', cost structure, key networks, channels, etc.

1. How have business models for your chosen product/service changed? How might they change?
2. How could you provide different ways of creating the core value proposition?
3. Could you expand the target market segments?
4. Which alternative channels might you use to reach them?
5. Which new technologies might you take advantage of?
6. Which new partners might you link with to improve the way value is delivered?
7. How can you cut costs?
8. How can you add or improve revenue streams?
9. Using these and other questions develop business model which represents a better way of delivering value.
10. Prepare a short presentation to 'pitch' your idea to potential investors.

DELIVERABLES
One Business Model Canvas of a service that you have used recently. One business model canvas of an improved service

CONSIDER THE FOLLOWING

CUSTOMER SEGMENTS
1. Who is the customer?
2. What's the customer's major need?
3. What job must the customer accomplish?

Total Market Size
4. Segmented by:
   - Geography
   - Age
   - Income
   - Substitutes
5. Competitors.

6. Early Adopters.
7. Large base free/small base?
8. Niche community.
9. Mass Market.
10. Regulatory approved product.

VALUE PROPOSITION
1. New product category.
2. Enabler.
3. Highest performance.
4. Ease of Customization.
5. Best design.
6. Disruptive price.
7. Cost Reduction.
Risk Reduction.
8. Convenience.
9. Security and Safety.
10. Rent or lease instead of sell.
11. Disruption in service.
12. What unmet need is being met?

CHANNELS
1. How you contact the customer?
2. Deliver the value.
3. Promote the value.
4. Improve his position and more.
5. Direct versus Indirect.
6. Direct.
7. Salesforce.
8. Web.
9. Retail store.
10. Key opinion leaders.
11. Mobile platforms.
12. Direct email/mailings/spam.
13. Franchise.
14. Indirect.
15. Partners.
16. OEM / embedded.
17. Wholesale.
18. Mobile Platform

CUSTOMER RELATIONSHIPS
1. What is the customer retaining cost?
2. Acquisition cost?
3. Lifetime value?
4. Switching cost?
5. Personal assistance.
6. Dedicated Personal Assistance.
7. Self Service.

8. Automated Services.
9. Communities Co-creation.
10. Revenue Streams.
11. Why will customers pay?
12. How do customers prefer to pay?
13. What's the retail price?
14. How many paying customers will there be?

KEY RESOURCES
1. What resources required to maintain the business model
2. Platform.
3. Infrastructure.
4. People.
5. Skills.
6. Patents.
7. Specialists.
8. Content creators.
9. Software rights.
10. Content library.

KEY ACTIVITIES
1. Key activities necessary to build the business.
2. Maintaining the platform
3. Brand building.
4. Reducing cost.
5. Innovation.
6. R&D.
7. Selling.
8. Regulatory approval.
9. Reimbursement.
10. Signing Partnerships.
11. Acquiring content.
12. Logistics.
13. Managing inventory.
14. Managing a community/niche.

KEY PARTNERS
1. Strategic partner needed to build the business model.
2. Outsourced coding.
3. Reseller of software.
4. Social Networking Platform.
5. OEM Partner.

6. Research Partner.
7. Manufacturer.
8. Retailer.
9. Crowds.

COST STRUCTURE
1. How much it costs to build the business.
2. Fixed Costs.
3. Variable costs.
4. Engineering cost.
5. Manufacturing cost.
6. HR cost.
7. Revenue Streams.
8. Channels.
9. Customer Relationships.
10. Customer Segments.
11. Key Partners Key Activities.
12. Value Propositions.
13. Key Resources.
14. Cost Structure.

06
AFFINITY DIAGRAMS

JIRO KAWAKITA AND AFFINITY DIAGRAMS

Jiro Kawakita, Born on November 11 , 1920 - died July 8 , 2009, is a Japanese ethnographer , the first person in ethnogeography in Japan and a researcher in Nepal, inventor of the Affinity diagram.

He studied geography at Kyoto University , and also obtained a degree in literature. His achievements have immensely contributed to design thinking, research, ethnography, innovation and solving complex human problems. His work allows designers to make sense from the chaos of real-world complex or wicked problems. His method is perhaps the most basic tool of design thinking.

In the 1950s, he did field work in the Sikha Valley in South-Eastern Annapurna, Nepal. Jiro Kawakita was a pioneer in participation of remote Nepalese villagers in researching their problems, to improve water supplies and transport across mountain gorges. He developed empathy by working with the villagers. He practiced what he called a "Key Problem Approach". His approach is what design thinking calls co-design today. This work was the starting point of the KJ method and diagram , which he developed in Japan. Affinity diagrams were introduced to the western world by Shoji Shiba as as one of seven total quality management tools from 1985.

USE AN AFFINITY DIAGRAM WHEN:
1. You are confronted with many facts or ideas in apparent chaos.
2. Issues seem too large and complex to grasp.

Anyone who uses brainstorming can use an affinity diagram. Affinity diagrams, allow large numbers of ideas to be sorted into groups for review and analysis. These, simple diagrams are useful with large group where ideas which are generated at a fast pace need to be organized. The best results are achieved when the activity is completed by a cross-functional team, including key stakeholders. The process requires becoming deeply immersed in the data

BOOKS
- His two books entitled "Journals of Expedition to the Nepali Kingdom" and "Land of Platform Burial" became best sellers in Japan.

Source: Adapted from Wikipedia.

AFFINITY DIAGRAMS

WHAT

An affinity diagram is a method used to organize many ideas into groups with common themes or relationships. Affinity diagrams are tools for analyzing large amounts of data and discovering relationships which allow a design direction to be established based on the associations. This method may uncover significant hidden relationships.

Traditional design methods struggle when dealing with complex or chaotic problems or with large amounts of data. The affinity diagram organizes a large quantity of information by natural relationships. This method taps a team's analytical thinking as well as creativity and intuition. It was invented in the 1960s by Japanese anthropologist Jiro Kawakita and is sometimes referred to as the KJ Method.

You can use an affinity diagram to:
1. Understand what is most important from ambiguous data.
2. Tame complexity.
3. Identify connections in data
4. Create hierarchies.
5. Identifying themes.

Identify what factors to focus on that will support the most successful design possible from a customer's perspective.

Most groups that use this technique are amazed at how powerful and valuable a tool it is. Try it once with an open mind and you'll be another convert."

Nancy R. Tague

For around 50 years affinity diagrams have been an essential pillar of what is known as the Seven Management and Planning Tools, used in Japan. The seven management and planning tools are used in leading global organizations for making and implementing better team decisions.

Jiro Kawakita developed the method, and so it was sometimes referred to as the K-J method.

The affinity diagram is a method that an individual or team can use for problem-solving. Affinity diagrams encourage creative input by everyone on the team.

The tool is used in project

management to sort brainstorming ideas into groups, based on their natural relationships and for synthesis and analysis. It is also used in design research to synthesize insights from field research. Affinity diagrams are built through consensus of a design team on how the information should be grouped in logical ways.

WHY USE AFFINITY DIAGRAMS?

Traditional design methods do not work when dealing with complex or chaotic problems with large amounts of data. This tool helps to establish relationships or similarities between many pieces of information. From these relationships, insights can be determined which are the starting point of design solutions. It is possible using this method to reach consensus faster than many other methods.

You can use an affinity diagram to:
1. Understand what is most important from a large amount of complex or ambiguous data.
2. Tame complexity.
3. Understand connections between ideas.
4. Identify relationships in data.
5. Create hierarchies.
6. Exercise team decisio-making.
7. Make sense from brainstorming ideas.
8. Support design and data workshops.
9. Identifying themes from data
10. Identify patterns from data.
11. It helps to reduce "team paralysis," from too many options and lack of consensus.

HISTORY OF AFFINITY DIAGRAMS

Affinity diagrams were created in the 1950s by Japanese anthropologist Jiro Kawakita It is sometimes called the K-J Method. Jiro Kawakita worked in remote Nepalese villages researching problems, related to water supplies and transportation. He was awarded the Ramon Magsaysay Award in 1984.

Affinity diagrams were part of the Seven Management and Planning Tools, used in Total Quality Control in Japan. Jiro Kawakita named the method around 1967 and published a comprehensive description of the KJ method in 1986. Since 1969, Kawakita has presented KJ method workshops in Japan.

WHEN SHOULD WE USE AFFINITY DIAGRAMS?

An Affinity Diagram is useful when you want to:
1. Make sense out of large volumes of chaotic data.
2. Encourage new patterns of thinking. An affinity diagram can break through traditional or entrenched thinking.

STRENGTHS
1. It is a simple method.

2. Supports innovation.
3. Causes breakthroughs to emerge
4. Helps groups come to a consensus about most important issues
5. Multiple people can combine their ideas by on post-it notes and be organizing them.
6. Organizing generates useful discussions.
7. Builds critical thinking skills.
8. Allows for involvement of each team member
9. Helps your team to see the big picture and where the biggest problems are.
10. Post-it notes are a flexible method to organize ideas into various levels of groups and sub-groups.
11. It is both a creative and analytical method
12. Promotes the emergence of breakthrough thinking
13. Most effective when applied to a team with varied perspectives and open-mindedness.
14. Is useful to make sense of complex apparently unrelated ambiguous or chaotic data
15. It makes your analysis highly visible to others in the company.

WEAKNESSES
1. Good facilitation is required to when there is a lot of data.
2. Affinity diagrams are not portable or mobile.
3. Affinity diagrams occupy a large space for a period.
4. Can be time-consuming when there are a large number of pieces of data.
5. The small size of post-it notes and the effort of writing forces you to be brief,
6. It is an analog or physical activity
7. the rationale behind particular groupings can be lost.
8. Affinity diagrams are temporary and must be photographed to keep a permanent record.
9. It may be difficult find individual pieces of information.

USE AN AFFINITY DIAGRAM WHEN:
1. You have a large body of information in apparent chaos.
2. To uncover hidden connections between pieces of information or ideas
3. When issues seem too broad and complex to grasp.
4. There is no clear solution evident to your team.
5. When group consensus is necessary.
6. You wish to move beyond habitual thinking and preconceived categories.
7. When other solutions to a problem have failed.
8. To rethink how issues are connected.
9. To brainstorm root causes and solutions to problems, especially when little or no data is available
10. Organize qualitative data from stakeholders to uncover insights and themes

11. The solution requires consensus amongst the team members to work effectively
12. Extract requirements from user research
13. To organize ideas from brainstorming.
14. To brainstorm root causes of problems, especially when data is confusing or ambiguous.

DO NOT USE AN AFFINITY DIAGRAM WHEN
if less than 15 items of data.

PROCESS
SELECT YOUR TEAM
Care should be taken in choosing your team. As many groups and diverse points of view involved in design delivery and use of the service as possible should be represented.
1. Keep groups to six people or less.
2. Break large groups into smaller groups of six or fewer people.
3. Have a diverse team with different genders, age, occupations and status represented.
4. Have at least two or three "T" shaped team members. That is people with two or more areas of expertise such as technology and management or administration and design. T-shaped team members make the team more flexible and help group collaboration.
5. Involve external and internal stakeholders such as customers, suppliers, internal business management, engineering, design, and sales.
6. Have customer-facing people where possible because they better see the client's perspective.

APPOINT YOUR MODERATOR
1. Create handouts with clear instructions
2. Provide copies of research summaries
3. Take breaks every 90-minutes
4. Photograph the map as it is being built.

MODERATOR SKILLS
1. Effective Listening Skills
2. Flexibility
3. Customer empathy
4. Sincerely Interested in People
5. Enthusiasm
6. People management skills
7. Able to establishing common direction and buy-in.
8. Understands Group Dynamics
9. Authority
10. Neutral and Objective
11. Patient and Persistent
12. Guide discussion promptly.

RESOURCES
White-board
Large wall spaces or tables
Dry-erase markers
Sharpies
Post-it notes

There are two ways to use affinity diagrams:

GATHER YOUR DATA SPREAD IT OVER A WALL

Spread the data on a wall or Whiteboard

Gather more than 100 pieces of data

MOVE THE DATA INTO RELATED GROUPS

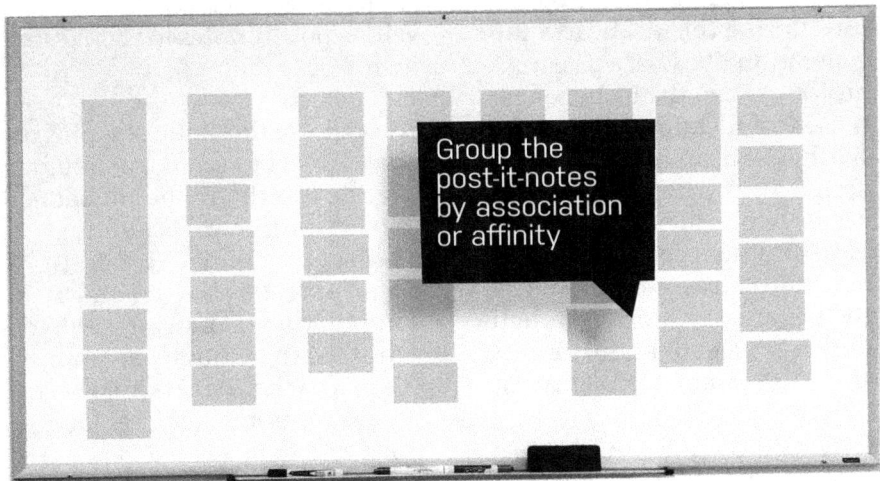

Group the post-it-notes by association or affinity

RESEARCH TOOL

To make sense of a large body of research data. This approach can be used to establish connections between different pieces of research, to uncover insights from the data that can then be used to develop design concepts. With this approach, the team can develop a hierarchy of significance of the connections or themes and the insights. This hierarchy helps to establish the levels of focus for different ideas and themes uncovered by the research for the ideation design phase.

BRAINSTORMING TOOL

Affinity diagrams can also be used during the ideation or idea generation phase of a design project. When the technique is used for ideation it helps synthesize a large number of design ideas. The design team can decide which ideas are the best ideas and then combine features of various ideas to develop themes and variations through iterative cycles of brainstorming, affinity diagrams and synthesis.

GATHER YOUR DATA

First gather your data. Break the data down into pieces. For example, if an interview subject has raised several interesting points during an interview transcribe the interview, highlight the interesting points then copy each point onto a separate post-it-note. Use only one color post-it notes at this stage. The most common color used at this phase for the raw data is yellow.

FIND YOUR SPACE

Once you have selected your team, your moderator, and space to work, spread the ideas randomly across a wall, a Whiteboard or large table. A floor in a little traffic area also can work for this stage of the process. You need plenty of space.

Affinity diagrams work best with more than 100 discrete pieces of information and work efficiently up to several thousand pieces of data.

CLUSTERING

Hand a block of blank 2" x 3" yellow post-it notes to each team member.

You can use the "Rule of 7 plus or minus 2". The summary should have no less than 5 and no more than 9 words in it, including a verb and a noun. Use also simple cartoon sketches and a combination of drawings and words. Gather your team around the place where you have placed the post-it notes. Look for ideas that seem to be related.

Go for volume, suspend judgment, build on each other's ideas and set a strict time limit. Allow 30 or 40-minutes for brainstorming ideas.

The moderator then asks the team to take two ideas that seem to belong together and place them together, at least, three feet away from the other post-it notes. Keep moving post-it notes into the groups until all the post-its have been placed into groups. It is OK to replace another person's group if it doesn't make sense to you. Some groups may have only a small number of items.

The type of relationship that you see will depend on your background, your profession your personality and your life experience.

Move related ideas into groups and continue moving the post-it notes until all notes are in groups. Some ideas may not seem to fit a group. Place those ideas into a group. If a note belongs in two groups, make a second note.

It is best that no one speaks at this stage, so different perspectives are represented.
Work silently. Ask the team to move the ideas into groups based on their gut instincts and without talking. This approach encourages unconventional thinking and discourages one person from steering the affinity. It is important to maintain silence at this stage, as it ensures that each member has an equal opportunity to apply their perspective without being influenced to conform to others' thinking.

Ask your team not to struggle over placing the data into groups, use gut instincts.
If consensus is not reached, make a duplicate of the idea and place one copy in two groups. The idea written on each post-it should be a phrase or sentence that clearly conveys the meaning to people who are not on the team. Make the notes large enough to be readable from 10 feet distance.

HEADERS

Hand out a block of blank 2" x 3" blue post-it notes to each team member. Using the second color of post-it notes, ask each participant to assign a name to each group. Write a header above each cluster that describes what connects the data in the group. Use a different color post-it notes for the headers. Blue is a color that is often used for headers. You can use any color, but it should be the same color for all headers and a different color than the color utilized in the previous phase. The most efficient use of space is to position the post-it notes in a group vertically with the header above the group.

To create headers ask for each grouping: "What key words summarize the central idea that this grouping communicates?" Sometimes a post it from within the group can be used as a header.

Create a heading for each group that captures the theme of each group. Place it above the group. A header should capture the association or affinity among the ideas contained in a group.
The team develops headers by discussing and agreeing on the wording of the header post-it notes.

MOVE THE DATA INTO RELATED GROUPS

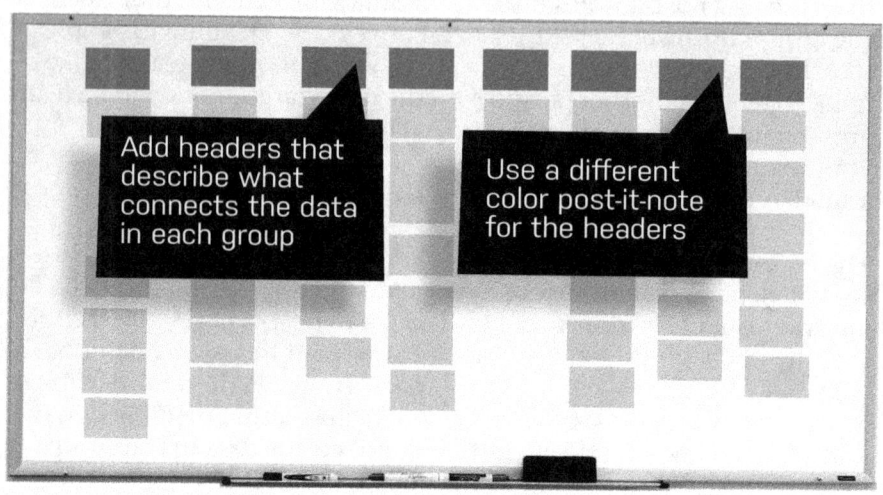

GROUP ASSOCIATED GROUPS AND SUPERGROUPS WITH HEADERS

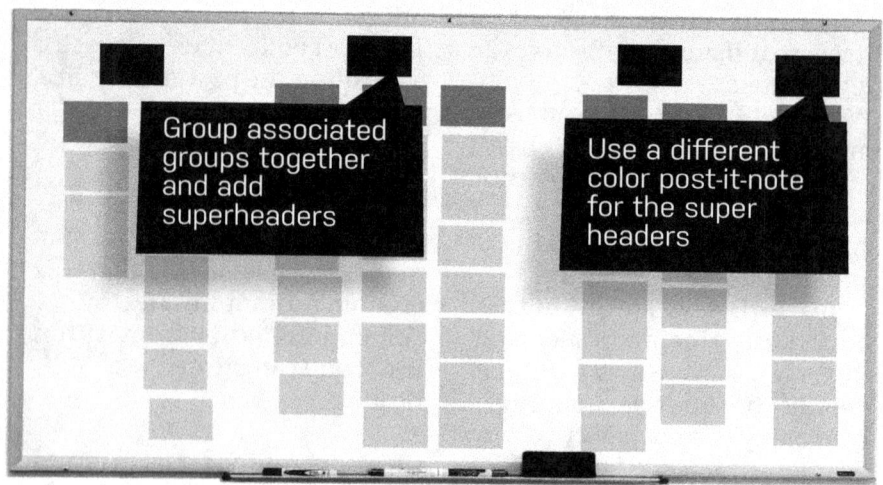

Review each group and write down a name that best represents each cluster on the new set of sticky notes. Do not use full sentences for headers but summarize the association with just one or two words.

If a group has two themes, then split the group into two groups. If two groups share the same theme combine the two groups into one or move the two groups near to each other and place a header above the headers of the two groups that define the association of the two groups.

Making a simple title involves abductive thinking, which is the best form of problem-solving for complex, changing and ambiguous problems. Some notes will not fit into any group. Put these in a separate group.

When people slow down it is time to break the silence, and start discussing the groups that have emerged. When consensus is reached, move on to the next step.

SUPERHEADERS

If two groups have the same theme then place an additional header in a third color above those two groups. Leave the previous headers in place. Pink is commonly used for a combined header of two groups. This type of header is sometimes called a super header. Repeat the process until the number of groupings is between 5 and 9 groups. Ask each participant to read through the post-it notes in each group.

The moderator should then say "We will now see if we can combine some groups. Please nominate two groups that you think we can combine. Only combine groups that have the same theme but not groups that are subsets of one another"

DOT VOTING

Give each participant 3 adhesive dots and ask them to place the dots next to the header of the three groups that they think are most important in relation to the design goals.
1. What are the user needs?
2. What are the needs of the business?
3. What technologies are most appropriate?

After each person has voted tally the number of votes for each group.

This gives you a hierarchy of importance for the themes in order to address these themes in the next phase of the design process, the ideation phase.

This is a way of efficiently selecting from a large number of ideas the preferred ideas to carry forward in the design process.

WHY USE DOT VOTING?

It is a method of selecting a favored idea by collective rather than individual judgment. It is a fast method that allows a design to progress. It leverages the strengths of diverse team member viewpoints and experiences

CHALLENGES
1. The assessment is subjective.
2. Group-think
3. Not enough good ideas
4. Inhibition
5. Lack of critical thinking

HOW
1. Gather your team of 4 to 12 participants.
2. Brainstorm ideas, for example, ask each team member to generate ten ideas as sketches.
3. Each idea should be presented on one post-it-note or page.
4. Each designer should quickly explain each idea to the group before the group votes.
5. Spread the ideas on a wall or table.
6. Ask the team to vote on their two or three favorite ideas and total the votes. You can use sticky dots or colored pins to indicate a vote or a moderator can tally the scores.
7. Rearrange the ideas so that the ideas with the dots are ranked from most dots to least.
8. Refine the preferred ideas.

VOTE FOR GROUPS

Each team member is given 3 votes

AFFINITY DIAGRAM EXERCISE

WHAT IS AN AFFINITY DIAGRAM?
An affinity diagram is a method of brainstorming, in which

seemingly random ideas or suggestions are eventually organized within natural groupings.

WHY USE AN AFFINITY DIAGRAM?
1. Affinity diagrams are a great way to make sense of a large volume of chaotic information that might otherwise seem overwhelming.
2. Affinity diagrams also allow a group to see connections in ways that might not seem obvious at first.
3. Affinity diagrams can help groups reach consensus.
4. Affinity diagrams can also help team members to build upon each other's knowledge.
5. Each member of a team can contribute.
6. An affinity diagram can have anywhere from 50 to 1000 ideas many ideas may be combined with one another if they're similar, or discarded.

TIMING
Anticipate the process taking between 409 minutes and one hour to the stage of clustering ideas and associating headers.

MATERIALS
Two pads of sticky notes in three colors. One color can be used for ideas, while other can be used for the titles of the groups.

RULES
1. Go for quantity quantity breeds quality.
2. Withhold criticism for a later 'critical stage' of the process.
3. Welcome wild ideas. Wild ideas are encouraged.
4. Combine and improve ideas.

PROCESS
1. Select a target user group and a need or problem they have to solve.
2. State the problem in the form of a need statement xxxx needs to solve xxxx because xxxx.
3. Divide your team into groups of 4 to 8 people and generate possible solutions to the needs statement.
4. Record the ideas, suggestions, and opinions of each team member on sticky notes. Team members should only write one idea/suggestion/opinion per sticky note and should be encouraged to create at least five sticky notes.
5. Post everyone's sticky notes on a wall
6. Ask all team members to come to the wall and quietly look for ideas/suggestions/opinions that seem to be related
7. Ask team members to sort the related sticky notes into

groups
8. Ask a team member to write the titles of each group on different colored sticky notes, which will be the team's Affinity Diagram Titles.
9. Give everyone three votes and vote on the best idea.

07
EMPATHY MAPS

EMPATHY MAPS

WHAT
A mapping method that analyzes each part of a user experience. An Empathy Map gives a high-level view of where an experience is good or bad. Used to improve a customer experience.

The biggest single cause of failure of new products and services in the marketplace is that the organization creating the product or service did not thoroughly understand the customer's perspective. This method helps draw out the main components of the client's experience so that problems can be identified and fixed.

Empathy Map is a tool that helps the design team empathize with the end users. You can create an empathy map for a group of customers or a persona.

WHAT IS EMPATHY?
The identification with the feelings, thoughts, or attitudes of another. Keep in mind, empathy and sympathy are different things

WHO
Scott Matthews and Dave Gray at XPLANE now Dachis Group.

HOW LONG DOES IT TAKE?
One to three hours per persona.

WHY
This tool helps a design team understand the customers and their context. It is an outside-in technique.

CHALLENGES
1. Emotions must be inferred by observing clues.
2. This method is not as rigorous as traditional personas but requires less investment.

RESOURCES
Empathy map template
White-board
or chalkboard
or video projector
or Large sheet of paper
Dry-erase markers
Post-it-notes
Pens
Video Camera

HOW
1. A team of 4 to 12 people is a good number for this method.
2. The best people to involve are individuals who have direct interaction with customers.
3. The team should represent various functions in your organization such as management, design, marketing, sales, and engineering. It is helpful also to include some stakeholders such as customers and others affected by the end design.

The process will help draw out useful information from them.
4. This method can be used with personas.
5. The map should be based on real information from customers. Research can be gathered from sources such as interviews, observation, web analytics, customer service departments and focus groups.
6. Segment your market then create a persona representing an average customer in each segment. Create four to six personas.
7. Draw a circle. The circle will represent your target persona.
8. Create some radial boxes around the circle to represent aspects of that person's sensory experience. It is common to have boxes for seeing and hearing. Some experiences such as drinking coffee could include boxes for other senses such as taste and smell.
9. Place two boxes at the bottom of the map and label them "Pain" and "Gain".
10. Ask your team to describe from the persona's point of view their experience.
11. Populate the map by using the research gathers through your fieldwork: What are they thinking, feeling, saying, doing, hearing, seeing?
12. Once you have filled all of the top boxes move the post-it notes for negative components of the experience into the lower pain box and positive into the gain box.
13. The pain box can serve as a start for identifying the problems to fix in the ideation phase.

On a large White-board draw a circle about 6 inches to one foot in diameter near the center of the board.

Inside this circle describe the persona that you are about to map. This persona represents a significant segment of your customers.

Fill in the persona's name, age, gender, occupation, income, location and any other important information.

Write down the answers to the following questions:
• What's their role i.e. how do they spend their day?
• What are their goals? How do they measure success?
• What are their top hopes and hurdles?
• What's their age, marital status, income and location.
Select an appropriate name for your persona.

For your product or service, what are the most important sensory inputs? For example, sight sound smell and taste may be essential for a coffee shop. Now divide the top three-quarters of the board

ON A WHITE-BOARD DRAW A CIRCLE THEN 4 RADIATING BOXES

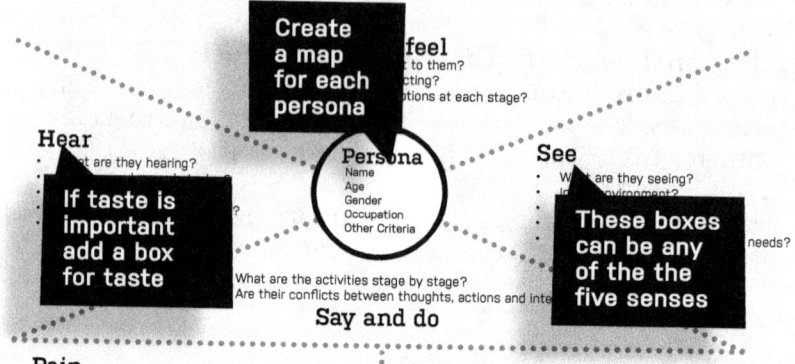

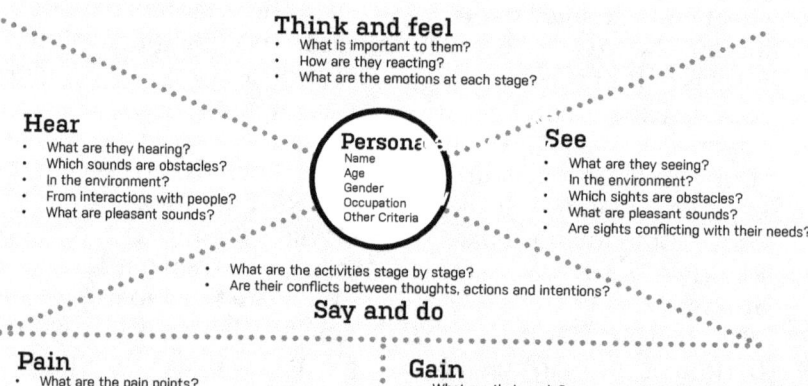

Think and feel
- What is important to them?
- How are they reacting?
- What are the emotions at each stage?

Hear
- What are they hearing?
- Which sounds are obstacles?
- In the environment?
- From interactions with people?
- What are pleasant sounds?

Persona
Name
Age
Gender
Occupation
Other Criteria

See
- What are they seeing?
- In the environment?
- Which sights are obstacles?
- What are pleasant sounds?
- Are sights conflicting with their needs?

Say and do
- What are the activities stage by stage?
- Are their conflicts between thoughts, actions and intentions?

Pain
- What are the pain points?
- What are the frustrations?
- What are the obstacles?
- What are the fears?
- What are the risks?

Gain
- What are their goals?
- What are they trying to achieve?
- What are their needs?
- What are their desires?
- How do they measure success?

space into a number of boxes radiating from your persona circle. Name these boxes "Think and Feel", "Say and Do" and the appropriate senses selected from the five senses

1. See
2. Hear
3. Touch
4. Taste
5. Smell

With your team seated around the board populate the boxes one box at a time.

What is the perspective of your customer? Take a walk in her shoes?
What are your customer segments?
1. List all customer segments
2. Pick one to work on
3. Give the customer a name
4. Develop some demographic characteristics
5. Income, marital status, etc.
6. Create Story

SEE
1. What does he see in his Environment that influences him?
2. What is the persona seeing in their surroundings?
3. Who surrounds them?
4. Who are their friends?
5. What visual problems do they encounter?

HEAR
1. What does your customer hear in the context of the experience?
2. What do their friends say?
3. What does their partner say?
4. Which media channels do they access?
5. What friends say
6. What work colleagues say?
7. What news says
8. What influences say

THINK AND FEEL
1. What matters most to your customers?
2. What is your client thinking?
3. Talk to them and ask them what they are thinking.
4. What concerns them most?
5. What are their dreams, desires and aspirations?
6. What doesn't your customer articulate?
7. What things move her?

SAY AND DO
Some questions:
1. What do they say when experiencing your product or service?
2. What do they say when experiencing competitor's goods or services?
3. What do they say to their friends or colleagues?
4. What do they do? What are the activities?
5. How do they behave?
6. Are there differences between what they say and do?
7. What is common for her to say?
8. How does she behave?
9. What are her hobbies?
10. What does he like to say?
11. How is the world in which he lives?

START BY LISTING WHAT YOUR PERSONA SEES

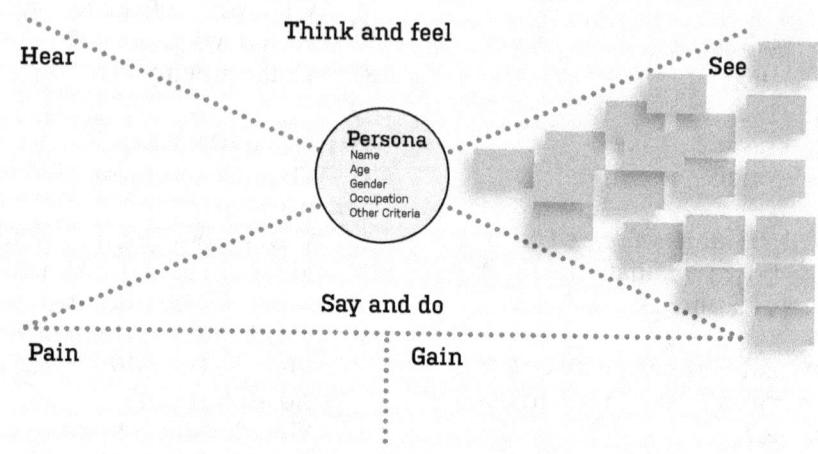

THEN WHAT YOUR PERSONA SAYS AND DOES

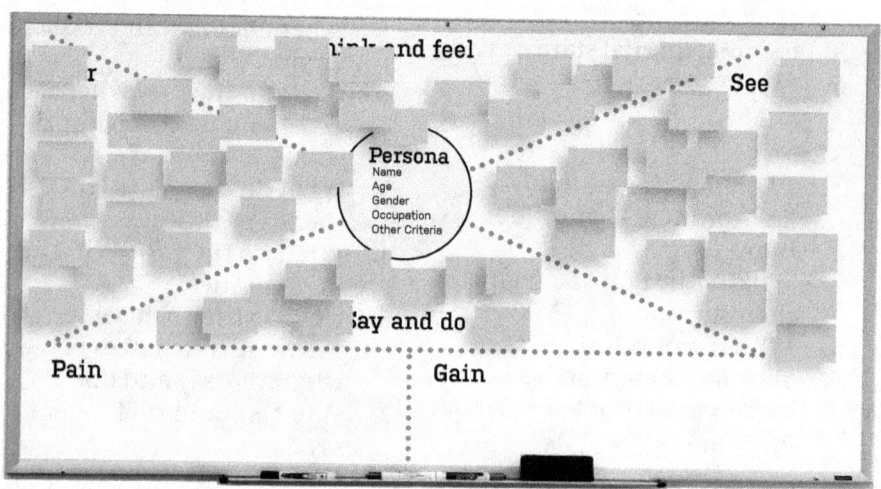

12. What do people around him/her do?
13. Who are her friends?
14. What is popular in his daily life?
15. What people and ideas influence her?
16. What do the important people in his life say?
17. What are her favorite brands?
18. Who are his role models?
19. What does he want to achieve?
20. How does she measure success?
21. What would make it a better experience?
22. What are his aspirations?
23. Imagine what the customer might say, or how they might behave in public
24. What is her attitude?
25. What could she be telling others?
26. Pay particular attention to potential conflicts between what a customer might say and what the customer truly thinks and feels.
27. What is his attitude?
28. What could he be telling others?
29. What does he say that normally contradicts to what he thinks and feels?

PAIN

What are the fears, frustrations, and the obstacles that concern your customer most? What obstacles stand in the way of your customer reaching their goals?
1. What are the pain points?
2. What does the persona fear?
3. What is the persona frustrated by in relation to the experience?
4. Why doesn't the customer come back?
5. What is standing in the way of your client reaching their goals?
6. What does your customer need?
7. What does your customer desire?
8. What do competitors do better?
9. When is your customer most unhappy?
10. Where is your customer most unhappy?
11. Here are some questions:
12. What are their fears? What do they worry about?
13. What are their aspirations? What do they dream about?
14. What else do they think about during the day?
15. Do they love or hate what they do?
16. What are the differences between what they say/do and think/feel?
17. • How do they feel about using your product or alternative solution?
18. What are the customer's biggest frustrations?
19. What obstacles stand between the customer and what they want or need to achieve?
20. Which risk might she fear taking?
21. What are his biggest frustrations?

MOVE ALL THE NEGATIVE EXPERIENCES TO THE PAIN BOX

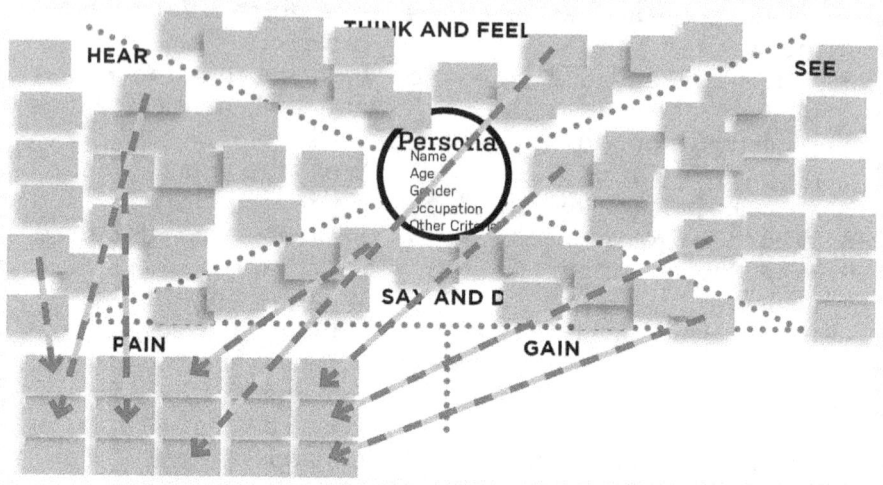

MOVE ALL THE POSITIVE EXPERIENCES TO THE GAIN BOX

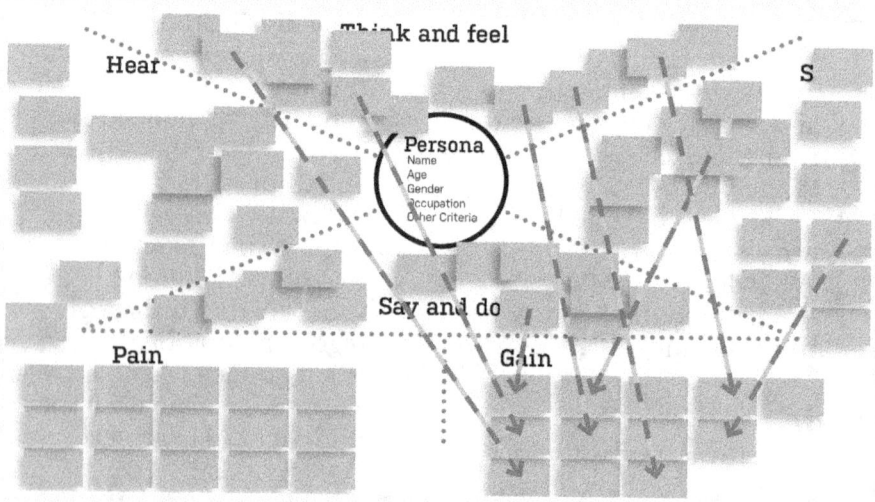

GAIN

What are their goals, desires, and needs; how do they work towards these goals?

1. How does your customer measure success?
2. Is the customer satisfied?
3. What short-term goals does your customer have?
4. What long-term goals does your customer have?
5. When is your customer happy?
6. What do you do better than your competitors?
7. When is your customer happy
8. Where is your customer happy?
9. What is ultimate dream? What are they desperately hoping to achieve?
10. Why is getting that outcome so important? What would that mean for them?
11. What have you learned by building the empathy map? What are the themes and insights? How can you improve your customer's holistic experience?
12. What does the customer want or need to achieve?
13. How does your customer measure success?
14. What are the strategies the customer might use to achieve their goals.

Reading is an exercise in empathy; an exercise in walking in someone else's shoes for a while."

Malorie Blackman

"Empathy is key in the design process, especially when you start expanding outside of your comfort zone to new languages, cultures, and age groups. If you try to assume what those people want, you're likely to get it wrong.

Mike Krieger

Studying design has made me a much, much more astute observer of this aspect of business. And I'm working mightily to improve my empathic skills. I've dramatically improved my ability to read facial expressions and I'm trying to be a better, more attentive listener.

Daniel H. Pink

EMPATHY MAP EXERCISE

BACKGROUND
The Empathy Map is a tool intended to help you to systematically consider the perspectives of those who a service may affect. Empathy maps can be created to help understand and improve the customer experience. Empathy maps can be completed by individuals or as a team. Invite real stakeholders to complete first-person empathy maps.

INSTRUCTIONS
Select a service experience to map. A period of around 30-minutes of customer experience is a good length of time to study.
Draw the empathy map framework or use a template.
3. Identify the group of people your design will serve. Choose a Persona that represents a market segment, Define the gender and age for this persona. What culture do they come from? Where do they live? How are they employed? What is their income? What are their interests?
Add observations on post-it notes to the empathy map in the appropriate sections.

Think about their experience about a particular service:
1. What does she see?
2. Describe what the customer sees in her environment:
3. What does it look like?
4. Who surrounds her?
5. Who are her friends?
6. What problems does she encounter?
7. What does she hear?
8. Describe how the environment influences the customer.
9. What do her friends say? Her family?
10. Who really influences her, and how?
11. Which media Channels are influential?
12. 3- What does she really think and feel?
13. What is really important to her (which she might not say publicly)?
14. Imagine her emotions. What moves her?
15. What might keep her up at night?
16. What are her dreams and aspirations?
17. What does she say and do?
18. Imagine what the customer might say, or how she might behave in public:
19. What is her attitude?
20. What could she be telling others?
21. Pay particular attention to potential conflicts between what a customer might say and what she may truly think or feel.
22. What is the customer's pain?
23. What are her biggest frustrations?
24. What obstacles stand between her and what she wants or needs to achieve?

25. Which risks might she fear taking?
26. 6- What does the customer gain?
27. What does she truly want or need to achieve?
28. How does she measure success?
29. Think of some strategies she might use to achieve her goals.
30. Populate each area in the template with 6 or more observations.
31. Analyze the completed map. What have you learned about this stakeholder group?
32. What patterns do you see?
33. How can you best serve their needs?
34. Move the appropriate post-it-notes into the pain and gain boxes.

PAIN:
1. What are their frustrations?
2. What obstacles and challenges stand in their way?
3. What keeps the customer up at night?
4. Where are they unhappy?

GAIN:
1. What do they want to achieve?
2. What are their hopes and dreams?
3. How do they measure success?
4. What strategies could help them reach their goals?

DELIVERABLES
One Empathy Map

Humans aren't as good as we should be in our capacity to empathize with feelings and thoughts of others, be they humans or other animals on Earth. So maybe part of our formal education should be training in empathy. Imagine how different the world would be if, in fact, that were 'reading, writing, arithmetic, empathy.'

Neil deGrasse Tyson

"We need somebody who's got the heart, the empathy, to recognize what it's like to be a young teenage mom, the empathy to understand what it's like to be poor or African-American or gay or disabled or old and that's the criterion by which I'll be selecting my judges."

Barack Obama

08
EXPERIENCE MAPS

ELEMENTS OF AN EXPERIENCE MAP

Here are some of the lanes that may be included in an experience map. Maps do not usually contain every lane described here but are build based on the elements that you are most interested in understanding when your team constructs the map.

PHASE
Journey and experience mapping can be used for the following purposes:

TOUCHPOINTS
A touchpoint is any point of contact between a customer and the provider of a service, product or experience. A touchpoint is where a potential customer or customer comes in contact with your brand before, during and after a transaction.

Identifying your touchpoints is an important step toward creating an experience map. Each touchpoint is an opportunity to create a better customer experience. A touchpoint can be a physical, virtual or human point of interaction. Chris Risdon from Adaptive Path defines touchpoints in this way. 'A touchpoint is a point of interaction involving a specific human need in a specific time and place.'

PHYSICAL EVIDENCE CHANNEL 1
Journey and experience mapping can be used for the following purposes:

PHYSICAL EVIDENCE CHANNEL 1
Journey and experience mapping can be used for the following purposes:

CUSTOMER ACTIONS
Customer actions are those actions a user performs during an experience in chronological order left to right. Include steps that don't have visible actions, like waiting to receive a quote.

THINKING
Journey and experience mapping can be used for the following purposes:

SAYING
Journey and experience mapping can be used for the following purposes:

FEELING
Journey and experience mapping can be used for the following purposes:

GOALS
Journey and experience mapping can be used for the following purposes:

PAIN POINTS
Journey and experience mapping can be used for the following purposes:

FRUSTRATIONS
What is frustrating the user?

CHALLENGES
What difficulties is the customer trying to overcome?

BARRIERS
What is standing in the way of the user achieving their goal?

MOMENTS OF TRUTH
The phrase 'moment of truth' (MOT) was first introduced by Richard Norman and popularized by Jan Carlzon in his 1987 book of that name. CEO of Scandinavian Airlines (SAS) He used the term to mean those moments in which there is an opportunity for an organization to make a difference when interacting with a customer. Moments of truth are the instances of contact or interaction between a customer and a firm that gives the customer an opportunity to form or change an impression about the firm. They are the moments that leave a lasting impression. These are the customer interactions where you should focus your resources.

ACTOR 1
Journey and experience mapping can be used for the following purposes:

ACTOR 2

Journey and experience mapping can be used for the following purposes:

CUSTOMER QUOTES
Customer quotes from interviews, observation, or workshops will show what customers think, feel, and experience step-by-step..

ENVIRONMENTS
Journey and experience mapping can be used for the following purposes:

EXPECTATIONS
Journey and experience mapping can be used for the following purposes:

RISKS
Journey and experience mapping can be used for the following purposes:

OPPORTUNITIES
Journey and experience mapping can be used for the following purposes:

EMOTIONAL JOURNEY
Journey and experience mapping can be used for the following purposes:

EXPERIENCE MAPS

WHAT

Experience maps are diagrams that allow a designer or manager to describe the elements of a customer experience in concise terms.

A journey map focuses on identifying touch points, An experience map focuses on the emotions your customer experiences. In practice, many people use these terms interchangeably. The particular lanes included can be mixed and matched to your goals.

Customer journeys depict what customers really want. These methods help us to understand interactions from users' point of view. They must be developed from your customers' perspective. They are a framework to craft a better customer experience. With these tools you can identify problem areas and opportunities for improvement.

Maps are usually created to help understand a particular segment or persona. The more complex your service or customer experience, the more value there is in mapping the customer journey and experience.

HISTORY

The origin of journey and experience mapping is less apparent than Service Blueprints, but they have been used at least since 1991 (Whittle & Foster, 1991).

Several sources mention these methods from 2006 (Parker & Heapy, 2006; Voss & Zomerdijk, 2007). The detailed application is still evolving (Følstad et al., 2013). Følstad defines a customer journey as the process a customer goes through to reach a particular goal. The value of these techniques is greatest when the complexity of the route is higher. Customer journey maps describe not only what a customer experiences but also the customer's response to those experiences.

Wechsler (2012) describes internal workshops for creating customer journey maps. The analysis of customer journeys may also concern quantitative measurement of the customer's experience. In the scientific literature, such analysis is

EXAMPLE OF AN EXPERIENCE MAP

STAGES	EVALUATE	ENTER		USE/ENGAGE				EXIT	
TOUCH POINTS	Home Internet Laptop	Car	Car park Coffee shop exterior	Coffee shop interior Menu board	Counter Coffee cup	Coffee shop interior Chair table	Laptop Power socket Internet	Laptop Internet chair table Cup	Car Taxi to coffee shop interior	Car Bar Car
DOING	Customer at home decides to go out to have a coffee	Checks location of coffee shop on internet	Drives car to coffee shop	Parks and enters coffee shop	Selects drink and waits in line to order	Pays and picks up coffee	Finds a table and sits down	Writes and sends some emails. Tops up coffee	Finishes coffee and puts cup in trashcan	Returned to car
THINKING	Should I call a friend? Will I have a long wait to be served?	Which coffee shop should I go to?	Will there be a long queue?	Will there be a long queue?	Should I have a latte or a drip coffee?	The coffee is more expensive than last time	Is there a seat available at the window?	Not a plug seat table. How long will my battery last?	Where is the trashcan?	Will the traffic be heavy?
FEELING	Should I call a friend? Will I have a long wait to be served?	Which coffee shop should I go to?	Will be able to park close to the coffee shop?	Will there be a long queue?	Should I have a latte or a drip coffee?	The coffee is more expensive than last time	Is there a seat available at the window?	The coffee is very hot. Is there a plug for my laptop?	Where is the trashcan?	Will the traffic be heavy?
PAIN POINTS		No parking places available close to coffee shop	Queue takes 20 minutes	Too many choices on menu	Prices have increased	Replace chairs. Open up second room	Coffee too hot to drink. Coffee shop cold.	No plug available for laptop. Music too loud.	No visible trashcan	Long walk back to car. Traffic heavy
OPPORTUNITIES	Improve website	Differentiate coffee shop from other coffee shops	Make more parking available.	Order coffee Online. Add second cash register.	Reduce number of options	Different level priced menu items		Add a coffee temperature. Be busy with own.	Add power points	Relocate trash cans. Increase number of trashcans.

EXPERIENCE MAPS

typically conducted as part of the mapping process to quantify changes in experiential quality during the customer journey (Trischler & Zehrer, 2012). Kankainen et al. (2012) describe the use of customer journeys for co-design, where customers formulate "dream journeys". In 2007 the British Government published guidelines on customer journey mapping (HM Government, 2007).

WHY
Experience mapping can be used for the following purposes:
1. Understand the collective experiences of customer segments
2. To create a more streamlined, consistent, and efficient customer experience.
3. Create a more seamless customer experience across business departments and channels.
4. Design a new service or product customer experience
5. Allocate people and resources more effectively.
6. Develop alignment across departments of an organization.
7. Craft a better customer experience.
8. Expose places where your service or customer experience may fail.
9. Craft a better customer experience
10. Strategic and tactical innovation
11. Building and sharing knowledge
12. Designing the moments of truth
13. Understand competitive positioning
14. Understanding the ideal experience
15. Reveal the truth from your customer's perspective
16. Identify opportunities
17. Empathize with your custom
18. Designing and improving Systems
19. Develop a better product road map
20. Take cost & complexity out of the system
21. Prioritize competing deliverables
22. Plan for hiring
23. Bring different parts of your business together to work to improve the customer experience
24. Build knowledge of customer behaviors and needs across channels
25. Identify specific areas of opportunity to drive ideation and innovation
26. Make intangible services tangible.
27. Develop customer insights
28. Understand where friction exists between the needs of different market segments
29. Introduce metrics for what matters most for your customers.
30. Align your offerings to brand promise.
31. Identify failure points.
32. Improve efficiency.
33. Imagine future product and service experiences.

34. More Holistic thinking.
35. Making better decisions.
36. A living document that can evolve with your business.
37. Is a holistic view of key touch points and interactions personas have with the brand.
38. Communicate the experience visually.
39. Promotes better coordination of across channels.

A MAP HELPS YOU

1. Plan your product or service offering most efficiently for various customer segments.
2. Evaluate customer experience gaps or fail points before they occur.
3. Identify opportunities to improve you customer experience.
4. identify ways to improve your touchpoints and remove duplication.
5. You can create a map as a concept for a customer's ideal future experience.
6. Put all stakeholders on the same page so that you can reach a common understanding and agreement on how to move forward towards your organizational goals.
7. Helps make measures of success clear.
8. From analyzing your map recommendations and a plan to reach your objectives can be put into place.

HOW

Here is a list of stages that you can complete creating a Service Blueprint. Consider the blueprint to be a living document that will develop and improve, so it doesn't have to be perfect first time. Concentrate on your customers and their point of view.

SELECT YOUR TEAM

Care should be taken in choosing your team. As many groups and diverse points of view involved in design delivery and use of the service as possible should be represented.

1. Keep groups to six people or less.
2. If your total group size is larger than six break the large group into smaller groups of six or less.
3. Have a diverse team with different genders, age, occupations and seniority represented.
4. Have at least two or three "T" shaped people. That is, people with two or more areas of expertise such as technology and management or management and design. This makes the team more flexible and helps group collaboration. This experience can be gained through education or work. Look for people with at least 10,000 hours of experience in each of two areas. That corresponds to three or four years of work experience in each area.
5. Involve external and internal stakeholders such as

1. customers, suppliers, internal business management, engineering, design, marketing, distribution, IT and sales. Have customer-facing people where possible because they better understand the customer's perspective.

CREATE YOUR GOAL STATEMENT

1. What is the problem, unmet needs or opportunities that you wish to analyze?
2. Create a clear outline of customer goals and needs that is compatible with your goals and with an outcome that satisfies them.
3. Who are the stakeholders?
4. Where is the service or experience delivered?
5. When is the service or experience provided?
6. What are the channels?
7. Why is there a need for a new design solution?
8. Do you want to enhance the customer experience?
9. Do you wish to engage your customers more effectively?
10. Do you wish to create a more efficient process?
11. Define your goals in a statement.

DEFINE YOUR TARGET AUDIENCE SEGMENT AND THEIR NEEDS

The most successful products services and experiences target precise customer segments.

GATHER YOUR EXISTING RESEARCH

Start by auditing internal customer experience data that has been previously gathered. Do you have existing research? Where are the gaps in your knowledge?

Interviews are one of the most usual methods used to gather data. Ask them to walk you through their experience and talk about their problems, needs desires and feelings at each stage. Start by talking to between five and twenty people as a minimum sample size. Ask them what touch points they are engaging at each phase. Ask them where they are experiencing problems or frustrations in achieving their goals. Document your interviews or observations by using video or a digital recorder.

To be useful, your map needs to be based on real and truthful information.

REVIEW YOUR EXISTING RESEARCH

Review existing research Identify gaps in data and create a list of recurring customer experience problems.

CREATE A RESEARCH PLAN TO FILL THE GAPS

1. What do you still need to know?
2. What questions do you need to ask?
3. How many people will you study?

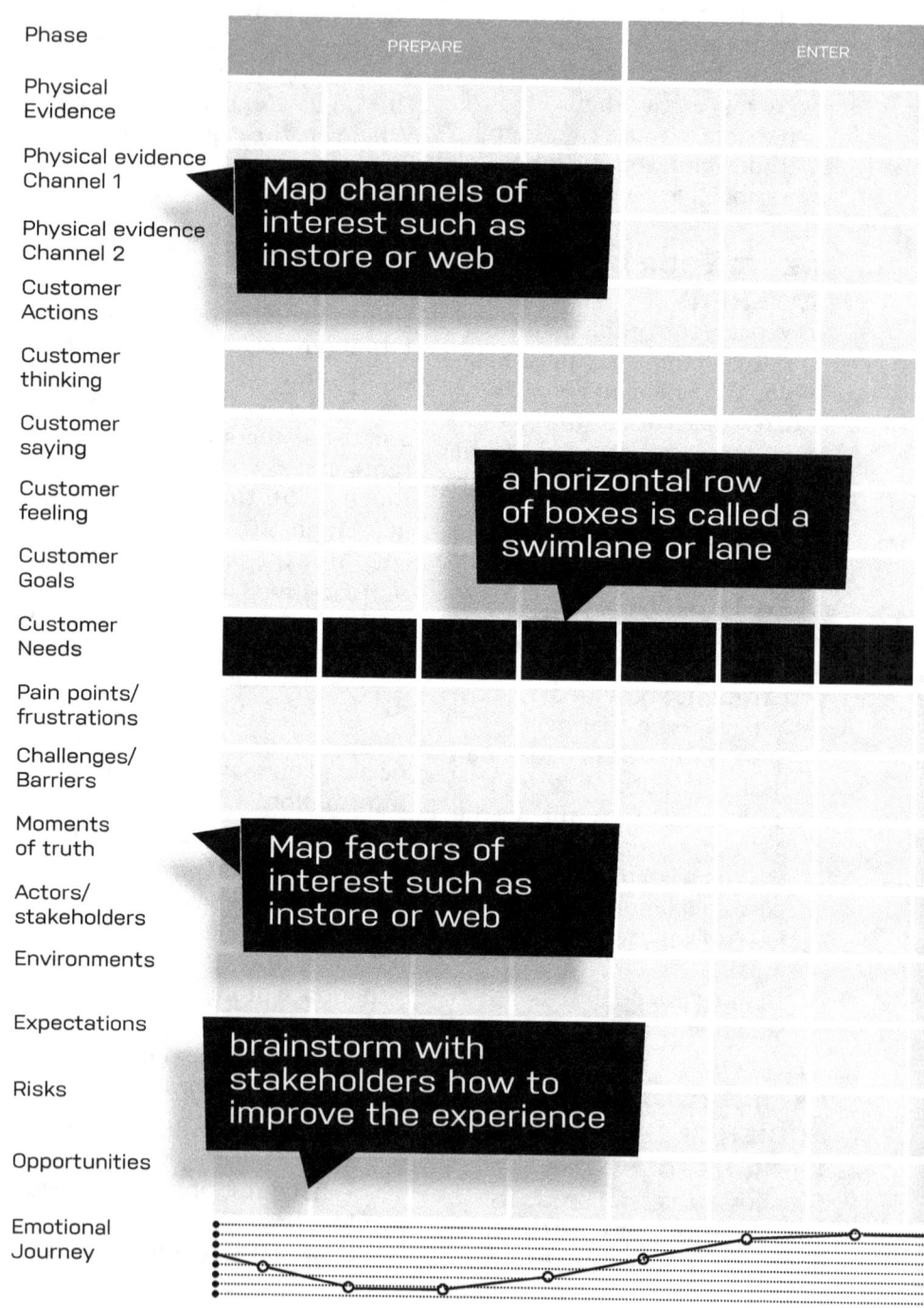

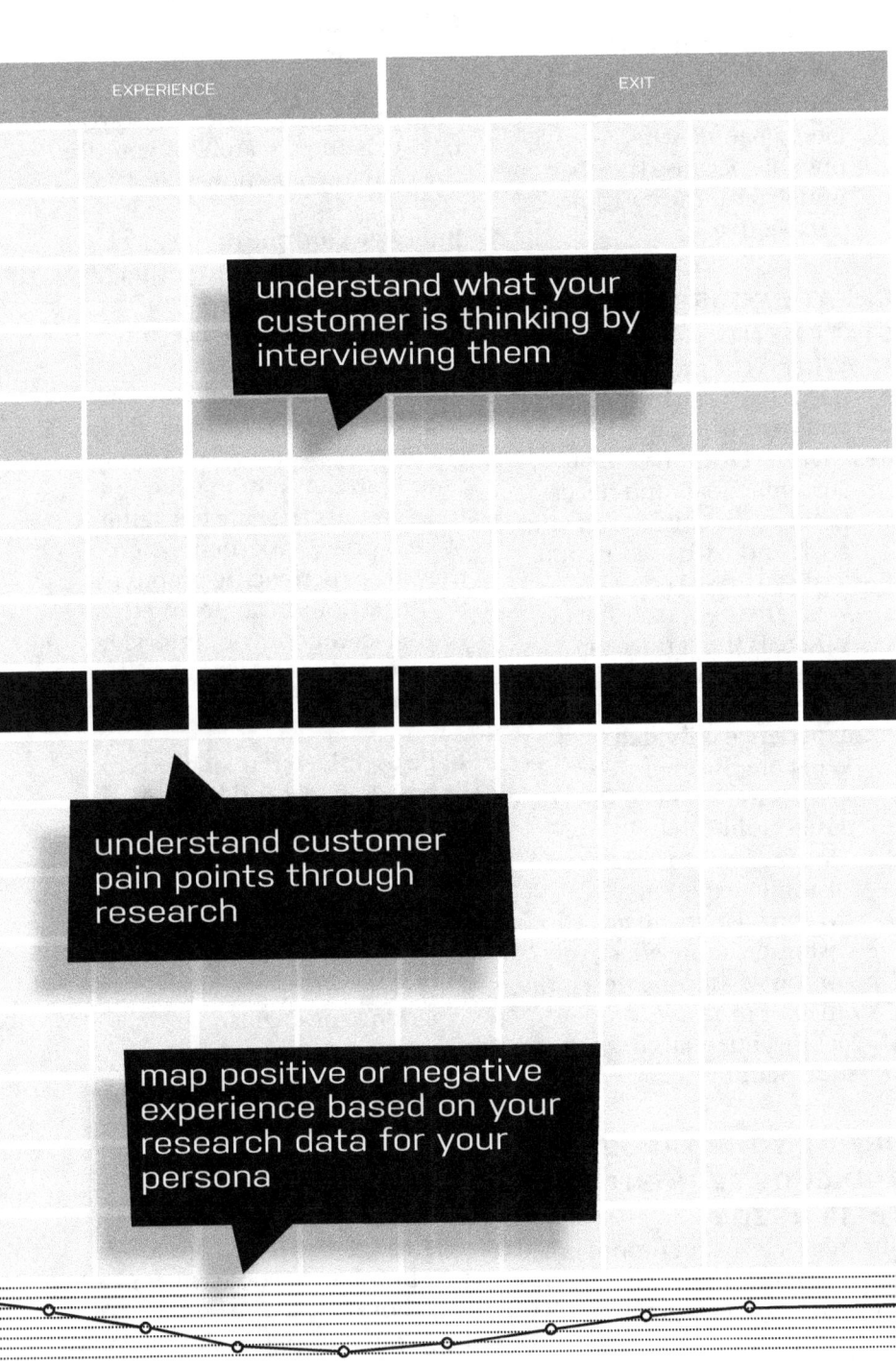

customers, suppliers, internal business management, engineering, design, marketing, distribution, IT and sales. Have customer-facing people where possible because they better understand the customer's perspective.

CREATE YOUR GOAL STATEMENT

1. What is the problem, unmet needs or opportunities that you wish to analyze?
2. Create a clear outline of customer goals and needs that is compatible with your goals and with an outcome that satisfies them.
3. Who are the stakeholders?
4. Where is the service or experience delivered?
5. When is the service or experience provided?
6. What are the channels?
7. Why is there a need for a new design solution?
8. Do you want to enhance the customer experience?
9. Do you wish to engage your customers more effectively?
10. Do you wish to create a more efficient process?
11. Define your goals in a statement.

DEFINE YOUR TARGET AUDIENCE SEGMENT AND THEIR NEEDS

The most successful products services and experiences target precise customer segments.

GATHER YOUR EXISTING RESEARCH

Start by auditing internal customer experience data that has been previously gathered. Do you have existing research? Where are the gaps in your knowledge?

Interviews are one of the most usual methods used to gather data. Ask them to walk you through their experience and talk about their problems, needs desires and feelings at each stage. Start by talking to between five and twenty people as a minimum sample size. Ask them what touch points they are engaging at each phase. Ask them where they are experiencing problems or frustrations in achieving their goals. Document your interviews or observations by using video or a digital recorder.

To be useful, your map needs to be based on real and truthful information.

REVIEW YOUR EXISTING RESEARCH

Review existing research Identify gaps in data and create a list of recurring customer experience problems.

CREATE A RESEARCH PLAN TO FILL THE GAPS

1. What do you still need to know?
2. What questions do you need to ask?
3. How many people will you study?
4. What type of people will you

research?
5. What will be the context of the research?
6. What methods will you use?
7. When will you select and screen the subjects, conduct the research and report on findings?

SYNTHESIZE YOUR RESEARCH

Put each potentially useful piece of information on a separate post-it note. Put the post-it notes on a wall and ask your team to organize the customer's comments into related groups or themes. Which issues are most significant to more customers? Build a hierarchy of issues.

APPOINT YOUR MODERATOR

SELECT AND PREPARE YOUR WORKSPACE

A safe space is a large room with plenty of natural light with a large table and sufficient chairs for your team.
Some useful materials
1. A large wall
2. Butcher paper
3. Masking tape
4. Mobile dry erase boards
5. Dry erase markers
6. Sharpies
7. Adhesive notes in 5 colors
8. Digital camera
9. Tripod

IDENTIFY YOUR TARGET SEGMENT/S TO MAP

Identifying customer segments.

CREATE A PERSONA FOR EACH TARGET SEGMENT

Create 3 to 6 personas to cover all your customers.

IDENTIFY STAKEHOLDERS

A stakeholder is someone who may be in some way influenced by your design when it is complete and marketed.

HOLD STAKEHOLDER WORKSHOPS

Organize a workshop, and guide internal and external stakeholders through the process of creating the first draft. Go over the user experience in detail and discuss the experience from the perspective of customers and diverse stakeholders,

SELECT THE SERVICE TO BE MAPPED

Select your journey or experience to map. We suggest starting small with part of an experience that is important or problematic. For example rather than mapping an entire customer journey for air travel from New York to London, map a part of it that is important such as selecting the airline and booking the travel online. Then explore several challenging sub-journeys before tackling the whole journey.

DECIDE PRESENT OR FUTURE SERVICE TO MAP

It is most usual to first map your existing customer experience. A current state map can help identify ways to make your existing customer experience better or more efficient.

After mapping your existing service you may be interested in creating a map as a scenario for a future service or customer experience.

SELECT START AND END POINTS OF THE CUSTOMER EXPERIENCE

Define the scope in terms of time and customer activities.

SELECT CHANNELS TO MAP

Some examples of channels include
1. In-store experience
2. Face to face
3. Print
4. Web
5. Call center
6. Tablet app
7. TV
8. Mobile phone

The channel defines the opportunities and constraints of a touchpoint. You can map all channels on one map in parallel lanes. This type of map is called a multichannel map. You can map just one channel per map and create as m,any separate maps as you have channels.

START SMALL

Consider picking a specific scenario or sub-activity of your entire customer experience.

DRAFT THE MAP

Use a large wall or table. Create your first rough draft using post-it notes. When it is complete photograph and share it with as many internal and external stakeholders as possible and ask for their feedback. If insights don't fit on a single map, keep maps simple by creating one map for each persona.

CREATE THE STORY

What are the main elements of the customer experience from a customer perspective? What parts of their experience leave a lasting impression on them either positive or negative.

MAP USER ACTIONS & ACTIVITIES STEP-BY-STEP

Start at the beginning of the service or experience and list each thing a customer commonly does step by step. Put each sub-activity on a separate post-it note. For example, if the activity is visiting a coffee shop the activities may include.
1. At work decide to get a coffee on the way home
2. Check the location of coffee shops on the Internet.
3. Select coffee shop
4. Go to car
5. Drive to coffee shop
6. Park
7. Enter coffee shop

activities into four or six phases of sub-activities. Some examples of phases of activities are:

1. Explore
2. Evaluate
3. Engage
4. Experience

1. Aware
2. Join
3. Use
4. Develop
5. Leave

1. Research
2. Evaluate and compare
3. Commit
4. Use and Monitor
5. Refine and review

MAP THE PHYSICAL EVIDENCE STEP-BY-STEP

Physical evidence is usually the lane shown at the top of a blueprint. Services consist of the interactions with people, the processes, and the physical proof of the experience. Designed objects in the service environment are sometimes referred to as "physical evidence" because they are physical proof of service that has taken place. Physical evidence is the tangible things that help to communicate and perform the service and influence a customer's perception of a service.

Physical evidence is the visible manifestation of service. It conveys to customers whether the service provider cares about their customers and whether they

8. Stand in line
9. Order
10. Pick up coffee
11. Find table
12. Sit down
13. Drink coffee
14. Read news on tablet
15. Pack up
16. Return to car
17. Drive home
18. Reflect on the experience.

Describe each activity on a separate post-it note and place them in a line on your wall or table. Continue till your team is happy that all important activities have been included.

MAP TIME

How long does each customer activity usually take? Does a stage usually last ten seconds or ten minutes. Place the time taken on a post-it note above each stage of customer activity.
Time to consider:
1. Critical periods service actions, such as response to a proposal.
2. Duration of each service step, such as airline check-in
3. Time between service steps such as walking to a hotel room after check-in.
4. End to end service experience.

BUILD THE MAP

Now you are ready to create the map.

MAP USER ACTION PHASES

Break the list of customer

LIST THE PHASES OF CUSTOMER ACTIONS

PHASES	EVALUATE	ENTER	USE/ENGAGE	EXIT
TOUCH POINTS				
DOING				
THINKING				
FEELING				
PAIN POINTS				
OPPORTUNITIES				

> Review customer activities. Identify 4 to 6 phases

LIST THE STAGE-BY-STAGE TOUCHPOINTS FOR EACH CHANNEL

STAGES	EVALUATE		ENTER		USE/ENGAGE					EXIT		
TOUCH POINTS	Home interior	Internet Laptop	Car	Car park Coffee shop exterior	Coffee shop interior Menu board	Counter Coffee cup	Coffee shop interior Chair table	Laptop Power socket Internet	Laptop Internet chair table Cup	Cup Trashcan coffee shop interior	Car Par Car	Car
DOING												
THINKING												
FEELING												
PAIN POINTS												
OPPORTUNITIES												

trust their customers. Physical evidence cues are what customers use to evaluate service quality.

Physical evidence can convey intended and unintended messages to customers. Physical evidence is the interface between a service provider and a customer. Key to delivering a successful service is to clearly identify a simple, consistent message, and then manage the evidence to support that message.

" Well-prepared small details represent sincerity in serving guests which reflects the hotel's good service spirit. For example, welcome fruit, an electric kettle and fresh flowers in hotel rooms are service evidence that often evoked delight as they show the hotel's thoughtfulness"

"For example, a research participant talked about disappointment caused by "fake" hangers in a hotel room's closet. She complained: They're not real hangers, because they're attached to the railing. So
if you want to take out a hanger and then hang it on a chair or hang it on a door, you can't, because there's no hook... That's kind of a fake hanger. It shows that they think I'm going to steal the hangers. So it makes me feel not trusted."

Source: Kathy Pui Ying Lo Loughborough University

Physical evidence includes the service providers building/facilities and staff appearance; and uniforms. Physical evidence should be considered important by the customer and the promise implied by these tangible objects should be delivered. A bank card is an example of physical evidence of a service. It helps a bank differentiate their service from another bank. It separates the service from the seller.

Other examples of physical evidence are
1. The building
2. The interior
3. The car park
4. Internal signs.
5. Packaging.
6. Promotional materials
7. Web pages.
8. Paperwork
9. Brochures.
10. Stationery
11. Billing statement
12. Furnishings.
13. Signs
14. Uniforms and employee dress.
15. Business cards.
16. Mailboxes.

MAP THE PAIN POINTS
A pain point is any part of the customer experience that they find people disturbing, frustrating, urgent or uncomfortable. Many customer needs are for things the end users don't clearly understand or can articulate. A pain point is a problem for your customer and a problem and an opportunity for you. Solving pain points create value for you and your customer.

EXPERIENCE MAPS 207

LIST THE STAGE-BY-STAGE CUSTOMER ACTIONS

STAGES	EVALUATE		ENTER		USE/ENGAGE						EXIT		
TOUCH POINTS	Home Interior	Internet Laptop	Car	Car park Coffee shop exterior	Coffee shop interior Menu board	Counter Coffee cup	Coffee shop interior Chair table	Laptop Power socket Internet	Laptop Internet chair table Cup	Cup Trashcan coffee shop Interior	Car Par Car	Car
DOING	Customer At home decides to go out to have a coffee	Checks location of coffee shop on internet	Drives car to coffee shop	Parks and enters coffee shop	Selects drink and waits in line to order	Pays and picks up coffee	Finds a table and sits down	Drinks coffee and reviews emails on laptop	Writes and sends some emails. Tops up coffee	Finishes coffee and puts cup in trashcan	Returns to car	Drives on to supermarket
THINKING												
FEELING												
PAIN POINTS												
OPPORTUNITIES												

LIST CUSTOMER THOUGHTS STAGE-BY-STAGE

STAGES	EVALUATE		ENTER		USE/ENGAGE						EXIT		
TOUCH POINTS	Home Interior	Internet Laptop	Car	Car park Coffee shop exterior	Coffee shop interior Menu board	Counter Coffee cup	Coffee shop interior Chair table	Laptop Power socket Internet	Laptop Internet chair table Cup	Cup Trashcan coffee shop Interior	Car Par Car	Car
DOING	Customer At home decides to go out to have a coffee	Checks location of coffee shop on internet	Drives car to coffee shop	Parks and enters coffee shop	Selects drink and waits in line to order	Pays and picks up coffee	Finds a table and sits down	Drinks coffee and reviews emails on laptop	Writes and sends some emails. Tops up coffee	Finishes coffee and puts cup in trashcan	Returns to car	Drives on to supermarket
THINKING	Should I call a friend? Will I have a long wait to be served?	Which coffee shop should I go to?	Will be able to park close to the coffee shop?	Will there be a long queue?	Should I have a latte or a drip coffee?	The coffee is more expensive than last time	Is there a seat available at the window?	The coffee is very hot. Is there a plug for my laptop?	Not a plug available. How long will my battery last?	Where is the trashcan?	Will the traffic be heavy?	There was a long queue. I will go to another coffee shop next time.
FEELING												
PAIN POINTS												
OPPORTUNITIES												

"customer pain" is a synonym for "customer needs". Customers spend money to combat pain or to pursue pleasure. Examples of service pain points are airport security lines, hospital directions, or the cost of travel. A pain point is the why customers choose you if you offer a solution to their need. If you engage your customers and listen, they'll tell you their pain points

To identify customer 'pain-points':
1. In-depth interviews with customer-facing internal employees
2. Requests from your most valuable customers.
3. Customer interviews.
4. Customer focus groups.
5. Review of customer support or warranty claims to identify persistent problems.
6. Review of competitor offerings.
7. You can list the root causes of pain for your customers at each stage.

CUSTOMER OR STAKEHOLDER COMMENTS
List significant or representative comments in a lane. What do customers think?

MAP BRAND IMPACT
List brand impact of touchpoints and customer comments in a lane.

KEY PEOPLE
Identify internal owners of experiences that support customer's needs.

CUSTOMER NEEDS
Do customers have unrecognized needs that could be addressed? What do customers want to accomplish at each stage of interaction?

MAP CONNECTIONS
Use arrows to illustrate the flow of responsibility who is driving the service at any moment and should be initiating service action:

1. Model expectations of "proactive" provider activity.
2. Model the customer responsibility for next steps.
3. Model partner expectations.
4. Define points of handoff between roles, such as from backstage to onstage.

MAP MOMENTS OF TRUTH
Map those interactions that have the most impact on the customer. A moment of truth is an interaction between a customer and a service provider that allows the end user to form an impression of the organization. For example waiting in line in a coffee shop. A moment of truth is a point in time when a customer can make a judgment about the value of a service delivery and a business relationship. Identifying moments of truth and improving their outcomes is a focus of service blueprinting.

1. training.
2. Map upcoming product launches or your desired future state

MEASURE YOUR PROGRESS TOWARDS YOUR GOALS
Define ways of tracking your progress towards measurable goals. Metrics will help you measure the quality of your customer experience, now and in the future.
1. Net Promoter Score and customer loyalty measures
2. Customer satisfaction measures
3. Quantitative assessments of the customer emotions.
4. Metrics of customer effort
5. The measure of the performance of each touchpoint.
6. New sales.
7. Increased loyalty and retention of customers
8. The increase in revenue per customer.
9. More sales.
10. Reduced costs
11. Better delivery processes.
12. Better quality
13. Increased competitiveness

MULTI-CHANNEL MAP

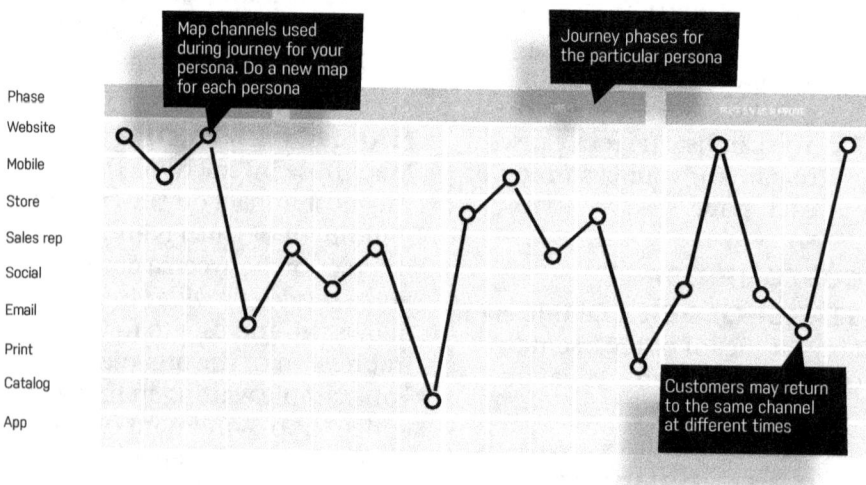

LIST HOW THE CUSTOMER IS FEELING STAGE-BY-STAGE

STAGES	EVALUATE		ENTER		USE/ENGAGE					EXIT		
TOUCH POINTS	Home Interior	Internet Laptop	Car	Car park Coffee shop exterior	Coffee shop interior Menu board	Counter Coffee cup	Coffee shop interior Chair table	Laptop Power socket Internet	Laptop Internet chair table Cup	Cup Trashcan coffee shop interior	Car Par Car	Car
DOING	Customer At home decides to go out to have a coffee	Checks location of coffee shop on internet	Drives car to coffee shop	Parks and enters coffee shop	Selects drink and waits in line to order	Pays and picks up coffee	Finds a table and sits down	Drinks coffee and reviews emails on laptop	Writes and sends some emails. Tops up coffee	Finishes coffee and puts cup in trashcan	Returns to car	Drives on to supermarket
THINKING	Should I call a friend? Will I have a long wait to be served?	Which coffee shop should I go to?	Will be able to park close to the coffee shop?	Will there be a long queue?	Should I have a latte or a drip coffee?	The coffee is more expensive than last time	Is there a seat available at the window?	The coffee is very hot. Is there a plug for my laptop?	Not a plug available. How long will my battery last?	Where is the trashcan?	Will the traffic be heavy?	There was a long queue. I will go to another coffee shop next time.
FEELING	Should I call a friend? Will I have a long wait to be served?	Which coffee shop should I go to?	Will be able to park close to the coffee shop?	Will there be a long queue?	Should I have a latte or a drip coffee?	The coffee is more expensive than last time	Is there a seat available at the window?	The coffee is very hot. Is there a plug for my laptop?	Not a plug available. How long will my battery last?	Where is the trashcan?	Will the traffic be heavy?	I will go to another coffee shop next time.
PAIN POINTS												
OPPORTUNITIES												

LIST PAIN POINTS STAGE-BY-STAGE

STAGES	EVALUATE		ENTER		USE/ENGAGE					EXIT		
TOUCH POINTS	Home Interior	Internet Laptop	Car	Car park Coffee shop exterior	Coffee shop interior Menu board	Counter Coffee cup	Coffee shop interior Chair table	Laptop Power socket Internet	Laptop Internet chair table Cup	Cup Trashcan coffee shop interior	Car Par Car	Car
DOING	Customer At home decides to go out to have a coffee	Checks location of coffee shop on internet	Drives car to coffee shop	Parks and enters coffee shop	Selects drink and waits in line to order	Pays and picks up coffee	Finds a table and sits down	Drinks coffee and reviews emails on laptop	Writes and sends some emails. Tops up coffee	Finishes coffee and puts cup in trashcan	Returns to car	Drives on to supermarket
THINKING	Should I call a friend? Will I have a long wait to be served?	Which coffee shop should I go to?	Will be able to park close to the coffee shop?	Will there be a long queue?	Should I have a latte or a drip coffee?	The coffee is more expensive than last time	Is there a seat available at the window?	The coffee is very hot. Is there a plug for my laptop?	Not a plug available. How long will my battery last?	Where is the trashcan?	Will the traffic be heavy?	There was a long queue. I will go to another coffee shop next time.
FEELING	Should I call a friend? Will I have a long wait to be served?	Which coffee shop should I go to?	Will be able to park close to the coffee shop?	Will there be a long queue?	Should I have a latte or a drip coffee?	The coffee is more expensive than last time	Is there a seat available at the window?	The coffee is very hot. Is there a plug for my laptop?	Not a plug available. How long will my battery last?	Where is the trashcan?	Will the traffic be heavy?	I will go to another coffee shop next time.
PAIN POINTS	Should I call a friend? Will I have a long wait to be served?	Hard to park at best coffee shop	No parking place available close to coffee shop	Queue takes 20-minutes	Too many choices on menu	Price has increased	Needs to wait for an available table. Chairs uncomfortable.	Coffee too hot to drink Coffee shop cold.	No plug available for laptop. Music too loud.	No visible trashcan	Long walk back to car Traffic heavy	
OPPORTUNITIES												

ROOT CAUSE OF PAIN POINT
Ask why the experience is painful for the customer. If necessary, ask why several times to understand the cause of the pain.

MAP BARRIERS
What are the obstacles to the optimal experience for the customer at each stage of their interaction?

ADD PHOTOS OR PICTURES WHERE POSSIBLE
Maps sometimes have a lane of photographs that show pain points or other aspects of customer activities. Use pictures if they are the best way of communicating something. For example lack of cleanliness on a train platform.

IDENTIFY POINTS OF FAILURE
Where is the experience failing or likely to fail?

OPPORTUNITIES
Brainstorm ways to change to better meet customer needs.
1. Brainstorm ways to change to meet better customer needs.
2. Bullet these ideas in a separate lane stage by stage.
3. What is the ideal customer experience
4. Analyze every touch point
5. Identify physical evidence at each phase - moment of truth
6. Simplify and refine the process
7. Remove pain points and surprises.
8. Add touchpoints that are missing
9. Build scenarios.
10. Think about extreme users, new users, average users.

PHOTOGRAPH THE DRAFT
Photograph the whole blueprint and photograph the blueprint in sections with sufficient resolution to enable you to transfer the map into a graphics program such as Adobe Illustrator or InDesign.

CREATE A PRESENTATION COPY
Photograph the whole map and photograph the map in sections with sufficient resolution to enable you to transfer the map into a graphics program such as Adobe Illustrator or InDesign. Templates can be used for future maps.

DISTRIBUTE TO STAKEHOLDERS FOR FEEDBACK
Distribute draft to internal and external stakeholders for feedback. Circulate you map as widely as possible to get feedback from internal departments, executives, external customers and stakeholders.

REFINE THE MAP BASED ON THE FEEDBACK
Does it tell the story of your customer's experience that is complete, from beginning to end? Is it understandable to

people outside the team? Are the insights actionable? Does it inspire and support a change in strategy? Does it communicate the necessary information, without further explanation? Simplify the map. Identify gaps and do further research to fill the gaps. Gaps in touchpoints may suggest opportunities to add new touchpoints.

ITERATE
Distribute the refined map to other stakeholders and refine the map again.

BRAINSTORM THE IDEAL EXPERIENCE
Put together what you have learned to generate a better experience for your customers that you can implement. Develop step-by-step corrective actions for fail points.

RAPID PROTOTYPING
Experience prototyping is the most efficient way to implement an improved service. The goal is to observe customers interacting with the new experience and obtain their feedback about the experience. Use methods such as:
1. Video prototyping
2. Role-playing
3. Desktop walkthroughs
4. Bodystorming
5. Paper prototyping
6. Empathy tools
7. Wireframing
8. Service staging
9. Wizard of Oz
10. Start with low-fidelity methods and move to higher fidelity prototyping methods as you find clarity with the best design direction.

SERVICE STAGING
Test the refinements in a staged setting. Sets up space that imitates the real environment, but with simple props to represent physical objects.

CONDUCT USER STUDIES IN THE TARGET CONTEXT
Test with target users iteratively and refine the service until the pain points have become points of pleasure for customers.
1. Do people understand the service
2. Do people see the value of the service?
3. Do people understand how to use it?
4. Is the experience positive?
5. What ideas do the customers have that could improve the service?

IMPLEMENT THE SERVICE
The end purpose of a blueprint is to take action and improve the journey and drive the ROI to justify the investment. After the new service design is tested, the design team documents the new experience and creates implementation guidelines to roll out of the new service across the organization. The service blueprint is now a tool to communicate the new design.

1. Use your map for employee

BRAINSTORM OPPORTUNITIES TO IMPROVE THE EXPERIENCE

STAGES	EVALUATE		ENTER		USE/ENGAGE						EXIT	
TOUCH POINTS	Home Interior	Internet Laptop	Car	Car park Coffee shop exterior	Coffee shop interior Menu board	Counter Coffee cup	Coffee shop interior Chair table	Laptop Power socket Internet	Laptop Internet chair table Cup	Cup Trashcan coffee shop interior	Car Par Car	Car
DOING	Customer At home decides to go out to have a coffee	Checks location of coffee shop on Internet	Drives car to coffee shop	Parks and enters coffee shop	Selects drink and waits in line to order	Pays and picks up coffee	Finds a table and sits down	Drinks coffee and reviews emails on laptop	Writes and sends some emails. Tops up coffee	Finishes coffee and puts cup in trashcan	Returns to car	Drives on to supermarket
THINKING	Should I call a friend? Will I have a long wait to be served?	Which coffee shop should I go to?	Will be able to park close to the coffee shop?	Will there be a long queue?	Should I have a latte or a drip coffee?	The coffee is more expensive than last time	Is there a seat available at the window?	The coffee is very hot. Is there a plug for my laptop?	Not a plug available. How long will my battery last?	Where is the trashcan?	Will the traffic be heavy?	There was a long queue. I will go to another coffee shop next time.
FEELING	Should I call a friend? Will I have a long wait to be served?	Which coffee shop should I go to?	Will be able to park close to the coffee shop?	Will there be a long queue?	Should I have a latte or a drip coffee?	The coffee is more expensive than last time	Is there a seat available at the window?	The coffee is very hot. Is there a plug for my laptop?	Not a plug available. How long will my battery last?	Where is the trashcan?	Will the traffic be heavy?	I will go to another coffee shop next time.
PAIN POINTS	Should I call a friend? Will I have a long wait to be served?	Hard to park at best coffee shop	No parking place available close to coffee shop	Queue takes 20-minutes	Too many choices on menu	Price has increased	Needs to wait for an available table. Chairs uncomfortable.	Coffee too hot to drink	No plug available for laptop. Coffee shop cold.	No visible trashcan	Long walk back to car Traffic heavy	
OPPORTUNITIES	Improve website	Differentiate coffee shop from other coffee shops	Make more parking available.	Order coffee Online. Add second cash register.	Reduce number of options	Offer some lower priced menu items	Replace chairs. Open up second room	Adjust coffee temperature. Fix leaky windows.	Add power points	Relocate trash cans. Increase number of trashcans.	Make more parking available.	

training.
2. Map upcoming product launches or your desired future state

MEASURE YOUR PROGRESS TOWARDS YOUR GOALS

Define ways of tracking your progress towards measurable goals. Metrics will help you measure the quality of your customer experience, now and in the future.
1. Net Promoter Score and customer loyalty measures
2. Customer satisfaction measures
3. Quantitative assessments of the customer emotions.
4. Metrics of customer effort
5. The measure of the performance of each touchpoint.
6. New sales.
7. Increased loyalty and retention of customers
8. The increase in revenue per customer.
9. More sales.
10. Reduced costs
11. Better delivery processes.
12. Better quality
13. Increased competitiveness

EMOTIONAL JOURNEY MAP

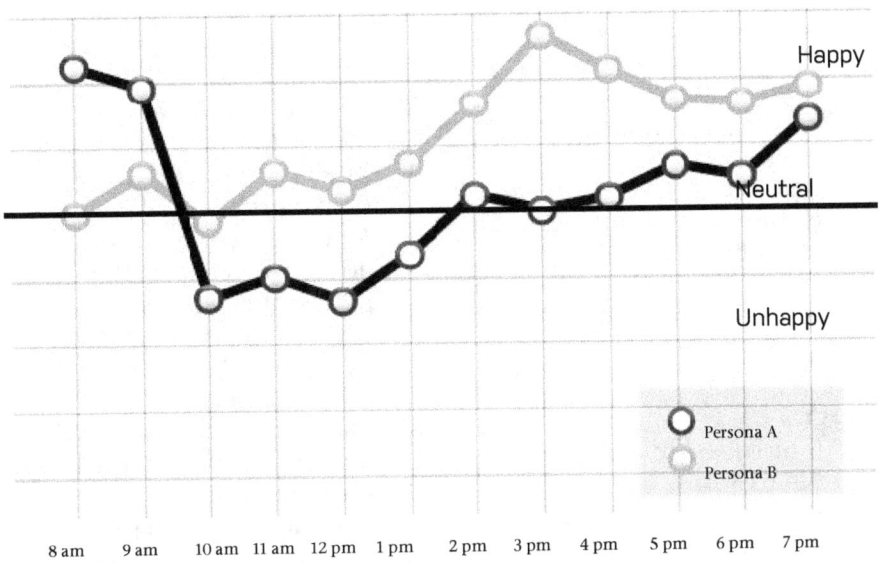

EMOTIONAL JOURNEY MAP

> **WHAT**
>
> An emotional journey map is a map that visually illustrates people's emotional experience throughout an interaction with an organization or brand.

WHY
1. It provides a focus for discussion.
2. It focuses on what may make your customers unhappy
3. Provides a visually compelling story of customer experience.
4. Customer experience is more than interaction with a product.
5. By understanding the journey that your customers are making, you will be in a position to make informed improvements.

CHALLENGES
1. Customers often do not take the route in an interaction that the designer expects.
2. Failure to manage experiences can lead to lost customers.

HOW
1. Define the activity of your map. For example, it could be a ride on the underground train.
2. Collect internal insights.
3. Research customer perceptions.
4. Analyze research.
5. Map journey.
6. Across the top of the page do a timeline Break the journey into stages using your customer's point of view
7. Capture each persona's unique experience.
8. Use a scale from 0 to 10. The higher the number, the better the experience.
9. Plot the emotional journey.
10. Analyze the lease pleasant emotional periods and create ideas for improving the experience during those periods.
11. Create a map for each persona.

MULTI-CHANNEL MAP
Interactions can cross channels, touchpoints or physical evidence and take place in multiple contexts. More than 50% of companies according to one study have little understanding of the complex nature of their customer's typical purchase routes. Customers desire seamless interactions across channels and touchpoints. A multichannel map can help uncover opportunities for your business to improve the customer experience.

EXPERIENCE MAP EXERCISE

Experience mapping is a strategic process of capturing and communicating complex interactions and experiences. The activity of mapping builds knowledge and consensus across your organization, and the map helps build seamless customer, user or employee experiences.

INSTRUCTIONS

1. 1. Choose a service, customer, user, or employee experience you find interesting, that you will be able to find people to interview about, and that you believe can be improved by some intervention. It should involve at least 12 steps and take at least 30-minutes on average.
2. Interview 5 end users: Discover user's emotional state throughout the experience. Try to understand what they feel, what they care about, and what that implies.
3. Create an experience map to describe the customer or employee journey.
4. What is the customer or employee doing? Break the experience down into at least one dozen activities that take place over at least 30-minutes
5. List the touchpoints that the employee or customer engages through the activities at each stage of their activity. These can be websites, vehicles, buildings, devices, interior spaces, people or other tangible physical things.
6. What does the person want or need at each stage?
7. List how the average customer is feeling at each stage, are they happy, frustrated, bored, confused or experiencing some other emotions.
8. What are the pain points at each stage where the person has negative feelings?
9. What are the opportunities to improve the experience or pain points at each stage?
10. Plot the most important points within the experience. The most successful experience maps will communicate creatively, demonstrate emotional insights, and clearly identify where lapses can be prevented or repaired by providing people with a better solution.

DELIVERABLES

One experience map of one to two pages as a PDF file.

09
JOURNEY MAPS

A CUSTOMER JOURNEY MAP

CUSTOMER LENS

PERSONA IMAGE

PERSONA NAME	SCENARIO	GOALS	EXPECTATIONS
• Persona details • Persona details • Persona details • Persona details	• Goal one • Goal two • Goal three • Goal four	• Goal one • Goal two • Goal three • Goal four	• Expectation one • Expectation two • Expectation three • Expectation four

CUSTOMER JOURNEY

JOURNEY PHASE	REACH	ENGAGE	ACTIVATE	NUTURE
TOUCHPOINTS	**TOUCHPOINTS** • Touchpoint one • Touchpoint two • Touchpoint three • Touchpoint four	**TOUCHPOINTS** • Touchpoint one • Touchpoint two • Touchpoint three • Touchpoint four	**TOUCHPOINTS** • Touchpoint one • Touchpoint two • Touchpoint three • Touchpoint four	**TOUCHPOINTS** • Touchpoint one • Touchpoint two • Touchpoint three • Touchpoint four
USER ACTIVITIES	**USER ACTIONS** • Action one • Action two • Action three • Action four	**USER ACTIONS** • Action one • Action two • Action three • Action four	**USER ACTIONS** • Action one • Action two • Action three • Action four	**USER ACTIONS** • Action one • Action two • Action three • Action four

CHANNELS

- CHANNEL 1
- CHANNEL 2
- CHANNEL 3
- CHANNEL 4

EMOTIONAL JOURNEY

Happy / Neutral / Unhappy

RECOMMENDATIONS

METRICS	METRICS	METRICS	METRICS	METRICS
	• Metric one • Metric two • Metric three • Metric four	• Metric one • Metric two • Metric three • Metric four	• Metric one • Metric two • Metric three • Metric four	• Metric one • Metric two • Metric three • Metric four
OPPORTUNITIES	**IDEAS FOR IMPROVEMENT** • Idea one • Idea two • Idea three • Idea four • Idea five	**IDEAS FOR IMPROVEMENT** • Idea one • Idea two • Idea three • Idea four • Idea five	**IDEAS FOR IMPROVEMENT** • Idea one • Idea two • Idea three • Idea four • Idea five	**IDEAS FOR IMPROVEMENT** • Idea one • Idea two • Idea three • Idea four • Idea five

JOURNEY MAPS

WHAT

Customer or user journey maps focus on a specific customer's interaction with a product or service. Best used when you are focused on a specific target such as the journey for one type of target persona or one specific product, service, or product or line.

It is a visualization of a particular persona journey in order to accomplish a goal tied to a specific business or product.

FEATURES
1. Based on a specific persona, product or service.
2. Four lanes: phases, actions, thoughts, mindsets/emotions.
3. It reflects the user's point of view:
4. Omits some process details.
5. Activities described in chronological order.

> **86% of senior-level marketers say it's critical to create a cohesive customer journey**
>
> **26% of companies currently employ future journey maps**
>
> **36% of companies have a process to map current customer journeys**

Sources: business2community.com, Forrester, Aberdeen Group

> **Companies see an average of 24.9% YOY increase in incremental revenue associated with marketing campaigns, a 21.2% reduction in service costs, and a 16.8% shrinkage in the sales cycle when the customer journey is mapped and managed successfully."**

Aberdeen Group - Customer Journey Mapping: Lead the Way to Advocacy.

IDEO AND JOURNEY MAPS

The customer journey map for service design was first introduced through the Acela high-speed rail project of IDEO (1999). The developers of this project wanted to visualize the customer experience and their interactions and feelings between them and the rail system. This project was managed by Richard Eisermann who headed a team of 25 internal and external designers at IDEO. In this project the team broke the customer journey into three phases, before use, use and after use. The use of this visual mapping technique has been adopted and developed by companies worldwide. A customer journey map tells the story of the customer's experience. "Mapping the customer journey helps organisations understand how prospects and customers use the various channels and touchpoints, how the organisation's is perceived and how the organisation would like its customers and prospects' experiences to be. By understanding the latter, it is possible to design an optimal experience that meets the expectations of major customer groups, achieves competitive advantage and supports attainment of desired customer experience objectives."

IDEO is an international design and consulting firm founded in Palo Alto in 1991, The company uses the design thinking methodology to design products, services, environments, and digital experiences. The firm employs over 600 people in a number of disciplines including: Behavioral Science, Branding, Business Design, Communication Design, Design Research, Digital Design, Education, Electrical Engineering, Environments Design, Food Science, Healthcare Services, Industrial Design, Interaction Design, Mechanical Engineering, Organizational Design, and Software Engineering. The current CEO is Tim Brown.

Source: Adapted from Wikipedia.

COMMON JOURNEY PHASES

1. Awareness: Customer becomes aware of their need and the product category.
2. Research: customers research solutions to their need
3. Evaluation: Customers evaluate alternatives and make a purchase decision.
4. Purchase: Customer purchase the product or service.
5. Onboarding Customers learn to interact with the product or service
6. Retention: Customers decide to stay with the product or service or to purchase a competitive product or service.
7. Advocacy: Customers recommend the product or service to others.

WHY

1. Used for understanding customer needs and pain points.
2. Used to identify specific customer journey touchpoints and the quality of experiences in relation to those touchpoints.
3. Used to develop one organization-wide understanding of the customer journey.

WHEN

Use journey mapping after building an experience map to describe a specific persona or customer segment perspective. Can be used an any point in the design process.

BENEFITS OF JOURNEY MAPS

1. Increases your revenue from marketing campaigns.
2. Reduces your service costs.
3. Helps build a consistently good brand experience.
4. Increases customer engagement.
5. Eliminates duplicated or ineffective touchpoints.
6. Shift to a customer-focused perspective.
7. Break down silos between departments.
8. Target specific customer segments.
9. Assign ownership of customer touchpoints.

HOW

1. One map per persona or user segment.
2. Talk to your customers.
3. Make your first draft of a customer journey map based on your hypothesis, and continue to build it out as you get more customer information
4. choose just one persona and one customer scenario to research and visualize at a time.
5. Build the map with a group of stakeholders from multiple departments.
6. Gather research from sources including:
   - Interviews.
   - Observations of customers using your product.

- Talk to customer-facing employees that regularly interact with customers.
- Customer surveys.
- customer support logs.
- Social media discussions.
- Conduct market research.
- Web analytics.
- Customer satisfaction data.

7. Assemble your team
8. Build the map
    - Touchpoints
    - Moments of truth
    - Actions taken by the customer
    - Channels
    - Opportunities to improve your CX
    - Assigned ownership of a touchpoint
9. Identify gaps or poor transitions between stages.
10. Present your findings company-wide.
11. Make mapping part of your company culture.
12. Assign responsible parties
13. Implement

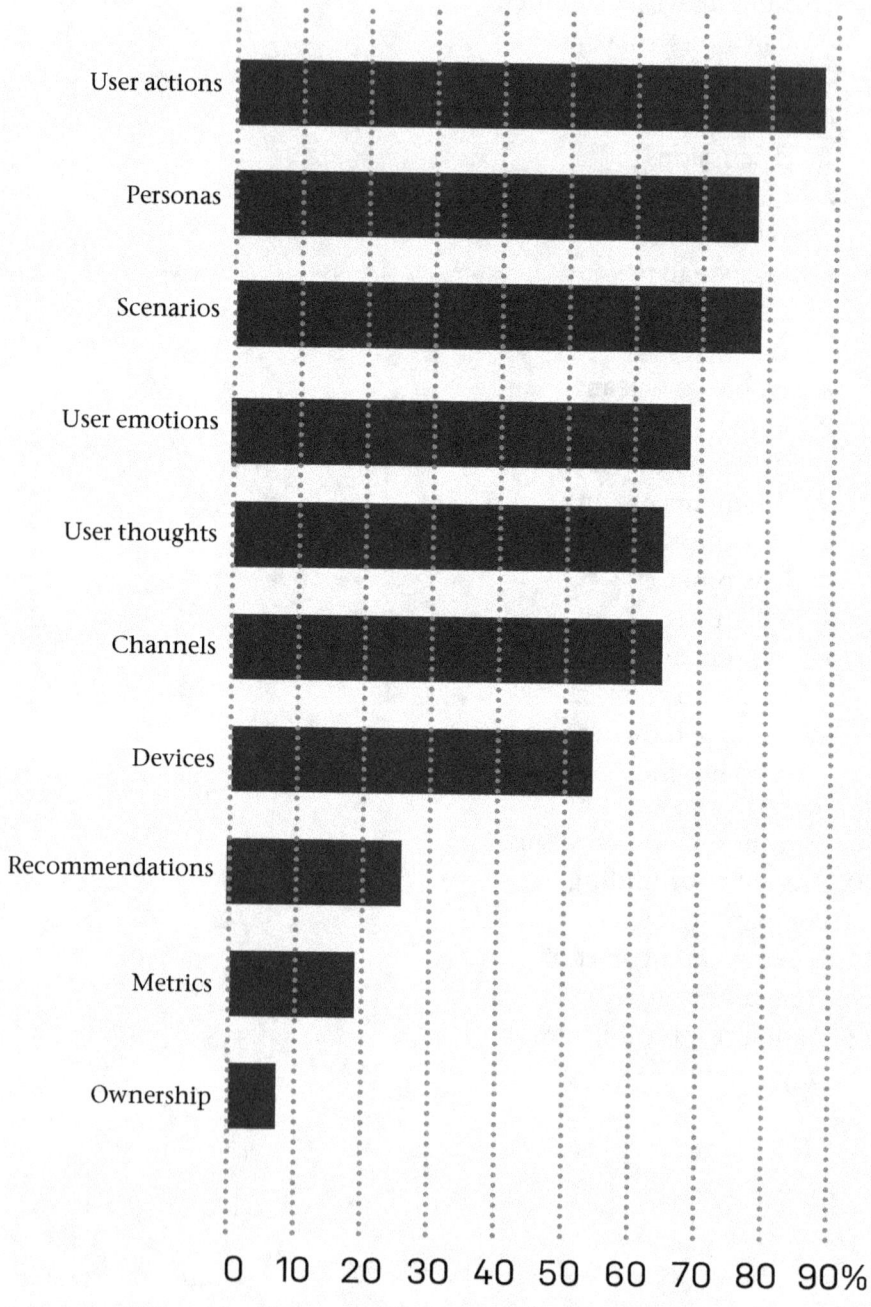

10
SERVICE BLUEPRINTS

ELEMENTS OF A SERVICE BLUEPRINT

PHYSICAL EVIDENCE
Tangible elements associated with each step that has the potential to influence customer perceptions of the service sch as the web site, .

CUSTOMER ACTIONS
List the customer activities as they happen most of the time in order stage by stage from left to right

LINE OF INTERACTION
Separates customer actions from service provider actions.

FRONTSTAGE STAFF
Visible Contact Employee Actions: Steps taken by contact employees as part of the face-to-face service encounter.

LINE OF VISIBILITY
Separates the front-stage and back-stage actions.

BACKSTAGE STAFF
Non-visible steps taken by contact employees for example taking a hotel or restaurant reservation by telephone.

LINE OF IMPLEMENTATION
Separates management zone from the support zone.

SUPPORT PROCESSES
Activities carried out by employees who are not contact employees, but whose actions are required for the service to be delivered.

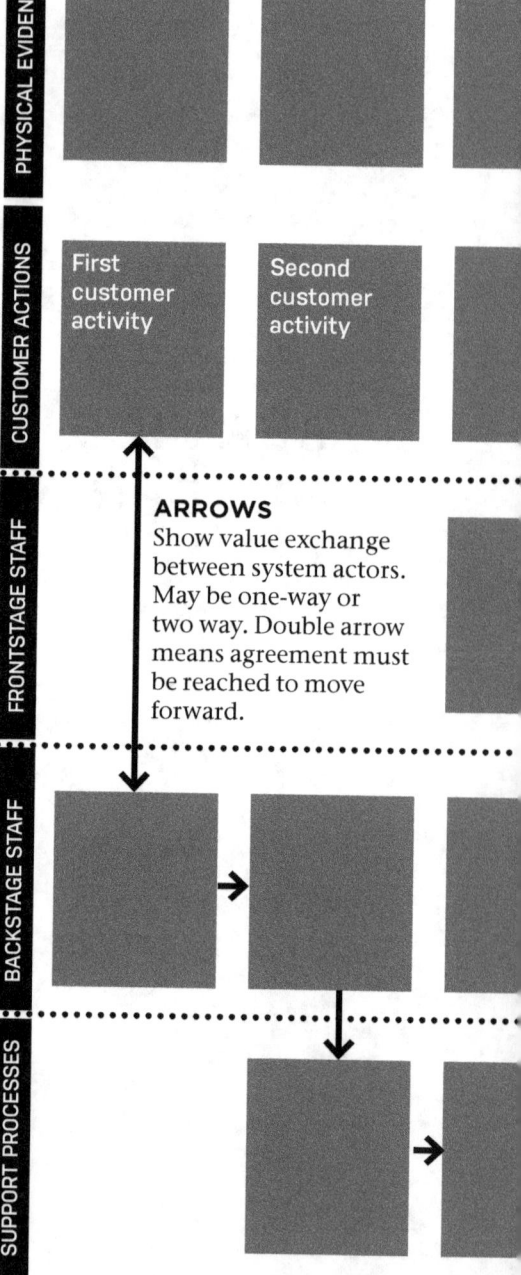

ARROWS
Show value exchange between system actors. May be one-way or two way. Double arrow means agreement must be reached to move forward.

SERVICE BLUEPRINTS

WHAT

A service blueprint is a map showing the structure of a service. It shows how a service will be provided, what physical and virtual elements customers will interact with, employee actions, and support systems to deliver the service across channels.

WHY

Service blueprints can be used for the following purposes

1. Understand the structure of a service or experience system.
2. Understand the collective experiences of customer segments
3. To create an improved customer service or experience.
4. Create a more seamless customer experience across business departments, and channels.
5. Design a new service or product customer experience
6. Allocate people and resources efficiently.
7. Develop alignment across departments of an organization.
8. Craft a better customer experience.
9. Expose places where your service or customer experience may fail.
10. Craft a better customer experience
11. Strategic and tactical innovation
12. Building and sharing knowledge
13. Understand competitive positioning
14. Understanding the ideal experience
15. Identify opportunities
16. Empathize with your end users
17. Designing and improving Systems
18. Develop a better product road map
19. Take cost & complexity out of the system
20. Prioritize competing deliverables
21. Plan for hiring
22. Bring different parts of your business together to work to improve the customer experience
23. Identify specific areas of opportunity to drive ideation and innovation
24. Make intangible services tangible
25. Develop customer insights
26. Introduce metrics for what matters most to your customers
27. Align your offerings to brand promise
28. Improve efficiency
29. Imagine future product and service experiences
30. Making better decisions
31. A living document that can evolve with your business

LYNN SHOSTACK AND SERVICE BLUEPRINTS

The technique was introduced by G. Lynn Shostack, a bank executive, in the Harvard Business Review in 1984. The service blueprint has become one of the most widely used tools to manage service operations, service design and service positioning.

Since its original development, a number of contributors have proposed improvements Zeithaml and Bitner recommend adding four lines to the map.

1. The Line of Visibility.
2. The Line of Interaction which separates customer actions from service provider actions
3. The Line of Internal Interaction which separates the front office and the back office
4. The Line of Implementation which separates management zone from the support zone.

The addition of these lines helps to separate the functions of planning and controlling from support activities including preparation. Other practitioners have recommended adding the Line of Order Penetration which separates customer-induced activities from customer-independent activities.

Zeithaml, Bitner and Gremler (2006) recommended adding bottlenecks and fail points to the map. A bottleneck is a point in the system at which consumers waiting time is likely to exceed average or minimum tolerable expectations. A fail point is any point within the encounter that has potential to affect customer satisfaction or quality. These additions increase the usefulness of the service blueprint.

Source: Adapted from Wikipedia.

SERVICE BLUEPRINT FOR HOTEL CHECK-IN

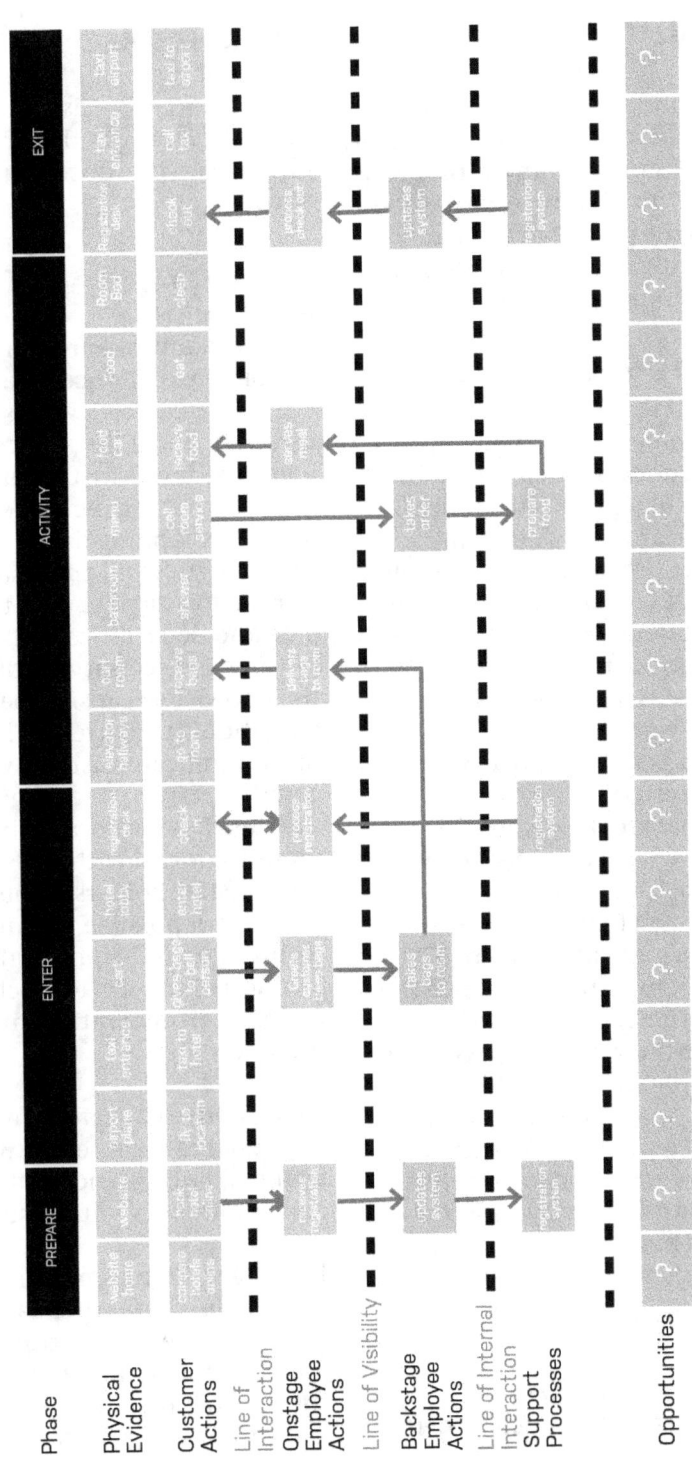

SERVICE BLUEPRINTS 229

HOW

Here is a list of stages that you can complete creating a service blueprint. Consider the blueprint to be a living document that will develop and improve, so it doesn't have to be perfect first time. Concentrate on your customers and their point of view.

CREATE YOUR GOAL STATEMENT

1. What is the problem, unmet needs or opportunities that the blueprint is to realize?
2. A clear map of customer needs should be compatible with your goals and with an outcome that satisfies them.
3. Who are the stakeholders?
4. Where is the service delivered?
5. When is the service delivered?
6. What are the channels?
7. Why is there a need for a new design solution?
8. Are you looking to address issues already identified?
9. Do you want to enhance the customer experience?
10. Do you want to engage your customers more effectively? Do you want to create a more efficient process? Define your goals in a statement and return to that statement as you build your map to ensure that your efforts contribute to reaching the goal.

DEFINE YOUR TARGET AUDIENCE SEGMENT AND THEIR NEEDS

The most successful products and services target precise customer segments. Designs that try to please everyone do not satisfy anyone.

GATHER YOUR EXISTING RESEARCH

Start by auditing internal customer experience data that was gathered. Review existing user data, including call center logs, customer satisfaction surveys, existing personas, mystery shopping data, web analytics and customer satisfaction data. Review the data and determine what new research is necessary to fill in the knowledge gaps. To be useful data should be current. The most significant insights will come directly from engaging the stakeholders located in their natural context with the service. Engage stakeholders through a variety of possible research techniques in the physical location of the service such as contextual observation and interviews.

Quantitative data is less useful than qualitative research when trying to understand the feelings and emotions of your customers.

Interviews are a common method used to gather data. Ask them to walk you through their experience and talk about their problems, needs desires and feelings at each stage. Start by talking to between five and twenty people as a minimum sample size. Focus your questions on the areas relevant to the lanes of the service blueprint. If you are creating a journey map, ask what are they doing, thinking, and feeling at each stage of the activity. Ask them what touch points they are engaging at each stage. Ask them where they are experiencing problems or frustrations in achieving their goals. Document your interviews or observations by using video or a digital recorder. Quantitative data with a larger sample size is also useful. Create a survey for existing or prospective customers.

To be useful, your service blueprint needs to be based on real and truthful information. Use prototype maps in focus group discussions to validate findings directly with customers..

REVIEW YOUR EXISTING RESEARCH
Review existing research. Identify gaps in data and create a list of recurring customer experience problems.

CREATE A RESEARCH PLAN TO FILL THE GAPS.
1. Create a research plan to fill the gaps.
2. What do you still need to know?
3. What questions do you need to ask?
4. How many people will you involve?
5. What type of people will you research?
6. What will be the context of the customer?
7. What methods will you use?
8. When will you select and screen the subjects, conduct the research and report on findings?

SYNTHESIZE YOUR RESEARCH
Put each potentially useful piece of information on separate post-it notes. Put the post-it notes on a wall and ask your team to organize the customer's comments into related groups or themes. Which issues are most significant to more customers? Build a hierarchy of problems. Identify themes and patterns from the interviews.
What are your customers' needs and goals at each stage of their activity? What touchpoints are they engaging at each step?

SELECT YOUR TEAM
Care should be taken in selecting your team. As many groups and diverse points of view involved in design delivery and use of the service as possible should be represented.
1. Keep groups to six people or less.
2. If your total group size is larger than twelve people, break the large group into smaller groups of six or fewer people.
3. Have a diverse team with different genders, age,

occupations and status represented.
4. Have at least two or three "T" shaped people. "T" shaped people are individuals with two or more areas of expertise such as technology and management or design. This makes the team more flexible and helps group collaboration.
5. Involve external and internal stakeholders such as customers, suppliers, internal business management, engineering, design, and sales.
6. Have customer-facing people where possible because they better understand the customer's perspective.

APPOINT YOUR MODERATOR

Create handouts with clear instructions. Provide copies of research summaries. Take breaks every 90-minutes. Photograph the map as it is being built.

MODERATOR SKILLS
1. Effective Listening Skills
2. Flexibility
3. Customer empathy
4. Sincerely Interested in People
5. Enthusiasm
6. People management skills
7. Able to establishing common direction and buy-in.
8. Understands Group Dynamics
9. Authority
10. Neutral and Objective
11. Patient and Persistent
12. Curious
13. Guide discussion promptly.
14. Able to draw our quieter group members.
15. Able to read between the lines and understand what is not said.
16. Beginner's mind
17. Get Panelists to talk to each other.
18. Get the audience involved early.
19. Able to read body language
20. Able to create an atmosphere where divergent views can be explored
21. Encourage all participants to share their views openly.
22. Keep the conversation focused and relevant
23. Track and record the key themes and ideas expressed by the group.
24. Make sure the best and needed people are in the room.
25. Make sure all roles are clearly defined.
26. State the meeting purpose before or at the start of the meeting
27. Set objectives for the meeting.
28. Define next steps and action items at the conclusion of the meeting.

SELECT AND PREPARE YOUR WORKSPACE

A good space is a large room with plenty of natural light with a large table and sufficient chairs for your team.
Useful materials
1. A large wall

2. Butcher paper
3. Masking tape
4. Mobile White-boards
5. Dry erase markers
6. Sharpies
7. Adhesive notes in 5 colors
8. Digital camera
9. Tripod

IDENTIFY YOUR TARGET SEGMENT TO MAP
Identifying customer segments.

CREATE PERSONAS
Create your customer personas. Personas are archetypal characters created to represent the different user types that might use a product or service in a similar way. Create 3 to 6 personas to cover all your customers.

IDENTIFY STAKEHOLDERS
A stakeholder is someone who may be in some way influenced by your design. For example in a hospital stakeholders may be patients, relatives of patients, hospital workers, doctors, nurses, health insurance workers. Stakeholders are also people who represent various areas within your organization such as technology, design, business management, sales, customer experience.

HOLD STAKEHOLDER WORKSHOPS
Organize a workshop, and guide internal and external stakeholders through the process of creating the first draft. Go over the user experience and discuss the the perspective of customers and diverse interested parties,

SELECT THE SERVICE TO BE BLUEPRINTED
Choose your experience to map. We suggest starting small with part of an experience that is important or problematic. For example rather than mapping an entire customer journey for air travel from New York to London, map a part of it that is important su8ch as selecting the airline and booking online. Explore several challenging sub-journeys before tackling the whole journey.

DECIDE PRESENT OR FUTURE SERVICE TO MAP
It is most usual first to map your existing customer experience. A current state map can help identify ways to make your existing customer experience better or more efficient.

After mapping your current service you may be interested in creating a map as a concept for a future service or customer experience. You may not have a current service in which case go straight to a map of a future service or experience.

SELECT START AND END POINTS OF THE CUSTOMER EXPERIENCE
Define the scope in terms of time ad customer activities.

SELECT CHANNELS TO MAP
Typical examples of channels include
1. In-store experience
2. Print,
3. Web,
4. Mobile

The channel defines the opportunities and constraints of a touchpoint.

START SMALL
Consider picking a particular scenario or sub-activity of your entire customer experience.

DRAFT THE MAP
Use a large wall or table. Create your first rough draft using post-it notes. Share the first blueprint with as many internal and external stakeholders as possible and ask for their feedback. If insights don't fit on a single map, keep maps simple by creating building one map for each persona.

CREATE THE STORY
What are the main elements of the customer experience from their perspective? What parts of their experience leave a lasting impression on them either positive or negative.

MAP USER ACTIONS & ACTIVITIES STEP-BY-STEP
Start at the beginning of the service or experience and list each thing a customer commonly does step by step. Put each sub-activity on a separate post-it note. For example, if the activity is visiting a coffee shop the activities may include.
1. At work decide to get a coffee on the way home
2. Check the location of coffee shops on the Internet.
3. Select coffee shop
4. Go to car
5. Drive to coffee shop
6. Park
7. Enter coffee shop
8. Stand in line
9. Order
10. Pick up coffee
11. Find table
12. Sit down
13. Drink coffee
14. Read news on tablet
15. Pack up
16. Return to car
17. Drive home
18. Reflect on the experience.

Describe each activity on a separate post-it note and place them in a line on your wall or table. Continue till your team is happy that all important events are included

MAP TIME
How long does each customer activity usually take? Does a stage usually last ten seconds or ten minutes. Place the time required on a post-it note above each stage of customer activity.
Time to consider:
1. Critical periods service actions, such as response to a proposal.
2. Duration of each service steps, such as airline check-in
3. The time between service

SERVICE BLUEPRINT FOR VISIT TO A COFFEE SHOP

Phase	PREPARE			ENTER				ACTIVITY				EXIT	REFLECT
Physical Evidence	work building	Internet computer	car	car park	building	chalkboard menu	cash register	coffee machine	table chair	computer	table chair	car park	car
Customer Actions	Decide to have a coffee	Locate coffee shop	Drive to coffee shop	Park	Enter coffee shop	Stand in line	Order	Picks up coffee	Sit down	Drink & Work	Pack up	Finish & return to car	Drive home
Line of Interaction													
Onstage Employee Actions					Greet customer		Take order	Make order	Escort to table			Ask if they need refill	Pick up empty cup
Line of Visibility													
Backstage Employee Actions						Accounting	Order supplies					Cleans room	
Line of Internal Interaction													
Support Processes													
Opportunities													

steps such as walking to a hotel room after check-in.
4. End to end service experience.

BUILD THE BLUEPRINT
Now you are ready to create the map.

MAP USER ACTION PHASES
Break the list of customer activities into four or six phases of sub-activities. Some examples of sets of phases of activities are:
Example One
1. Explore
2. Evaluate
3. Engage
4. Experience

Example two
1. Aware
2. Join
3. Use
4. Develop
5. Leave

Example Three
1. Research
2. Evaluate and compare
3. Commit
4. Use and Monitor
5. Refine and review

MAP THE PHYSICAL EVIDENCE STEP-BY-STEP
Physical evidence is usually the lane shown at the top of a blueprint. Services consist of the interactions with people, the processes, and the physical evidence of the experience. Objects in the service environment that customers engage are sometimes referred to as "physical evidence" because they are proof of the service that has taken place. Physical evidence is the tangible things that help to communicate and perform the service and influence a customer's perception of a service.

Physical evidence is the tangible manifestation of service. It conveys to customers whether the service provider cares about their customers and whether they trust their customers. Physical evidence cues are what customers use to evaluate service quality.

Physical evidence can convey intended and unintended messages to customers. Physical evidence is the interface between a service provider and a customer.

The key to delivering a successful service is to identify clearly a simple, consistent message, and then manage the evidence to support that message.

" *Well-prepared small details represent sincerity in serving guests which reflect the hotel's good service spirit. For example, welcome fruit, an electric kettle and fresh flowers in hotel rooms are service evidence that often evoked delight as they show the hotel's thoughtfulness."*

For example, a research

participant talked about disappointment caused by "fake" hangers in a hotel room's closet. She complained: They're not real hangers, because they're attached to the railing. So if you want to take out a hanger and then hang it on a chair or hang it on a door, you can't, because there's no hook... That's kind of a fake hanger. It shows that they think I'm going to steal the hangers. So it makes me feel not trusted."

Source: Kathy Pui Ying Lo Designing Service Evidence for Positive Relational Messages, http://www.ijdesign.org/ojs/index.php/IJDesign/article/viewFile/898/333 (accessed March 23, 2016).

The physical evidence lane on the blueprint appears above the "line of visibility" in a service blueprint. Physical evidence includes the service providers building/facilities and staff appearance; and uniforms. Physical evidence should be considered important by the customer and the promise implied by these tangible objects should be delivered. A bank card is an example of physical evidence of a service. It helps a bank differentiate their service from another bank. It separates the service from the seller.

Other examples of physical evidence are
1. The building
2. The interior
3. The car park
4. Internal signage,
5. Packaging.
6. Promotional materials
7. Web pages.
8. Paperwork (such as invoices, tickets and dispatch notes).
9. Brochures.
10. Stationery
11. Billing statement
12. Furnishings.
13. Signage
14. Uniforms and employee dress.
15. Business cards.
16. Mailboxes.

Blueprint the physical evidence of service. Physical evidence should be refined developed and improved over time. Work cross-functionally.

DRAW THE LINE OF INTERACTION
Separates customer activities from face-to-face onstage and unseen backstage actions.

MAP FRONT STAGE OR ONSTAGE EMPLOYEE ACTIONS
Onstage employee actions are separated from the customer by the line of interaction. Onstage or front stage employee actions are the things that your employees do during a face-to-face encounter with the customer. Examples are a waiter

in a restaurant taking your order or a hotel front desk employee checking you into a hotel.

DRAW THE LINE OF VISIBILITY
The line of visibility separates actions that are face-to-face from those that are not visible to the end user. Divides actions of onstage employees from backstage actions. Below the line of visibility, actions that involve non-visible interaction with customers such as contact by telephone is described

MAP BACKSTAGE OR OFFSTAGE EMPLOYEE ACTIONS
Backstage actions are the activities by your employees to provide the service that the end user doesn't see.

DRAW THE LINE OF INTERNAL INTERACTION
This line separates contact employees activities from non-contact support actions.

SUPPORT PROCESSES
Support functions needed to support the employees. These are internal services, which help the contact employees in delivering the service.
An example is the registration computer system in a hotel.

Support processes are other actions, systems, and resources that the service provider relies upon that must be provided to deliver the service to the customer.

MAP THE PAIN POINTS
A pain point is any part of the customer experience that they find people disturbing, frustrating, urgent or uncomfortable. Some customer needs are needs which the customers themselves are not aware of and cannot articulate. A pain point is a problem for your customer and a problem and an opportunity for you. Solving pain points create value for you and your customer. "customer pain" is a synonym for "customer needs". Customers spend money to combat pain or to pursue pleasure.

Examples of service pain points are airport security lines, hospital directions, or the cost of travel.

A pain point is the why customers choose you if you offer a solution to their need. If you engage your customers and listen they'll tell you their pain points.

To identify customer 'pain-points':
17. In-depth interviews with customer-facing internal employees
18. Requests from your most valuable customers.
19. Customer interviews.
20. Customer focus groups.
21. Analysis of customer calls and

warranty claims to identify problems.
22. Review of competitor offerings.

You can list the root causes of pain for your customers at each stage.

CUSTOMER OR STAKEHOLDER COMMENTS
List significant or representative comments in a lane. What do customers think?

MAP BRAND IMPACT
List brand impact of touchpoints and customer comments in a lane.

KEY PEOPLE
Identify internal owners of experiences that support customer's needs.

CUSTOMER NEEDS
Do customers have unrecognized needs that could be addressed? What do customers want to accomplish at each stage of interaction?

MAP CONNECTIONS
Use arrows to illustrate the flow of responsibility—who is "driving" the service at any moment and should be initiating service action:
1. Model expectations of "proactive" provider activity.
2. Model the customer responsibility for next steps.
3. Model partner expectations.
4. Define points of handoff between roles, such as from backstage to onstage.

MAP MOMENTS OF TRUTH
Map those interactions that have the most impact on the customer. A moment of truth is a contact or interaction between a customer and a service provider that gives the customer an opportunity to form or change an impression about the organization.

For example waiting in line in a coffee shop. A moment of truth is a point in time when a customer has the opportunity to make a judgment about the value of a service delivery and a business relationship. Identifying moments of truth and improving their outcomes is a focus of service blueprinting.

ROOT CAUSE OF PAIN
Ask why the experience is painful for the customer. If necessary ask why several times to understand the underlying cause of the pain.

MAP BARRIERS
What obstacles are standing in the way of the optimal experience for the customer at each stage of their interaction?

PRIORITIZE TOUCHPOINTS TO IMPROVE OR DEVELOP ADD PHOTOS OR PICTURES WHERE POSSIBLE

Add photos or pictures where possible
Blueprints sometimes have a lane of photographs that show pain points of customer activities. Use pictures if they are the best way of communicating something. For example lack of cleanliness on a train platform.
Identify points of failure
Where is the service failing or likely to fail?

IDENTIFY POINTS OF FAILURE

Where is the service failing or likely to fail?

OPPORTUNITIES

Brainstorm ways to change to better meet customer needs.
1. Bullet point these ideas in a separate lane stage by stage.
2. Bullet points these ideas in a separate lane stage by stage.
3. What is the ideal customer experience
4. Analyze every touch point
5. Identify physical evidence at each stage - moment of truth
6. Simplify and refine the process
7. Remove pain points and surprises.
8. Add touchpoints that are missing
9. Build scenarios Think about extreme users, new users, average users.

PHOTOGRAPH THE DRAFT

Photograph the whole blueprint and photograph the blueprint in sections with sufficient resolution to enable you to transfer the map into a graphics program such as Adobe Illustrator or InDesign.

CREATE A PRESENTATION COPY

Transfer the map into a graphics program such as Adobe Illustrator or InDesign.

DISTRIBUTE TO STAKEHOLDERS FOR FEEDBACK

Distribute draft to internal and external stakeholders
for feedback. Circulate you map as widely as possible to get feedback from internal departments, executives, external customers, and stakeholders.

REFINE THE MAP BASED ON THE FEEDBACK

Does it tell the story of your customer's experience that is complete, from beginning to end? Is it understandable to people outside the team? Are the insights actionable? Does it inspire and support a change in strategy? Does it communicate the necessary information, without further explanation? Simplify the map. Identify gaps and do further research to fill the gaps. Gaps in touchpoints may suggest opportunities to add new touchpoints.

BRAINSTORM THE IDEAL EXPERIENCE

Put together what you have learned to generate a better experience for your customers that you can implement. Develop step-by-step corrective actions for fail points.

RAPID PROTOTYPING

Experience prototyping is the most efficient way to implement an improved service. The goal is to observe customers interacting with the new experience and obtain their feedback about the experience. Use methods such as:
1. Video prototyping,
2. Role-playing,
3. desktop walkthroughs
4. Bodystorming
5. Paper prototyping
6. Empathy tools
7. Wireframing
8. Service staging
9. Wizard of Oz

Start with low fidelity methods and move to higher fidelity prototyping methods as you find clarity with the best design direction.

SERVICE STAGING

Test the service refinements in a staged setting. Sets up a space that imitates the real environment, but with simple props to represent physical objects. For example cardboard boxes could be used to describe a counter. The design team can work through the experience "on stage" and adapt it based on feedback from customers.

CONDUCT USER STUDIES IN THE TARGET CONTEXT

Test with target users iteratively and refine the service until the pain points have become points of pleasure for customers.
1. Do people understand the service
2. Do people see the value of the service?
3. Do people understand how to use it?
4. Is the experience positive?
5. What ideas do the customers have that could improve the service?

IMPLEMENT THE EXPERIENCE

The end purpose of a blueprint is to take action and improve the journey and drive the ROI to justify the investment. After the new service design is tested, the design team documents the new experience and creates implementation guidelines to roll out of the new service across the organization. The service blueprint is now a tool to communicate the new design.
1. Use your map for employee training/
2. Map upcoming product launches or your desired future state

MEASURE YOUR PROGRESS TOWARDS YOUR GOALS

Define ways of tracking your progress towards measurable goals. Metrics will help you measure the quality of your customer experience, now and in

MAP THE PAIN POINTS

	RESEARCH RESERVATION						STAY					CHECK OUT		DEPART	
Phase															
Physical Evidence	hotel website	booking website			bag cart	elevator hallway		room	TV fridge bathroom		menu	food tray		lobby desk	car park
Customer activity	compare prices	make reservation	check in		give bags to bell person	go to room		picks up coffee	shower watch movie		order meal	receive meal		check out	return to car
Pain points	best hotel full		park full	long line	no one at desk		get lost		coffee stale	shower cold		argument next room	food cold	charged additional fees	
Line of interaction															
Onstage employee actions	reserve room	greet			process registration	take bags				refill coffee		take order prepare food	deliver food to room	process check out	
Line of visibility															
Backstage employee actions	maintain website		clean lobby	update system		deliver bags to room									clean room
Line of internal interaction															
Support processes	registration system		registration system						video system		food system			registration system	

pain points

the future.
1. Net Promoter Score and customer loyalty measures
2. Customer satisfaction measures
3. Quantitative assessments of the customer emotions.
4. Metrics of customer effort
5. Measure of performance of each touchpoint.
6. New sales.
7. Increased loyalty and retention of customers
8. Increase in revenue per customer.
9. More sales.
10. Reduced costs
11. Better delivery processes.
12. Better quality: i
13. Increased competitiveness

The idea behind services blueprinting is fairly simple: companies put themselves in their customers' shoes to find out what's working, what's not, and what needs to be changed." It's a very versatile technique that can be used for both innovation and services improvement."

Mary Jo Bitner

"A service blueprint allows a company to explore all the issues inherent in creating or managing a service."

Lyn Shostack

SERVICE BLUEPRINT EXERCISE

BACKGROUND
We all have a number of such encounters each week, including restaurants, banks, airlines, doctors, dentists, libraries, travel agencies, theaters, phone companies, mechanics, insurance companies, accountants, instructors. You are to keep a journal of your service encounter experiences. The purpose of this journal is to identify sources of customer satisfaction and dissatisfaction with services. A service blueprint visually describes and identifies the tasks, activities and means of achievement for a particular service. Key to the service blueprint is identifying the touch points (the front- and back-of-stage interactions the user experiences) and the supporting goods and other activities that make that service possible.

GOALS
To become more aware of critical aspects of the service encounter from a customer's perspective. The purpose of this assignment is for course participants to develop an understanding of service blueprinting.

TASKS
Choose a local service provider. Create a complete blueprint for the service that you have chosen. The blueprint should include the lanes

1. Physical evidence
2. Customer actions. List at least 14 steps in the customer journey
3. Line of visibility
4. Front stage employee actions
5. Backstage employee actions
6. Support processes
7. Pain points
8. Opportunities
9. Line of visibility

Identify and describe at least 3 potential service bottlenecks and/or fail-points
Suggest possible solutions/alternatives to address these potential problem areas that will enhance efficiency, appropriateness, overall value, or other attributes of the service.

DELIVERABLES
One service blueprint of one to two pages as a PDF file.

CONNECTING THE BOXES
Arrows show value exchanges through touchpoints

SINGLE ARROW
A single arrow shows a single direction value exchange

CUSTOMER EATS MEAL

WAITER BRINGS FOOD TO TABLE

DOUBLE ARROW
A double arrow indicates that two parties must agree

REGISTRATION EMPLOYEE GIVES CUSTOMER PRICE OF ROOM

CUSTOMER PAYS FOR ROOM

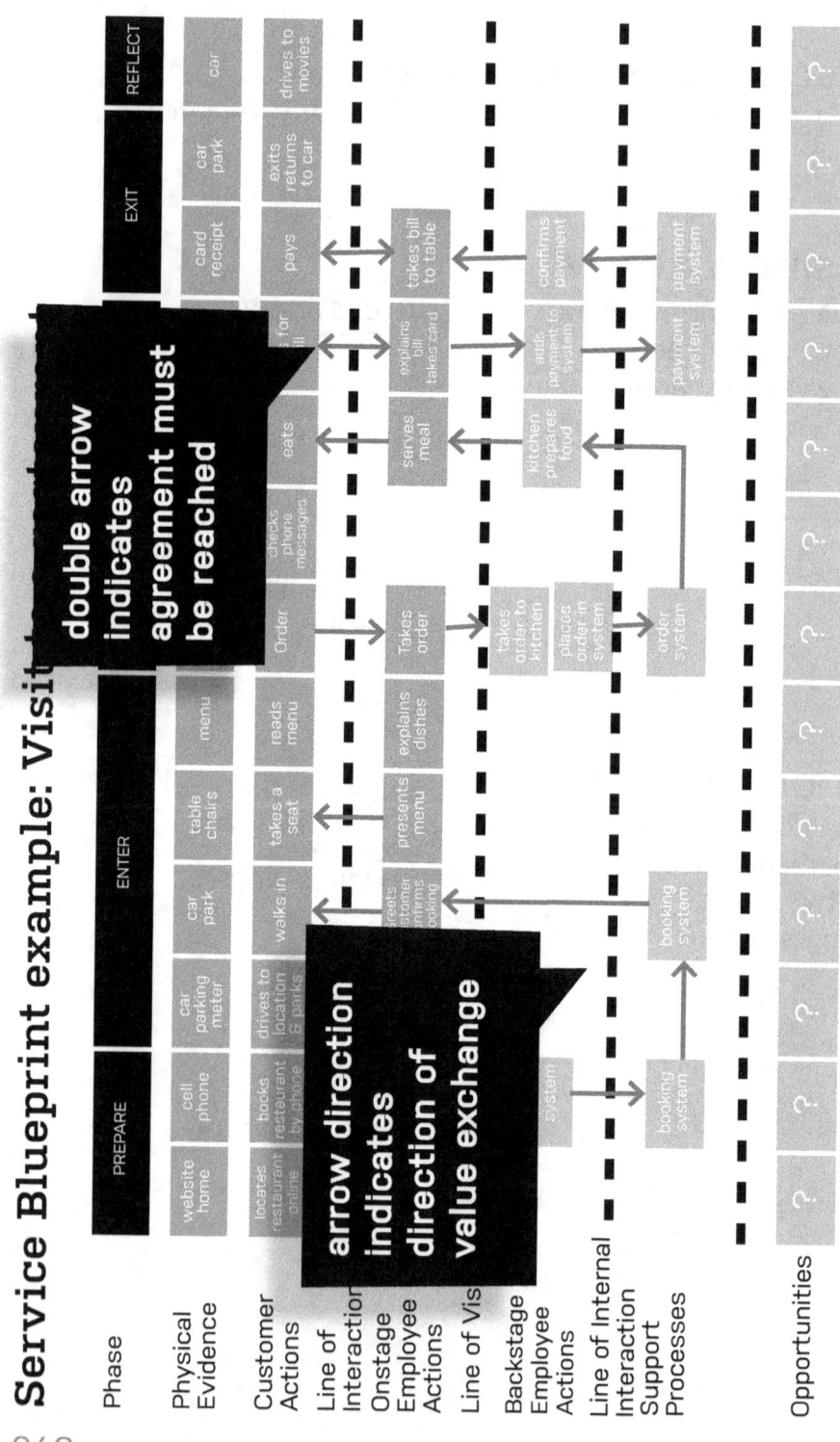

11 GLOSSARY

GLOSSARY

In this short glossary I have brought together a collection of terms used in Design Thinking, service design and user-centered design.

These fields are emerging areas of design and I believe will become the most significant areas of design this century. There are many terms that are used and these terms are still evolving.

At the back of this work you will find a list of my other publications if you would like more in-depth information about any of these fields.

I hope that you will find this collection useful.

A-B TEST
Testing technique where a percentage of site visitors are shown an alternate version of a design. The effectiveness of the two designs is then compared.

ACTOR
A person involved in the creation, delivery, support, or use of a service.

AFFINITY DIAGRAM
A tool used to organize a large number of ideas, sorting them into groups based on their natural relationships, for review and analysis

AFFORDANCES
The qualities of a design or material that affects or suggests how it can be used. For example, the affordances of a hammer (weight, handle and and grip, scribed head, etc) suggest it should be used for striking objects. Looking at affordances is especially useful when analyzing how designs or materials prompt certain behaviors. (eg. "When all you have is a hammer, everything looks like a nail."
Source dSchool Stanford

ANALOGOUS SITUATIONS
An analogous situation is a situation from another area or industry that may relate to an area of focus for a design and may suggests ways to improve it.

ANALYTIC INDUCTION
A qualitative research method that begins with a rough hypothesis, which is modified through the examination of cases that don't fit the hypothesis.

ANALYTICS
A broad term that encompasses a variety of tools, techniques and processes used for extracting useful information or meaningful

patterns from data.

ARTIFACTS
Physical service touchpoints. For example the New York Underground map

BACKSTAGE/ BACKOFFICE
Backstage activities are those taken by the service delivering company employees that are not visible to the customer. Backstage actions are actions that impact customers. Backstage actions are separated from onstage service delivery by the line of visibility. Activities above the line of visibility are seen by the client while everything below it is invisible. On an aircraft, the taking of an order for a meal is an onstage or front-stage action, and the preparation of the food is a backstage action if it is not seen by the traveler.

BETA LAUNCH
The limited launch of a software product with the goal of finding bugs before final launch.

BIAS
A one-sided viewpoint, inclination or a partial perspective. An interviewer might inadvertently bias an interviewee's answers by asking a "loaded" question, in which a desired answer is presupposed in the question.

BODYSTORMING
Prototyping method, Service situations are be acted out, for example for example at the hotel reception. The design team cast the roles, practice the situation. often with the input of end users The purpose is to prototype and test interactions to better understand and refine them.

BRAINSTORMING
Brainstorming is a group or individual creativity approach where design solutions are generated by members of the team in a collaborative session.

A method for generating ideas, intended to inspire the free-flowing sharing of thoughts of an individual or a group of people, typically while withholding criticism in order to promote uninhibited thinking.

CARD SORTING
A technique using either cards or software, whereby users generate an information hierarchy that can then form the basis of an information architecture or navigation menu.

A technique to investigate how users tend to group. The users are given a set of cards containing individual item names and are told to sort them into related piles and label the groups. Card sorting provides insight into the user's mental model and suggests the structure and placement of items on a Website.
Source: Human Factors

International

CAUSATION
A relationship between an event (the cause) and a second event (the effect), where the second event is a consequence of the first event.
Source: Human Factors International

CHANNEL
A medium for communication or delivery. Most services use more than one channel. For example phone, email, in-store or website.

CLOSED QUESTIONS
Questions that elicit a yes/no response.

CO-DESIGN
Process in which the design team directly engages end users to assist in the design to access knowledge that is crucial to develop successful design solutions.

The designers should provide ways for people to engage with each other as well as instruments to communicate, be creative, share insights and envision their own ideas. The co-design activities can support different levels of participation, from situation in which the external figures are involved just in specific moments to situations in which they take part to the entire process, building up the service together with the designers.

COGNITIVE DISSONANCE
A PET technique in changing impression. Cognitive dissonance refers to the discomfort caused by holding two or more conflicting (dissonant) beliefs at the same time. People seek to reduce the discomfort by changing one of the beliefs, thus returning to a state of 'consonance'. So, for example, someone holding the belief that "I am a smart consumer," may be faced with the dawning realization that "I paid too much for that car." The two beliefs are in conflict (dissonant) and therefore uncomfortable, so one of the beliefs must change. To avoid undermining positive self-belief, and because it is difficult to get a different car, the user's attitude about the car will change, so that it is seen as more valuable, and therefore worth the price paid.
Source: Human Factors International

COMPARISON TESTS
Usability test that compares two or more designs. Examples might be comparing alternative wireframes, comparing before and after designs, or a comparing a design against competitor designs.
Source: Human Factors International

CONCEPTUAL MODEL
A model constructed by the users in their mind to understand the working or the structure of objects, based on their mental

model and previous experience, to speed up their understanding. Also called mental model.
Source: Human Factors International

CONFIRMATION BIAS
The tendency to search for, notice, and interpret information in a way that confirms one's beliefs or opinions.
Source: Human Factors International

CONTEXTUAL INQUIRY
A semi-structured field interviewing method based on a set of principles that allow it to be molded to different situations. This technique is generally used at the beginning of the design process and is good for getting rich information, but can be complex and time-consuming.

CODE
a word chosen to represent an idea, topic, or event that is an important theme of the interviews. After these words are decided on, they are connected to colors or symbols used to mark passages of the transcripts.

CODING
The process of marking passages of the interview's transcript that are about the same thing. By same thing we mean-the passages have the same phrases repeated in them or they talk about the topic in the same way. These passages are marked with a name, the code, which is usually connected to a longer explanation of what the passages have in common. Codes stress what themes run through the interview or the collection of interviews.

COLLABORATIVE DESIGN
Inviting input from users, stakeholders and other project members.

COLLECTIVE INTELLIGENCE
Collective intelligence is shared knowledge that comes from the collaboration of a group of people and is expressed in consensus decisio-making. Collective intelligence requires openness, sharing ideas, experiences and perspectives.

CONTEXT
Context
The world the service belongs to. The context is the specific frame in which the service takes place. Exploring and defining the context means setting the project boundaries in terms of limits but also opportunities. Context is external elements that surround and influence design. These items can be physical and non-physical and cultural. The environmental context relates to the time, the day, the location, the type of place and any other physical aspect that could influence your design. The surrounding context influences the success of design.

CONTEXTUAL INQUIRY
Interviewing users in the location

that they use the product or service, to understand their tasks and challenges.

CONVERGENT
Process of Narrowing down ideas through synthesis.

CROSS-DISCIPLINARY COLLABORATION
Combines the wisdom and skills of different professional disciplines working in close and flexible collaboration. Each team member requires disciplinary empathy allowing them to work collaboratively with other discipline members. Design teams can include anthropologists, engineers, educators, doctors, lawyers, scientists, etc. in the innovative problem-solving process.

CULTURAL PROBE
Cultural probes are sets of simple artifacts (such as maps, postcards, cameras, or diaries) that are given to users for them to record specific events, feelings or interactions in their usual environment, in order to get to know them and their culture better. Cultural probes are used to uncover aspects of culture and human interaction like emotions, values, connections, and trust.

CUSTOMER JOURNEY
The customer journey is a graphical representation of how the customer perceives and experiences the service interface over time It often also shows the phases before and after the interaction with the service. A customer journey map is a tool to explore, visualize, understand and refine an end user experience.

DECOY STRATEGY
A PET technique in changing impression linked to the Contrast Principle. People want to compare things before making decisions and like to make easy comparisons. So you can persuade them to select one of a small number of easily compared choices by introducing another choice that can't easily be compared. For example, you are more likely to get people to purchase a front loader washing machine, if you give them two front loader choices (easily compared) by contrast to a third choice of a top-loader (less easy to compare). In another example, you can increase sales of an item, by offering a similar, but inferior item at about the same price. It's easy to compare them, recognize the contrast in quality, and conclude that the better quality item represents exceptional value.
Source: Human Factors International

DEDUCTIVE ANALYSIS
A type of analysis that begins with theoretically derived hypotheses then tests them with data that were collected in accordance with the theoretical context.

DIARY STUDY
Asking users to record their experiences and thoughts about a product or task in a journal over a set period of time.

DIVERGENT
Expansive idea generation and exploration of ideas.

EMPATHIZE
This term is sometimes used to encompass the Understand and Observe steps or as a replacement for them. The use of this emotional term helps remind designers that they must always consider the human experience of real people. It's more than just seeing it from their perspectives, it's about understanding how they feel about it all and what it means to them.
Source: dSchool Stanford

EMPATHY
Principle in the Design Thinking process and human- centered design, in which the user's perspective is always represented.
Source: Libraries Toolkit

ENTRY POINTS
Position of access to a service, where people are able to engage the service as customers, providers, or stakeholders.

ETHNOGRAPHY
The process of gathering information about users and tasks directly from users in their normal work, home or leisure environment.

EVIDENCE
Service evidences are touch-points that represent parts of a service experience.

EVIDENCE-BASED DESIGN
Evidence-based design is the approach of basing design decisions on credible research to achieve the best possible outcomes. Evidence-based design emphasizes the importance of basing decisions on the best possible data for the best possible outcomes. The design is not based just on the designer's opinion.

EXPERIENCE DESIGN
The application of design processes with the goal of creating an appropriate experience for the person interacting with the product. This process begins with understanding the needs and wants of the user. Analysis focuses on cognitive, emotional and motor aspects of the interaction and is completed when the quality of the experience is measured with the developed product.
Source: Human Factors International

EXPERIENCE PROTOTYPING
Service experiences have components that are intangible, and change over time and have multiple touch-points. Services are prototyped different ways then physical products. Experience Prototype is a representation, that is designed to help us understand,

explore or communicate what it feels like to engage with a product, space service or system.

EXIT POINTS
Point of disengagement of a service, by stakeholders.

EXTREME USER
A person who lies at the periphery of a group of users. Extremes can can include age, ability, occupation, experience, etc. Rather than designing for a composite or "average" user, a design team will oftentimes look to extreme users for surprising and actionable insights. Focusing on extreme users can lead to more innovative solutions, more profound insights about a group of users, and new, untapped markets for a product or service.
Source: dSchool Stanford

FIELD STUDY
A field study is a general method for collecting data about users, user needs, and product requirements that involves observation and interviewing. Data are collected about task flows, inefficiencies, and the organizational and physical environments of users.

FIVE WHYS
An analysis method used to uncover the root cause of a problem.

Example of the method:
A patient had the wrong leg amputated

1. Why: Patient gave consent for amputation the night before the proposed surgery to Registrar (who was not going to undertake procedure).
2. Why: Amputation site marked with a biro (wrong leg).
3. Why: Registrar unaware of hospital policy on amputation sites being marked with a skin pencil and with bodily part being fully visible to Doctor.
4. Why: The department had no induction procedures for new medical staff working in the department.
5. Why: Because "we've never been asked to". *Root Cause Analysis Tool Kit. NHS*

FOCUS GROUPS
A direct data gathering method in which a small group (8–10) of participants are led in a semi-structured, brainstorming session to elicit rapid feedback

FORMATIVE EVALUATION
Formative evaluation is a type of usability evaluation that helps to 'form' the design for a product or service. Formative evaluations involve evaluating a product or service during development, often iteratively, with the goal of detecting and eliminating usability problems.

FREE LISTING
Free listing is a technique for gathering data about a specific domain or topic by asking people

to list all the items they can think of that relate to the topic. It can be used to gather data in large group settings or in one-on-one interviews.

FRONTSTAGE/ FRONTOFFICE
These are face-to-face between customers and employees. These are separated from the customer by the line of interaction.

GAMBLER'S FALLACY
The mistaken belief that if an event has occurred more frequently than normal, it will happen less frequently in the future, and vice-versa.
Source: Human Factors International

GAP ANALYSIS
A technique used to determine the difference between a desired state and an actual state, often used in branding and marketing. Gap analysis may address performance issues or perception issues.
Source: Human Factors International

GESTALT PRINCIPLES
Set of principles developed by the Gestalt Psychology Movement that established rules governing how humans perceive order in a complex field of objects. Gestalt principles of visual organization state that objects near each other, with same background, connected to each other, or having similar appearance are perceived as belonging to a group.
Source: Human Factors International

GROUNDED THEORY
A qualitative research method in which theory is developed after data has been gathered and analyzed.

GROUPTHINK
Groupthink is consensus of opinion without critical reasoning or evaluation of consequences or alternatives. Employees may self-censor themselves for fear of upsetting the status quo.

HCI
Human Computer Interaction involves the study, planning, and design of the interaction between people (users) and computers.

HEURISTICS
Best practices, principles, or rules of thumb. Established principles of design and best practices in interface
design, used as a method of solving usability problems by using rules of thumb acquired from human factors experience.
Source: Human Factors International

HEURISTIC EVALUATION
A usability evaluation method in which one or more reviewers, preferably experts, compare a software, documentation, or hardware product to a list of

design principles, referred to as heuristics and identify where the product does not follow those principles. Evaluating a website or product and documenting usability flaws and other areas for improvement.

HICK-HYMAN LAW
Demonstrates the relationship between the time it takes someone to make a decision and the number of possible choices he or she has. More choices will increase decision time.
Source: Human Factors International

HIGH-FIDELITY PROTOTYPE
A prototype which is quite close to the final product, with lots of detail and a good indication of the final proposed aesthetics and functionality.

HORIZONTAL PROTOTYPE
Prototypes that display a wide range of features without fully implementing all of them. Horizontal prototypes provide insights into users' understanding of relationships across a range of features,
Source: Human Factors International

HOW MIGHT WE?
A positive, actionable question that frames the challenge but does not point to any one solution.
Source: Libraries Toolkit

HUMAN-CENTERED
An approach to design that adapts the solution to the end user through understanding the end user. The understanding is developed through engaging the end user and testing a variety of possible solutions through an iterative design process.

INDUCTIVE ANALYSIS
A type of analysis that begins with collecting and analyzing data, after which hypotheses are made.

Putting the user and user's perspective at the center of a solution. Human-centered or people-centric design requires having empathy with the user to solve for their specific needs. This philosophy involves starting with people and desirability first, before moving on to feasibility and viability.
Source: Libraries Toolkit

INTERACTION DESIGN
(IXD) Sometimes referred to as IxD, interaction design strives to create meaningful relationships between people and the products and services that they use.

INSIGHTS
Ideas or notions expressed as succinct statements that interpret patterns in your research and can provide new understanding or perspective on the issue.
Source: Libraries Toolkit

INTERCEPT
Spontaneous, casual and brief conversations with users in a natural context. Unplanned interviews that garner live feedback for your mini-pilot.
Source: Libraries toolkit

INTERVIEW GUIDE
A list of questions to direct conversation and make sure key issues get discussed. The guide should be flexible to move with conversation but at the same time its main purpose is to keep the interview on topic.

INTERVIEWER BIAS
the influence of the interviewer on the interviewee, which affects responses

I-SHAPED PERSON
Someone who has deep skills and knowledge in one area but not a broad competency across other areas.

ITERATIVE CONSULTATIVE PROCESS
An iterative consultative process is a design process of inviting diverse stakeholders to review a design and give feedback in order to improve the design from their point of view.

ITERATE
The act of repeating a process with the aim of approaching a desired goal, target or result. Each repetition of the process is also called an iteration.
In Design Thinking it refers to the cycles of prototyping, testing and revision.

ITERATIVE DESIGN PROCESS
Iterative design is the process of prototyping testing and refining a design in a series of repeated steps.

JOURNEY MAP
A visual representation of a particular person or persona's experience with a service. The experience is documented over time and often shows multiple channels.

LEADING QUESTION
a question that is phrased in a way that suggests to the interviewee an answer that the researcher prefers.

LEARNINGS
The most basic level of information you record from your research, including direct quotes, anecdotes, first impressions, notes on the environment, notes on what was most memorable or surprising, and more.
Source: Libraries Toolkit

LIKERT SCALE
A type of survey question where respondents are asked to rate the level on which they agree or disagree with a given statement on a numeric scale, e.g., 1–7, where 1 = strongly agree and 7 = strongly disagree. (Also see Rating Scale.)
Source: Human Factors International

LINE OF VISIBILITY
In a service blueprint this is a

line that separates face to face customer employee interactions from customer employee interactions that are remote or not face to face.

LOADED WORD
a word that has positive or negative connotations and can influence the interviewee's response to a question.

LOW-FIDELITY PROTOTYPE A quick and easy translation of high-level design concepts into tangible and testable artifacts, giving an indication of the direction that the product is heading. Prototypes that are simple, focused on one or two features. Low resolution prototyping allows a team to make their ideas tangible and gather feedback.

MASLOW'S HIERARCHY OF NEEDS
A theory of motivation, in which individuals' needs are described as a hierarchy, often illustrated as layers in a pyramid. Needs at each level must be met prior to an individual aspiring to the next level. Maslow's theory describes five levels: Physiological, Safety, Social, Esteem and Self-actualization. In PET we can design to meet needs at one or more of these levels. For example, a mobile phone may meet people's safety ('I need to contact you in an emergency'), social ('I like to keep in touch wherever I am') and self-esteem needs ('Look at my cool phone'), with somewhat different design considerations applying to each of these levels.
Source: Human Factors International

MINIMUM VIABLE PRODUCT
A minimum viable product is a simple version of a new product which allows a team to learn the maximum amount about customers with the least effort. The goal of an MVP is to test fundamental business hypotheses as efficiently in the real-world as possible.

MODERATOR
A person that works with a group to regulate, but not lead, a discussion. Whereas a facilitator might take charge of a discussion to shepherd it in a specific direction, a moderator remains passive, without explicitly leading the process or driving a desired outcome. A moderator takes the lead from the participants, listening and intervening only when necessary to encourage further discussion or ask for clarity for other participants or audiences.

NEEDS
A necessary function or condition. There are a wide variety of human needs such as food, shelter, security, affection and self fulfillment.

OUTSIDE-IN PERSPECTIVE
This is the perception that people

outside of an organization have of the organization and it's products and services such as customers and other stakeholders.

PAPER PROTOTYPE
Paper prototyping is the process of creating rough, often hand-sketched, drawings of a user interface, and using them in a usability test to gather feedback. A rough, often hand-sketched, drawing of a user interface, used in a usability test to gather feedback. Participants point to locations on the page that they would click, and screens are manually presented to the user based on the interactions they indicate.

PARADOX OF CHOICE
Limiting choice is a PET technique in changing impression. Paradoxically, people think they want many choices, but can, in fact, be overwhelmed by the complexities too many choices introduce to decision-making. So, people are more likely to be persuaded to make a purchase (or other decision) if you limit their choice to a small number, often no more than three or four.
Source: Human Factors International

PARTICIPATORY DESIGN
An approach that involves stakeholders such as clients, end users, community members in the design process to ensure that the design meets the needs of those it is serving as well as generating buy-in. A type of social research in which the people being studied have significant control over and participation in the research.

PERSONA
A persona is a fictitious identity that reflects one of the user groups for who you are designing. A representation of a user segment with shared needs and characteristics. In user-centered design and marketing, personas are archetypal characters that represent different user segments that might use a product or service in a similar way.

PLACEBO EFFECT
A PET technique in changing impression. In medicine, for example, you can achieve health improvements just by giving the impression you are treating patients with a drug, even if you are giving them a 'placebo', a neutral substance with no known medical properties. There is evidence that the more expensive patients think the drug to be, the greater the placebo effect.
Source: Human Factors International

POINT OF VIEW OR POV
In Design Thinking, a POV means the point of view of a very particular person. Creating a point of view involves synthesizing the data gained in the Understand and

Observe phases in order to create a common reference/inspiration for later ideation and prototyping. The idea is to focus on a real person, with many of the concrete details found during the Understand/Observe phases. One approach is to develop one or two concise sentences that express User+Need+Insight. Good: "Mark is a shy, recent college graduate who needs a way to stay connected with the college community because he feels that his life could be more exciting. Alumni newsletters and college reunions need not apply." Bad:"Mark needs a website to share pictures and news with the people he met in college because he feels lonely."
Source: dSchool Stanford

POWER OF EXPECTATION
A PET technique in changing impression. Presenting goods or services in a way that raises the expectation that they will be good, results in users perceiving them as better. A wellformatted report, for example will be seen as better written than a scruffy one, even if the text is exactly the same. Similarly, a well presented meal will not only be more tempting than the same food just thrown on the plate, but will also taste better (as every good chef knows!). So, in PET, if we design to give the expectation that goods and services will be good, they are more likely to be experienced as good.
Source: Human Factors International

PROBES
Areas you want to go more in-depth in an interview.

A technique used during in-depth interviews to explore the interviewee's emotions about the topic we're researching. The 'probing' questions asked gently nudge the interviewees to disclose their feelings and beliefs. For example: "How do you feel about shopping online?"
Source: Human Factors International

PROTOTYPE
A prototype is a model built to test a concept with end users in order to learn from. Prototyping helps understand real, working conditions rather than a theoretical conditions.

QUESTIONNAIRES
A research instrument consisting of a series of questions and other prompts for the purpose of gathering information from respondents.

REFRAMING
Reframe to create different perspectives and new ideas.

How to reframe:
1. Define the problem that you would like to address.
2. There is more than one way of looking at a problem. You could also define this problem in another way as."
3. What if a male or female used

it?
4. What if it was used in China or Argentina?
5. "The underlying reason for the problem is."
6. "I think that the best solution is."
7. "You could compare this problem to the problem of."
8. "Another, different way of thinking about it

RETURN ON INVESTMENT (ROI)
A monetary evaluation of benefits relative to the effort or expenditure invested; a measure of how much return, usually measured as profit or cost savings, results from a given use of money. In the context of usability, ROI is the monetary (or
other) benefit gained as a result of an investment in good usability design.
Source: Human Factors International

REVERSE CARD SORT
A usability testing technique, opposite to that of a card sort, where participants are given a list of items to see if they can figure out where to find them. Their success validates the self evidence
of the navigational structure of a design. Categories have already been made and labeled appropriately
Source: Human Factors International

ROLE-PLAY
Assign roles and act out scenarios with props and end users feedback to refine your design.

SATISFACTION SYSTEM
The satisfaction system is the system of how the products or services satisfy the customer's needs. It includes the product or service and its related products or service. It involves understanding how related products add value to the main product. Customers are interested in the entire system beyond the individual product.

RULE OF RECIPROCATION
The technique is built on a social rule where people given a gift feel compelled to give something back. For example: You give your customer a small gift. Later, they're likely to consider signing up for your new service.
Source: Human Factors International

SCALE
Service design considers micro and macro scales ,detailed interactions, and holistic overviews of an experience.

SCENARIOS
A scenario is a hypothetical narrative illustrating an event or series of events. It is a method of imagining a user experience in the real-world.

Use scenarios are a method of prototyping ideas in order to explore and refine them.

Scenarios are short stories about people and activities that describe typical usage and focus on goals, actions and objects.

Scenarios evoke reflection in design and provide a common reference point. Scenarios help express the requirements of the different stakeholders in a format that can be understood by the other stakeholders. They can be written, illustrated, acted or filmed. Scenario generating aims to predict how people could act in particular situations.

A concrete, often narrative, description of a user performing tasks in a specific context sufficiently detailed that design implications can be inferred. Source: Human Factors International

SENSORIAL DESIGN
Sensorial Design is a term used to include the presentation of an experience in all senses. For example, Visual Design only covers visual expression and presentation to the visual sense. Audio Design includes the creation of music, sound effects, and vocals to communicate and entertain in the aural sense (hearing). Likewise, all of the other human senses (touch, smell, taste, etc.) are elements of an experience that can be designed.

SERVICE DESIGN
Design for experiences that reach people through many different touch-points, and that happen over time.
British Standard for Service Design: BS 7000 -3, BS 7000 -10, BS EN ISO 9000

Service designs can be both tangible and intangible. Service design can involve artifacts, communication, context and behaviors. It should be consistent, easy to use and have the strategic alliance.

Gillian Hollins, Bill Hollins, Total Design: Managing The Design Process in the Service Sector

SERVICE ECOLOGY
A service ecology is a system of people, objects and the relationships between them that form a service.

System in which the service is integrated: i.e. a holistic visualization of the service system. All the factors are gathered, analyzed and visualized: politics, the economy, employees, law, societal trends, and technological development. The service ecology is thereby rendered, along with its attendant agents, processes, and relations. *Mager 2009*

Ultimately, sustainable service ecologies depend on a balance where the actors involved exchange value in ways that is mutually beneficial over time.
Live|work 2008

SENSUALIZATION
Sensualization is the approach of considering the experience to be the total of the individual experiences of the five senses.

SERVICE
An exchange of value, involving tangible and intangible elements A system of products spaces human interactions and experiences.

SERVICE MOMENTS
Discrete points of interaction between a user and a service, often mapped out in a user journey. An example of a service moment is a patron placing a hold on a book, which can be done at home via the website, in the library via the website, or at the reference desk.
Source: Libraries Toolkit

SERVICE SYSTEM
The ecology of relationships, interactions, and contexts of a service. channels, resources, and touchpoints, internal and external, that facilitate the delivering of a service.

STAKEHOLDER
A person, group, or organization directly or indirectly involved or affected by a product, service or experience.

Stakeholders include any individuals who are influence by the design. Specifically, the project team, end users, strategic partners, customers, alliances, vendors and senior management are project stakeholders

Possible stakeholders
1. Employees
2. Shareholders
3. Government
4. Customers
5. Suppliers
6. Prospective employees
7. Local communities
8. Global Community
9. Schools
10. Future generations
11. Ex-employees
12. Creditors
13. Professional associations
14. Competitors
15. Investors
16. Prospective customers
17. Communities

Why involve stakeholders?
1. Stakeholder analysis helps to identify:
2. Stakeholder interests
3. Ways to influence other stakeholders
4. Risks
5. Key people to be informed during the project
6. Negative stakeholders as well as their adverse effects on the project

SWIMLANES
An approach used in service design involving arranging descriptive boxes into rows (the "swim lanes") to provide additional context about how the steps are related. Work flow is represented over time and is usually read from left to right.

SYNTHESIS
The sense-making process in which research is translated and interpreted into insights that prompt design. Useful frameworks for synthesis include journeys, Venn diagrams, two by twos and maps.
Source: Libraries Toolkit

STAKEHOLDER MAP
A visual representation of the stakeholders in a service and the relationships between them.

SERVICE DESIGN
Service design is a form of conceptual design which involves the activity of planning and organizing people, infrastructure, communication and material components of a service in order to improve its quality and the interaction between service provider and customers.
Service design - Wikipedia, the free encyclopedia, https://en.wikipedia.org/wiki/Service_design (accessed March 20, 2016).

SOCIAL DESIGN
Design done for the social good or top positively impact society.

STRATEGIC DESIGN
Design that focuses on big picture systematic problems in order to increase an organization's future innovative and competitive advantage.

STORYBOARD
A storyboard is a graphic sequence of illustrations, words or images for the purpose of communicating a user scenario or experience. Storyboarding, was developed at Walt Disney during the early 1930s. A storyboard is a tool inspired by the film-making industry, where a visual sequence of events is used to capture a user's interactions. Depending on the audience, it may be an extremely rough sketch, purely for crystallizing your own ideas.

SUMMATIVE TESTING
Testing done to measure the success of the design in terms of human performance and preference.
Source: Human Factors International

THINK-ALOUD PROTOCOL
A direct observation method of user testing that involves asking users to think out loud as they are performing a task. Users are asked to say whatever they are looking at, thinking, doing, and feeling at each moment. This method is especially helpful for determining users' expectations and identifying what aspects of a system are confusing.

TOUCHPOINTS
A touchpoint is any point of contact between a customer and the provider of a service, product or experience. A touchpoint is where a potential customer or customer comes in contact with your brand before, during and after a transaction.

Identifying your touchpoints is an important step toward

creating a journey map or a service blueprint. Each touchpoint is an opportunity to create a better customer experience. A touchpoint can be a physical, virtual or human point of interaction. Chris Risdon from Adaptive Path defines touchpoints in this way. 'A touchpoint is a point of interaction involving a specific human need in a specific time and place.' Laura Patterson of VisionEdge defines a touchpoint as " any customer interaction or encounter that can influence the customer's perception of your product, service, or brand."

TRANSCRIPTION
The process of turning audio or video recordings into a typed format.

T-SHAPED PERSON
A person who has deep competency in a particular subject area and broad knowledge and skills across a range of disciplines.

TWO BY TWO MATRIX
A type of framework with opposing axes showing a spectrum along a particular dimension on each axis. This framework is used to organized ideas within the four quadrants, or to demonstrate mappings of ideas across several dimensions.
Source Libraries Handbook

UNIQUE SELLING PROPOSITION
An exclusive message that concisely describes a product against its competition, and which the business or brand can use consistently in its advertising and promotion to achieve a cutting edge in the market.
Source: Human Factors International

UNMET NEEDS
Six principles that will ensure a design is compatible with user needs:
1. The design is based upon an explicit understanding of users, tasks and environments.
2. Users are involved throughout design and development.
3. The design is driven and refined by user-centered evaluation.
4. The process is iterative.
5. The design addresses the whole user experience.
6. The design team includes multidisciplinary skills and perspectives.

Some Questions to ask:
1. Who are the users?
2. What are the users' tasks and goals?
3. What are the users' experience levels?
4. What functions do the users need from the design?
5. What information will be needed by end-users?,
6. In what form do they need it?
7. How do users think the design should work?

USABILITY
Is the ease of use and learning of an object, such as a book, software application, website, machine, tool or any object that a human interacts with.

USABILITY ROUND-TABLE
A meeting in which a group of end users is invited to bring specific work samples and discuss the validity of an early prototype.
Source: Human Factors International

USE CASES
A use case is a list of steps that define the interactions between a user and a system. Use cases, especially when used as requirements for software development, are often constructed in UML, with defined actors and roles.

USER-CENTERED DESIGN
A design process during which the needs of the user is considered at all times. Designers consider how a user is likely to use the product, and they then test the validity of their assumptions in real-world tests with actual users. Design that responds to user needs that is developed through engaging and understanding the point of view of users.

USER JOURNEY
The step by step journey that a user takes to reach their goal.

USER PROFILING
Based on research of user groups develop different character profiles to represent your users. These are also called personas.

USER VALIDATION
Process of testing to determine if the user's needs or requirements have been met

VALUE EXCHANGE
A service provider makes a promise to the service recipient in exchange for some form of value. The movement of value from the service provider to the recipient is the value exchange.

VANITY METRICS
Data that make you feel good, but is not very useful or actionable such as new users gained per day or number of downloads. Vanity metrics do not reflect the key drivers of a business.

VERTICAL PROTOTYPE
Prototypes that display just a few complex features of a product and almost completely implement only these features. Vertical prototype tests provide insights into users' understanding of the complexity, issues, and problems of a specific feature.
Source: Human Factors International

VISUAL HIERARCHY
Refers to the overall page layout and its ability to lead the users' attention through the page

elements. Effective visual hierarchies create an appropriate balance in composition that draws users to top levels of the hierarchy while optimizing visual access to important page level elements
Source: Human Factors International

WICKED PROBLEM
A wicked problem is a problem with contradictory, and changing requirements. The term 'wicked' is used, not in the sense of evil but rather its resistance to resolution.

Wicked problems are characterized by:
1. The solution depends on how the problem is framed.
2. Stakeholders have different world views and frames for understanding the problem.
3. The constraints of the problem and the resources needed to solve it change over time.
4. The problem is never solved definitively.

Source: Wicked problem:definition of wicked problem and synonyms http://brevard.ifas.ufl.edu/communities/pdf/SF_Wicked_Issues_Background_Defined_ (accessed March 20, 2016).

WIREFRAME
A rough guide for the layout of a website or app, either done with pen and paper or with wireframing software. The wireframe depicts the page layout and shows how the elements work functionally. It focuses on what a web interface does, not what it looks like. Wireframes can be sketches or computer images.

WIZARD OF OZ
A user-based evaluation of unimplemented technology where, generally unknown to the user, a human or team is simulating some or all the responses of the system.

WORKAROUND
A user's personal solution to a problem with a service or product, that circumvents the standard procedure. It is often temporary or makeshift. Observing these behaviors often leads to fruitful advances in insights and inspiration.
Source: Libraries Toolkit

12
INDEX

INDEX

SYMBOLS

2X2 matrix 133
5 Whys 106
10x10 107
50 Phrases that will prevent you from beating your competitors 129
101 brainstorming 107
635 Method 107

A

Abductive logic: 44
Abductive thinking 44
Abilities 37, 116
A-B test 248
action plan 62
activities 24, 161, 165, 166, 184, 204, 205, 206, 233, 249
activity 204, 205, 216, 242
actor 200, 248
acts 79
adaptability 37
adhesive notes 203
Adobe 212, 240
affinity diagram 106, 168, 169, 170, 171, 172, 174, 248
Affinity diagrams 113
affordance 248
age 59, 70, 72, 184, 186
Age 59, 70, 72, 74, 87, 115, 164, 184, 186
agile 96, 148
agreement 198, 246
Alam, I. 294
Alex F. Osborn 130
Allanwood, Gavin 294
Ambrose, Gavin 294
analogous situations 248
analytic induction 248

analytics 248
analyze 42, 57, 69, 216
Angelis. J. 309
Annapurna 168
Antonelli, Paola 294
Anu, Valtonen 295
Apaydin 128
Apple 11, 13
architectural charette 101
artifacts 249
Artifacts 249
association 173
attitudes 60, 73, 74
Australia 11
Autodesk 286
Availability 111

B

backoffice 249
backstage 249
backstory 35
Baines, T. 295
Balcioglu, Tevfik 295
Banerjee, Maithili 295
barriers 212, 239
Bate, Paul 295
Bateson, Gregory 42
Battarbee, K. 295, 301
behave 42, 53
behavior 42, 47, 53, 55, 65, 79, 83, 117, 118, 119, 144
Behavior segmentation 115
benchmarking 51, 106, 108, 114
benchmarking competitors 106
Benedettini, O. 295
Benefit segmentation 115
Berger, Warren 295
beta launch 249
Beta prototype 149
Beta testing 149

Bettencourt, Lance 295
Beyer, Hugh 295
bias 39, 49, 53, 81, 83, 114, 151, 249, 251, 257
Biemans, W. G 295
Bitner, M. J. 296
blank 174
Bleuel, William H. 296
block 134, 174
Blomkvist, J. 296
blue ocean 106
blueprint 212–311, 227–311, 241–311, 243–311, 265–311
Boas, Franz 42
body language 41, 63, 79, 112, 133, 232
body storming 127
bodystorming 107, 142, 213, 241, 249
Boucher, A. 299
Bowers, Micah 34
Brainstorm 116, 124
brainstorming 57, 69, 74, 96, 99, 107, 108, 120, 124, 130, 131, 132, 134, 168, 170, 172, 174, 178, 200, 212, 214, 240, 249, 254, 292
Brainstorming 130
brainstorms 101, 120
brand 43, 64, 193, 197, 198, 216, 264, 265
Brax, S. 296
Breakout groups 101
Brown, Tim 296
Bruere, Robert W. 48, 49
Buchanan, R. 296
Buchenau, M. 296
Business Model Canvas 161, 164
Bustinza, O 309
butcher paper 203
Buur, J. 310
Buxton, William (Bill) 296

C

camera 53, 134, 203
camera journal 106
Capital One Labs 141
cards 140
card sorting 107, 249
car park 207, 237, 242
Carroll, J. M. 296
cash flow 27
causation 250
Center for Universal Design at North Carolina State University 129
challenge 42, 48, 49, 53, 63, 64, 140, 178, 182
CHANNEL plans 155
channels 51, 56, 155, 158, 161, 162, 164, 185, 197, 198, 199, 200, 202, 204, 206, 210, 216, 227, 230, 234, 250, 257, 263
CHANNELS PRICING 155
CHANNEL STRATEGY 155
Charette 100, 101, 102
charrette 99, 100, 101, 102
Charter, Martin 296
checklist: environmentally responsible design 136
China 11, 25, 29, 261
choosing a technique 131
Christy Wampole 117
Chuck Close 128
Cipolla, Carla 297, 306
Cisco 286
Citizenship status 116
Clatworthy, S. 297
closed questions 250
clustering 108, 174
Clustering 133
CLUSTERING 150
Coate, Roger A. 65
Coates, Joseph F. 297
co-creation 55, 89, 93
code 251
co-design 107, 250
coding 150, 165, 251
coffee 134, 204, 205, 206, 208,

211, 214, 235, 242, 246
cognitive dissonance 250
collaboration 41, 83, 198
Collaboration 96, 153
collaborative 91, 99, 112, 249
collaborative design 251
collaborative spaces 41
collective intelligence 251
color 176
common ground 106
communication 137
communities 38, 55, 62, 263, 267
comparison tests 250
competitive advantage 66, 264
competitive positioning 51, 197, 227
competitive products 108
Competitor review 96
competitors 164, 263
Competitors 157
complex 34, 51, 110, 132, 168, 169, 170, 171, 177, 195, 216, 217, 251, 255, 266
complexity 50, 169, 170, 195, 197, 227, 266
concept 139
conceptual model 250
Condon, Patrick M. 297
confirmation bias 251
conflict 35
conflicting needs 51
connections 41, 134
consistency 66
constraints 108, 116
consumption 28, 136, 137
context 35, 42, 49, 53, 63, 74, 96, 100, 108, 113, 115, 118, 119, 122, 139, 142, 143, 182, 185, 203, 213, 230, 231, 241, 251, 252, 257, 261, 262, 263
contextual inquiry 251
continuous improvement 62
convenience 165
Convenience 111
convergent 106, 252

convergent thinking 46, 96
Cooper, Alan 57, 58, 69, 297
Corsten, Hans, 297
Cottam, H. 297
create a strategy 131
critical thinking 45
Crossan 128
cross-disciplinary collaboration 252
cross-disciplinary teams 87
cultural probe 252
cultural probes 252
culture 108
Curedale, Rob 287, 291
curiosity 37
curious 114
curiousity 39
customer 12, 43, 51, 52, 56, 58, 69, 93, 193, 195, 197, 198, 199, 201, 202, 203, 204, 205, 206, 207, 208, 209, 210, 211, 212, 214, 216, 233, 234, 235, 238, 240, 241, 243, 246, 264, 265
customer experience 50, 51, 52, 55, 77, 142, 182, 190, 193, 195, 197, 198, 199, 202, 204, 207, 210, 212, 214, 216, 227, 230, 231, 233, 234, 238, 240, 241, 265
customer journey 252
customers 43, 51, 56, 57, 58, 69, 71, 123, 195, 197, 199, 202, 203, 209, 213, 216, 227, 239, 241, 243
customer segments 114, 155, 185, 197, 198, 199, 202, 203, 227, 230, 233
customer's perspective 111, 169, 182, 197, 199, 202, 232, 244
Customer Traction 156
customization 28, 165

D

Danish Design Center 13, 32
Darden School of the University of Virginia 66
dark horse prototype 141
data 42, 48, 49, 57, 58, 69, 172, 173, 176, 199, 201, 202
Data analysis 150
data analyst 79
day in the life 106
DCC 285, 286
de Bono, E. 297
De Brentani, U. 297
decoy strategy 252
deductive analysis 252
deductive logic 44
defer judgment 133
DeFillippi, R. 301
Define next vision 159
De Jong, J. P. 297
deliverables 108
Dell 11
demographic segmentation 56
Demographic segmentation 115
Denmark 33
Dependability 111
desert island 106
Design charette 101, 102
design charrette 99, 101
Design Community College 2, 3, 287, 288, 289, 290, 291, 292
design problem 116
design process 46, 177
design sprint 95, 98
Design Sprint 96
design teams 11, 93, 112
design thinking process 89, 93, 106, 109, 111, 113, 115, 117, 119, 123, 125, 127, 129, 131, 133, 135, 137, 139, 141, 143, 145, 147, 149, 151, 153, 155, 157, 159, 160, 253
desktop walkthroughs 213
Despain, Wendy 297
development process 32, 33, 96
Dev Patnaik 136

diagram 168, 170
diaries 48
diary methods 64
diary study 253
Díaz-Kommonen, L 297
Dieter Rams 129
Dieter Rams Ten Principles of "Good Design" 129
differentiation 27, 37, 108, 111
digital camera 203
Dimitriadis, S. 308
Disabilities 116
disassembly 137
discovery 114, 118
Discovery 113, 114
Discovery Phase 66
Disney Method 107
disposable 136
distribution segmentation 56
divergent 46, 253
divergent thinking 46, 96
diversity 62
document 108
Donald Norman 64
Doorley, Scott 297
dot voting 107, 177
Dot voting 134
draft 203, 204
Druin, A. 297
dry erase markers 203
d.school 95
Duarte, Nancy 298

E

Easingwood, C. 306
Ecole des Beaux Arts 99
ecological 137
Edison 87, 91, 135
education 22, 54, 60, 70, 72, 74, 87
Education 116
Edvardsson, B. 298
emotional 216
emotional journey map 216

emotions 38, 42, 57, 69, 77, 115, 184, 190, 195, 210, 214, 217, 230, 243, 252, 260
empathy 53, 57, 63, 67, 69, 106, 115, 182, 190, 191, 197, 213, 227, 241, 253
empathy maps 182, 190
employees 12–311, 59, 71, 93–311
employee training 107
empowered teams 89
encourage wild ideas 133
end-of-life 137
end user 65, 114, 125, 209, 238, 252, 256
energy 136
engineering 199, 202
entrepreneurship 54
entry points 253
entry Points 253
environmental 137
environmentally responsible design 136
environments 200
ethnicity 60, 73
ethnographic methods 52, 53
ethnography 53, 58, 69, 253
Europe 11, 56
Evaluating an idea 136
evaluation matrix 107
Evelyn Huang 141
Evenson, S. 298, 300
Events 118, 155
evidence 200, 235, 237, 242, 246, 253
evidence-based design 253
exit points 254
expectations 27, 50, 51, 52, 74, 83, 100, 101, 111, 115, 149, 156, 209, 239, 264
experience 11, 34, 41, 43, 51, 64, 108, 115, 116, 193, 194, 195, 197, 198, 199, 200, 201, 202, 203, 204, 205, 210, 213, 214, 216, 234, 241, 264, 265
experience and journey maps 195

experience design 77, 253
experience mapping 106, 193, 194, 195, 217
experience maps 115, 142
experience problems 50, 199, 202, 231
experience prototyping 213, 241, 253
experiences 42, 52, 64, 70, 139, 140, 188, 195, 197, 199, 202, 216
Experiences 119
extreme user 254

F

facilitating 79, 87, 131
Facilitating 131
failure 51, 52, 65, 113, 135, 158, 182, 197, 212, 240
family size 60, 72
Fazlagic, Amir Jan 298
feedback 109, 204, 213
Feedback 140
feelings 200, 211
Feelings 119
field study 254
findings 49, 203
Fisher, A.G.B. 22
Fitzsimmons, James A. 298
Fitzsimmons, Mona J. 298
five whys 254
focus 12, 59, 60, 64, 71, 73, 93, 216
Focus 291, 292
focus groups 106, 183, 209, 238, 254, 291, 292
Focus groups 113
Følstad 195
Ford 13, 21, 286
formative evaluation 254
Foster 195
framework 23, 95, 96, 119, 164, 190, 195, 265
free association 106

free listing 254
Frei, Frances 298
frontstage 255
Frontstage 111
frustrations 58, 71
Fulton Suri, J. 298
future 45, 52, 197, 198, 204, 210, 214, 233, 241

G

gain 57, 69, 189
gambler's fallacy 255
gap analysis 255
Garcia, Fausto 298
Garrett, Jesse James. 298
Gaver, Bill 299
Gebauer, H., Krempl, R. 298
Gemmel, Paul 299
gender 60, 70, 72, 87, 108, 184, 186
Gender 116
generating ideas 99, 127, 128, 249
geographic segmentation 56
Geographic segmentation 115
Germany 46
Gestalt principles 255
global warming 137
glossary 248
goal 51, 199, 202, 230
goal grid 106
goals 32, 49, 51, 52, 53, 56, 57, 58, 62, 69, 71, 74, 76, 79, 83, 85, 95, 96, 99, 100, 101, 106, 108, 115, 126, 127, 143, 148, 152, 158, 164, 177, 183, 184, 187, 189, 191, 195, 198, 199, 200, 202, 210, 214, 230, 231, 241, 244, 262, 265
Goals 149
goal statemet 199, 202, 230
Goodwin, Kim 299
Google 39, 95, 98
government 197, 263, 286
Government 114

Gratton, Lynda 299
Gray, Dave 182, 299
Griffin, A. 295
Grönroos, Christian 299
grounded theory 255
group 11, 41, 43, 56, 57, 58, 59, 69, 71, 72, 108, 176, 177, 178, 198
groups 53, 56, 58, 60, 71, 73, 134, 173, 176, 178, 198
groupthink 178, 255

H

habitat 137
Halvorson, Kristina 299
Hamilton 11
Harris, Paul 294
Hasso Plattner 133
Hasso Plattner Institute 133
Hasso Plattner Institute of Design 133
HCI 255
headers 176
health 24, 55, 66
Health 116
Heapy, Joe 195, 299
hear 63, 185
Heath, Chip 299
Heskett, James L. 299
heuristic evaluation 255
heuristics 107, 255
Hick-Hyman Law 256
hierarchy 24, 108, 114, 132, 174, 177, 203, 231, 249, 258, 266, 267
high fidelity prototype 143, 256
high fidelity prototypes 141
history 170
Hohman, L. 299
holistic thinking 52, 198
Hollins, Bill 299
Hollins, Gillian 299
Holmlid, S. 296, 299, 300
Holtzblatt, Karen 300

Hong Kong University of Science and Technology 29
horizontal prototype 256
Horovitz, Jacques 300
hospital 59, 71
Hostetter, Chelsea 35
hotel 205, 207, 242
housing 60, 72
how might we? 256
HP 11, 21, 286
human-centered design 256
human factors 255
human needs 34, 65, 258
humor 34, 37, 132

I

IBM 13, 21
Icebreaker 112
idea 44, 108, 109, 140, 177, 178, 213, 216, 240, 241, 243
Ideate 96
ideation 51, 61, 117, 124, 125, 127, 174, 177, 183, 197, 227, 260
IDEO 66, 95, 127
Implement 158
implementaion 107
Implementation 148
implementation phase 153
improvement 195
income 60, 70, 72, 74, 164, 185
Income 116
inductive analysis 256, 256–311
inductive logic 44
information 41, 45, 48, 59, 72
inhibition 178
innovation 11, 13, 22, 27, 32, 39, 44, 50, 51, 53, 54, 55, 62, 65, 77, 95, 106, 119, 120, 128, 133, 135, 152, 165, 168, 171, 197, 227, 243
Innovation 118, 128, 135
insight 117, 118, 120, 121, 125, 139
insights 35, 41, 42, 43, 47, 57, 61, 69, 100, 106, 108, 117, 119, 125, 127, 153, 157, 170, 171, 174, 189, 197, 204, 213, 216, 217, 227, 230, 234, 240, 249, 250, 254, 256, 264, 266, 267
insignt 118, 120
in-store 204
intangible 51, 111, 127, 197, 227, 253, 262, 263
intangible elements. 111
Intel 286
intellectual property 109, 131
interaction design 256
interactions 41, 139, 140, 184, 195, 198, 216
intercept 257
internal communications 155
Internet device 61, 73
interviewer bias 257
interview guide 257
interviewing 251
interviews 42, 48, 58, 64, 69, 106, 107, 108, 183, 199, 202, 209, 230, 231, 238, 251, 255, 257, 260, 291, 291–311, 291–311, 292, 292–311, 292–311, 292–311
Interviews 97, 113
Intrigue/Surprise 157
Intuit 13, 77
intuition 37, 44, 53, 169
investment 139
Iqbal, Majid 300
I-shaped person 257
Iterate 102, 103, 140
iteration 109, 257
iterative consultative process 257
iterative design 257

J

Japan 25, 168, 169, 170
Jegou, François 302
Jehl, Francis 91
Johansson, M 300
Johne, A. 300

Johnson, Steven 300
journey 12–311, 93–311, 195, 203, 210, 215, 216, 241, 265
journey map 195, 215, 216, 257, 265
journey maps 220
judgment 24, 39, 63, 91, 114, 128, 133, 174, 177, 209, 239

K

Kalbach, Jim 300
Kallenberg, R. 304
Kaner, Sam 300
Kankainen, A. 197, 300
Kawakita, Jiro 168, 169, 170, 221
Kay, J. M. 295
Kelley, Tom 300
key differentiation 108
key participants 62
key problem approach 168
Kimbell, Lucie 301
King, Stanley 301
KJ method 168, 170
Kolko, Jon 301
Koskinen, I. 295, 301

L

laddering 64
language 87, 287, 288, 289, 290, 291, 292
Language 116
launch 109
Launch 153, 158, 159
LAUNCH PLAN 158
Leadbeater, C. 297
leading question 257
Lee, Fred 301
Lehrer, M. 301
Liedtka, Jeanne 66, 301
life cycle 137
life stage 60, 72
Lightfoot, H. W. 295
lightning talks 97
Likert scale 257

line of visibility 237, 238, 249, 257
Listen 114, 132, 158
listening 39, 53, 63, 76, 79, 81, 83, 85
listening skills 132
Lloyd, Vernon 301
loaded word 258
Lockton, Dan, 301
Lockwood, Thomas 301
lotus method 107
low fidelity prototyping 139, 143, 258
Low-fidelity prototyping 139
Lucero, A. 301
Lusch Robert F. 298, 302, 309, 311

M

Maffei, S. 302
Mager, Birgit 302
Malinowski, Bronisław 53
Malterud, K. 302
management 198, 199, 202
manager of logistics 79
Manning, Harley 302
manufacturing 109
Manzini, Ezio 302, 306
Mapping 98
mapping methods 42, 184, 193, 194, 195, 197, 198, 201, 203, 204, 205, 210, 212, 213, 215, 216, 227, 236, 240, 241, 265, 289
market 123, 137
marketing 11, 61, 73, 107, 123
MARKETING COMMUNICATIONS 154
market opportunities 137
Marquez, Joe 302
Martin, Roger L. 303
masking tape 203
Maslow's hierarchy of needs 258
materials 109, 140

Mathieu, V. 303
matrix 122, 124
Mattelmäki, Tuuli 295, 301, 303, 309
Matthews, Scott 182
McCarthy, J. 310
McQuilken, Lisa 303
Mead, Margaret 42
meaning 34, 67, 77
media 60, 73
Media 144
Menor L.J. 303
Meroni, Anna 303
methods 287–311
metrics 51, 54, 62, 152, 155, 158, 197, 210, 214, 227, 241, 243, 266
Metrics 98, 143, 150, 152
Mid-launch 158
Miettinen, Satu 295, 303
milestones 106
Milestones 144
Miller, Luke 304
mind maps 56
mind Maps 106
mini charette 100
minimum viable product 258
Miozzo, M. 301
mobile 40, 203, 204, 210
Mobility 116
MOCK-UPS 139
moderator 172, 178, 203, 232
Moenaert, R. K. 295
Moggridge, Bill 304
Möller, K. 304
moments of truth 197
Morelli, N. 304
Morgan, Michael 122
Moritz, Stefan 304
Moser, Christian 304
Motivations 119
multi-channel map 216
multidisciplinary 100, 115, 148, 265

N

narrative 34, 144, 261, 262
nationality 60, 73
Nationality 116
nature 137
need 112, 115, 116, 117, 137, 139
needs 34, 41, 42, 43, 51, 52, 53, 58, 59, 63, 65, 69, 71, 74, 81, 108, 177, 184, 193, 197, 199, 200, 202, 211, 212, 214, 235, 240, 243, 258, 265
Needs 121, 125, 127
negative stakeholders 263
Nestle 286
New York Times 21, 25
Nietzsche, Friedrich 89
Nike 13, 286
Norman, Donald A. 304
North America 11
notes 140, 178, 204, 205
Nudurupati, S. S. 304

O

objectives 109, 198
objects 236
observation 42, 48, 58, 69, 79, 85, 106, 115, 291, 292
Observation 97, 113
observe 39, 53, 63, 106, 108, 116, 253, 260
Observe 116
occupation 60, 70, 72, 184, 186
Occupation 116
Oliva, R. 304
Olsen 61, 73
Olsson, J. 298
opportunities 50, 55, 106, 175, 193, 195, 197, 198, 204, 207, 212, 214, 216, 227, 238, 239, 240, 265
opportunity 120, 147, 156, 157
Ordanini, A. 301, 304
O'Regan, N. 309

Osterwalder, Alexander 161, 304, 305
Ostrom, A. L. 296
outside-in perspective 258

P

Pacenti, E. 305
pain 187, 206, 207, 208, 211, 214, 238
Pain (+ Gain) 156
pain points 74, 184, 187, 201, 207, 209, 211, 212, 213, 217, 238, 240, 241, 242
Pang, S. 305
Papastathopoulou, P. 305
paper prototypes 127
paper prototyping 107, 213, 241, 259
paradox of choice 259
Park, Albert 29
Parker, Sophia 305
Park, Robert 42
Parry, G 309
Participant Recruitment Screener 146
participants 41, 62, 79, 81, 83, 85, 99, 100, 101, 102, 103, 112, 131, 132, 133, 134, 143, 144, 145, 146, 151, 152, 178, 232, 244, 254, 258, 261, 286
participation 62, 85, 168, 250, 259
participatory design 259
Patel, Raj 305
Patnaik, Dev 305
Patrício, L. 305, 307
Patton 47
Pennington, S. 299
PepsiCo 21
perceived risk 111
performance 108, 137
Perry, C. 294
person 41, 44, 56, 64, 70, 177, 242
persona 35, 57, 58, 59, 61, 69, 70, 71, 72, 73, 74, 106, 161, 182, 183, 184, 186, 190, 195, 198, 201, 203, 204, 210, 215, 216, 230, 233, 259, 266
personalization 40
Personalization 111
personas 114
Personas 149
perspective 49, 63, 195, 197, 199, 202, 203, 204, 234
phase 46, 177
photographs 212
physical evidence 205, 236
PICTIVES 107, 127
Pieter Baert 141
Pine, Joseph B. 305
Pinheiro, Tenny 305
Pink, Daniel H. 305
Pitch 153
PITCH 156
placebo effect 259
planning 169, 170
Planning 99, 100, 110
Plattner, Hasso 133
pleasure 213, 241
point of view 113, 114, 117, 124, 125, 142
Point of view 120, 125
point of view (POV) 34, 50, 53, 58, 63, 71, 106, 107, 108, 183, 195, 198, 216, 230, 257, 259, 266
Point of view statement 120
points of failure 212, 240
Polaine, Andrew 306
Polanyi, Michael 41
Pollak, L. 306
pollution 137
positive 201, 204, 213, 234, 241
Post-it-Notes 53–311, 134, 174, 204
post-it voting 133
Post-it voting 133
Post-launch 158
POST-LAUNCH PLAN 158

POV 117, 120, 124, 125, 128
power of expectation 260
Pre-launch 158
Preparing for brainstorming 131
presentation 212, 240
Presentation 100
Prestes Joly, M. 306
price 56, 211, 214
Price 111
PRICING analysis 155
Pricing structure 155
Priestner, Andy 306
primary research 48
print 204, 210
Prioritization 133
probes 260
problem 49, 108, 195
problems 43, 44, 45, 140, 199, 202
problem-solving 62, 93, 130, 169, 177, 252
problem statement 61, 116, 117, 124, 125, 127
process 13, 32, 43, 44, 45, 46, 74, 89, 177, 203, 242, 250, 252, 262, 266, 287, 288
Process 114, 117, 130
product 11, 11–311, 11–311, 34, 43, 52, 56, 57, 58, 59, 60, 64, 69, 71, 73, 109, 123, 136, 137, 141, 193, 197, 198, 210, 214, 216, 241, 264, 265
product design 11
product design charette 102
Product Manager 97
PRODUCT PROPOSITION 154
project goals 100, 106
prototype 35, 41, 44, 55, 77, 79, 96, 107, 109, 114, 135, 138, 139, 140, 141, 142, 143, 147, 148, 149, 231, 249, 253, 256, 258, 259, 260, 266
Prototype 96, 98, 134, 141, 153
prototypes 114, 127, 135, 140, 141, 142, 143, 149

Pruitt, John 306
Psychographic 115
psychographic segmentation 56, 60, 73
Psychographic segmentation 115

Q

qualitative research 108, 151, 230, 248, 255
quality 22, 23, 107, 170
Quality 111
quality assurance 107
quantitative research 108, 230, 243
Quesenbery, Whitney 306
question guides 109
questionnaire 145
questionnaires 48, 107, 260
Questionnaires 145
questions 49, 63, 139, 199, 202

R

Rada, J. 309
Radcliff-Brown, Alfred 42
Raddats, C. 306
rearrange 178
Reason, Ben 306
Recruitment Script 145
recycled 136
refine 109, 178, 205, 236
reframe 117
reframing 93, 260
reframing matrix 106, 122
Reframing matrix 122, 123
Reframing the problem 122
refreshments 131
Reinartz, W. J. 309
Religion 116
REPORT 151
report writer 79
Reputation 111
research 11, 41, 42, 47, 48, 49, 53, 58, 59, 64, 69, 71, 74, 77, 95, 97, 106, 108, 113, 114, 115,

116, 117, 125, 145, 148, 151, 152, 158, 168, 170, 172, 174, 183, 199, 201, 202, 203, 205, 207, 213, 216, 230, 231, 232, 236, 240, 248, 253, 255, 256, 257, 259, 260, 264, 266, 291
researcher 146, 151
research plan 106, 108, 114, 116, 152, 199, 202, 231
resources 42, 48, 49, 51, 53, 55, 58, 64, 69, 79, 96, 114, 125, 126, 133, 140, 158, 162, 165, 182, 197, 227, 238, 263, 267
responsible 136, 137
return on investment (ROI) 213, 241, 261
revenue 12–311, 93–311, 243
revenue streams 161
reverse 261
reverse card sort 261
Rickards 122
Rickards, Tudor 122
Ries, Eric 306
risks 108, 200, 263
Risks 148
Rizzo, F. 306
roadmap 50
Roam, Dan 306
Robinson, Ken 306
Roger Martin 44
ROI 159
role-play 261
role playing 107, 213, 241, 261
room 205, 207, 214, 235, 242
Rosati, Jerel A. 65
Royal Statistical Society 42
rule of reciprocation 261
RULES FOR BRAINSTORMING 133

S

Säde, S. 306

safety 66, 165, 258
Safety 111
Salvador, T. 307
Sampson S.E. 303
SAM/ Think Feel Do framework 119
Sandén, Bodil. 307
Sanders, E.B.-N. 307
Sangiorgi, D 305
Sangiorgi, D. 307, 311
Sangiorgi, Daniela 303
Sarmento, T. 307
satisfaction 12–311, 93–311, 243
satisfaction system 261
Sato, S. 307
say and do 185
scale 257, 261
SCAMPER 107
scenario 118, 141, 142, 144
scenarios 107, 108, 127, 142, 143, 144, 152, 204, 212, 234, 240, 261, 262, 264
Scenarios 143, 144, 152
schedule 83, 97, 100, 108, 110, 286
Scheduler 79
schools 263
Schrage, M. 307
Schwarz, Sven 307
scope 108, 204, 233
Screening SCRIPT 146
Script 145
secondary research 48, 49, 108
secondary users 59, 71
Seddon, John 308
see 185
Segelström, F. 296, 308
segmentation 51, 56, 58, 69, 199, 202, 230, 233
segments 51, 57, 59, 71, 114, 115, 150, 155, 161, 164, 185, 197, 198, 199, 202, 203, 227, 230, 233, 259
Seland, G. 308
sense of self 67

sensorial design 262
sensualization 262, 263
separate 204, 205, 240
service 110-311, 111-311, 114-311, 115-311, 123, 123-311, 123-311, 136-311, 137, 137-311, 137-311, 139-311, 142-311, 143-311, 147-311, 149-311, 150-311, 152-311, 153-311, 154-311, 157-311
Service 111, 114, 142, 148, 157
service blueprints 56, 106, 195, 227, 244
Service Blueprints 142
service design 30-311, 31-311, 54, 114, 261, 262, 264
service ecology 262
SERVICE LABORATORY 139
service package 111
Service prototyping 142
services 2, 10, 21, 22, 23, 24, 25, 26, 27, 28, 29, 32, 33, 34, 35, 41, 43, 50, 51, 52, 54, 55, 56, 57, 59, 60, 64, 69, 71, 73, 74, 77, 106, 109, 113, 114, 115, 128, 161, 164, 165, 172, 182, 183, 185, 190, 193, 195, 197, 198, 199, 202, 204, 205, 207, 209, 213, 217, 227, 230, 233, 236, 237, 238, 239, 240, 241, 243, 244, 246, 248, 249, 250, 251, 253, 254, 256, 257, 259, 260, 261, 262, 263, 264, 265, 266, 267, 290, 291, 292
service staging 213, 241
Service Staging & roleplay 142
service system 263
servitization 26, 27
Seth Godin 135
shareholders 263
sharpies 134, 203
Shoji Shiba 168
shoshin 39, 131, 132

Shostack, L. 308
Siemens 286
six thinking hats 107
sketches 101, 102, 103, 127, 135
sketching 35, 107, 174, 178, 267
Sketching 98
Sleeswijk Visser, F. 308
smart goals 106, 110
smell 185
social 70
Social context 119
social design 264
space 41
Spies, Marco 308
sprint 95, 97, 98
Sprint Master 97
Srinivasan, R. 308
stage 60, 72, 184, 205, 206, 208, 209, 211, 239, 240
stakeholder 59, 71, 106, 107, 113, 114, 121, 134, 191, 203, 209, 233, 239, 243, 263, 264
Stakeholder 97
stakeholder maps 243
stakeholders 50, 57, 59, 69, 71, 76, 93, 96, 97, 99, 100, 102, 103, 107, 108, 109, 110, 113, 114, 115, 116, 120, 122, 134, 142, 143, 144, 148, 149, 152, 153, 168, 171, 172, 182, 190, 198, 199, 200, 202, 203, 204, 212, 213, 230, 232, 233, 234, 240, 251, 253, 254, 257, 259, 262, 263, 264, 267
Stakeholders 99, 100, 142, 144
Stanford University 152, 286
Steelcase 11, 13, 286
STEP 46, 193, 204, 205, 264
Stevens, E. 308
Stickdorn, Marc 308
Storey, C. 300
story 34, 35, 144, 156, 212, 216, 240
Storyboard 96, 98, 141
storyboarding 161, 264

Storyboarding 98
storyboards 142, 264
storytelling 34
strategic 43, 50, 162, 165, 197, 227
Strategic 141
strategic design 264
strategies 100, 101, 136
strategy 55, 85, 108, 123, 189, 191
strengths 170
style guides 107
subject 53
subjects 42, 203
sub-journeys 203
success 58–311, 63–311, 71–311, 184–311, 198–311
summative testing 264
superheaders 177
suppliers 199, 202, 263
surveys 47, 107
Surveys 97, 145
Svanæs, D. 308
swimlane, lanes 195, 200, 204, 209, 240, 263
SWOT 114
synthesis 117, 125, 127, 142, 170, 174, 252, 263, 264
Synthesis 117
systems 50, 227

T

table 178, 204, 205, 206, 208, 211, 214, 235, 246
tablet 61, 73, 204
tacit knowledge 41, 42
Taffe, S. 309
Tague, Nancy R. 169
target audience 114, 115, 125, 127, 139, 154, 199, 202, 230
tasks 140
taste 185
Tatikonda, M.J. 303
team 95, 97, 98, 100, 110, 112, 113, 114, 115, 116, 120, 124, 125, 127, 128, 131, 132, 133, 134, 140, 142, 144, 148, 149, 152, 156, 159
teams 11, 26, 32, 33, 40, 57, 58, 63, 71, 76, 77, 79, 83, 87, 89, 91, 93, 102, 103, 106, 107, 108, 112, 115, 120, 132, 158, 168, 169, 170, 171, 172, 174, 175, 178, 182, 183, 185, 190, 198, 203, 205, 213, 231, 232, 234, 240, 241, 249, 250, 252, 254, 258, 263, 265, 267
techniques 53, 58, 69, 71, 243
technology 198
test 46, 109, 213, 241, 248
Test 115, 134, 143, 145, 151
testing 153, 158
testing plan 107
Tether, B. 309
Thackara, John 309
Thaler, Richard 309
The Design Ladder 31, 32
the environment 133
themes 79, 81, 119, 127, 150, 151, 169, 170, 171, 174, 177, 189, 203, 231, 232, 251
Themes 150, 151
think 41, 184, 186
think aloud protocol 264
think and feel 185
thinking 44, 45, 46, 52, 178, 198, 200, 201
THINK OUT LOAD SCRIPT 147
think out loud 107
Thomas A Edison 135
Tim Brown 66
time 11–311, 41, 48, 56, 185, 193, 204, 205, 208, 211, 214, 216, 233, 265
time segmentation 56
Tischner, Ursula 296
Titchener, E.B. 63
Tongur, S. 309
tools 41, 195
touchpoints 43, 51, 64, 193, 198,

204, 206, 209, 212, 213, 216, 217, 231, 239, 240, 243, 245, 249, 263, 264, 265
toxic 137
transcription 265
transformation 35
triangulation 47
Triangulation 151
tripod 203
Trischler 197
trust 34, 54, 55, 63, 91, 99, 139, 207, 236, 252
T-shaped people 87, 257
Tufte, Edward Rolf 309
TV 61, 73, 204, 242
two-by-two matrix 265
TYPES OF BRAINSTORMING 133
types of personas 59, 71

U

Ulaga, W. 309
underlying needs 113, 114
understand 140
understanding 53, 56, 57, 63, 64, 195, 198, 199, 201, 202, 213, 216, 241
understand people 42
unique selling proposition 265
United States 130
Universal design 129
UNIVERSAL DESIGN GUIDELINES 129
unmet needs 10, 35, 65, 106, 113, 114, 117, 127, 128, 199, 202, 230, 265
usability 143, 147, 250, 266
usability study 145
Usability testing 143
use cases 266
user 43, 57, 58, 59, 64, 69, 71, 72, 140, 177, 203
user-centered design 248, 259, 266
user experience 115

User Experience 118
user interviews 107
user journey 148, 266
user needs 177
user profiling 266
User Researcher 97
users 41, 43, 57, 58, 59, 69, 71, 140, 195, 213, 241
user validation 266
User validation 96
ux charette 102
UX designer 97
UX writer 97

V

Vaajakallio, K. 300, 309, 310
value exchange 266
value proposition 161, 165
values 27, 34, 37, 56, 74, 77, 113, 119, 154, 252
Vandermerwe, S. 309
vanity metrics 266
Vargo, S. L. 302, 309, 311
Vecchierini 294
Vendrell-Herrero, F. 309
Verganti, Roberto 309
Vermeulen, P. A. 297
vertical prototype 266
video 134, 242
video prototyping 213, 241
Viladàs, Xènia 310
vision 11, 34, 50, 95, 96, 108, 109, 110, 159
Vision 101
Visions 101
Visser, Froukje Sleeswijk 310
visual hierarchy 266
Voss 195
voting 177, 178
VW 11

W

Walker, B. 299
wall 173, 203, 204, 205

Walmart 21
want 43, 70, 195, 207
warming up 106
warming up exercise 112
Watanabe, Ken 310
Watkinson, Matt 310
weaknesses 171
web 49, 60, 61, 73, 204, 207, 237
web site 141
Wessels, G. 302
Westerlund, B. 310
Wetter-Edman, K. 310
What if and How might we questions 124
Whirlpool 13
white board 53
Whittle 195
wicked problems 267
wireframes 103, 127, 145
Wireframes 143
wireframing 107, 213, 241, 250, 267
withhold judgment 39, 63, 114
Wizard of Oz 107, 213, 241, 267
workarounds 116, 267
workflow 100
Wright, P. 310
WWWWWH 106

Y

Ylirisku, S. 310
Young, Indi. 311
Young, Laurie 311
Yu, E. 311

Z

Zehrer 197
Zeithaml, Valarie A., 311
zombie cats 106
Zomerdijk 195

13

**DCC ONLINE PROGRAMS
DCC WORKSHOPS
OTHER DCC TITLES**

DCC ONLINE COURSES
MORE INFORMATION HTTPS://DCC-EDU.ORG

OUR MISSION
Through our online programs, workshops and publications we provide skills to fulfill evolving work roles and to to create better solutions in a new economy. We provide quality education which is better value, more accessible, more flexible and more relevant for working global professionals. Online live, interactive continuing education courses that you can access from home, from work or anywhere with an internet connection.

ABOUT US
Our programs are for working designers and anyone seeking design and management training. Our online programs are presented direct from Los Angeles by some of the most experienced design professionals in the world. We offer introductory courses, five-week certificate programs and eight-week advanced certificate programs that meet once per week. The courses are delivered at a number at different times to fit your schedule and time zone. Our books have been specified as texts at many design and business schools including the University of California, Art Center Pasadena, Parsons Graduate Program, and Purdue University. We can present a custom program in your location anywhere in the world. We can tailor an online program to your schedule and needs. Contact us at info@curedale.com.

WHO HAS ATTENDED OUR COURSES?
Past participants in our on-line programs have included thousands of executives, design managers, designers from all design disciplines, architects, researchers, social scientists, engineers and other decision-makers from the following organizations including the following organizations. Tesla Motors, NASA, Kaleidoscope, Speckdesign, Intel, Nike, MillerCoors, Radiuspd, Gensler, Herman Miller, Trek bikes, Catalystnyc, Sylvania, Whipsaw, Berkeley University, Stanford University, Pininfarina, Inscape, Newbalance, MIT, Rhode Island School of Design, Tufts, Nokia, Steelcase, Mayo Clinic, Ocad, California State University Santa Barbara, University of Michigan, In Form, RIT, Honeywell, Columbia University, Nissan, Volkswagen, Sony, Nestle, Kraft Foods, Otterbox, Henry Ford Museum, Samsung, Ammunition, Siemens AG, Group, frog Design, Ziba Design, Plantronics, Luxion, Philips, Method, Visteon, Texas Instruments, Cisco, Mindspring, Hasbro, Dow Corning, Bressler Group, Reebok, Logitech, HP, CCS, Praxxis Design, Levi Strauss, NCSU, Design & Industry, Kensington, Symantec, Canberra University, Australian Government Department of Defence, Maya, Karten Design, Autodesk, Barco, Shutterstock, Lucid, Colgate, Starbucks, Sunbeam, Seimens.

OTHER TITLES
TO ORDER GO TO HTTPS://DCC-EDU.ORG

DESIGN THINKING

DESIGN THINKING PROCESS AND METHODS MANUAL 4TH EDITION
Author: Robert A Curedale
Published by:
Design Community College Inc.
August 21, 2016
Paperback: 600 pages
Language: English
ISBN-10: 194080535X
ISBN-13: 978-1940805351

DESIGN THINKING PROCESS AND METHODS MANUAL 1ST EDITION
Author: Robert A Curedale
Published by:
Design Community College Inc.
Edition 1 January 2013
Paperback: 400 pages
Language: English
ISBN-10: 0988236214
ISBN-13: 978-0-9882362-1-9

DESIGN THINKING PROCESS AND METHODS MANUAL 3RD EDITION
Author: Robert A Curedale
Published by:
Design Community College Inc.
August 21, 2016
Paperback: 690 pages
Language: English
ISBN-10: 194080549X
ISBN-13: 978-1940805498

DESIGN THINKING POCKET GUIDE 2ND EDITION
Author: Curedale, Robert A
Published by:
Design Community College, Inc
Jun 01 2013
Paperback: 228 pages
ISBN-10: 098924685X
ISBN-13: 9780989246859

DESIGN THINKING PROCESS & METHODS GUIDE 2ND EDITION
Author: Curedale, Robert A
Published by:
Design Community College, Inc
January 2016
Paperback: 422 pages
Language: English
ISBN-10: 1-940805-20-1
ISBN-13: 978-1-940805-20-7

DESIGN THINKING QUICK REFERENCE GUIDE
Plastic laminated
Loose leaf one page
Author: Curedale, Robert A
Published by:
Loose Leaf: 1 pages
Publisher: Design Community College Inc.; 1st edition (2015)
ISBN-10: 194080518X
ISBN-13: 978-1940805184

OTHER TITLES
TO ORDER GO TO HTTPS://DCC-EDU.ORG

BRIEFING CHECK LISTS

DESIGN THINKING POCKET GUIDE 2ND EDITION
Author: Curedale, Robert A
Published by:
Design Community College, Inc
Jun 01 2013
Paperback: 228 pages
ISBN-10: 098924685X
ISBN-13: 9780989246859

DESIGN THINKING QUICK REFERENCE GUIDE
Plastic laminated
Loose leaf one page
Author: Curedale, Robert A
Published by:
Loose Leaf: 1 pages
Publisher: Design Community College Inc.; 1st edition (2015)
ISBN-10: 194080518X
ISBN-13: 978-1940805184

DESIGN THINKING TEMPLATES & EXERCISES
Author: Curedale, Robert A
Published by:
Design Community College,Inc
2016
eBook 51 pages
ISBN-10: 1-940805-16-3
ISBN-13: 978-1-940805-16-0

PRODUCT DESIGN BRIEFING CHECKLIST
Author: Curedale, Robert A
Published by:
Design Community College, Inc.
Edition 1 2016
Paperback: 54 pages
Language: English
ISBN-10: 1940805317
ISBN-13: 978-1940805313

WEB DESIGN BRIEFING CHECKLIST
Author: Curedale, Robert A
Published by:
Design Community College, Inc.
Edition 1 November 2016
Paperback: 90 pages
Language: English
ISBN-10: 1940805287
ISBN-13: 978-1940805283

DESIGN THINKING PROCESS & METHODS GUIDE 2ND EDITION
Author: Curedale, Robert A
Published by:
Design Community College, Inc
January 2016
Paperback: 422 pages
Language: English
ISBN-10: 1-940805-20-1
ISBN-13: 978-1-940805-20-7

MAPPING METHODS

EXPERIENCE MAPS
JOURNEY MAPS
SERVICE BLUEPRINTS
EMPATHY MAPS
Author: Curedale, Robert
Published by:
Design Community College, Inc
March 2016
Paperback: 402 pages
ISBN-10: 194080521X
ISBN-13: 978-1940805214

SERVICE BLUEPRINTS
Author: Curedale, Robert
Published by:
Design Community College, Inc
March 2016
Paperback: 152 pages
ISBN-10: 1940805198
ISBN-13: 978-1940805191

JOURNEY MAPS
Author: Curedale, Robert
Published by:
Design Community College, Inc
March 2016
Paperback: 152 pages
Language: English
ISBN-10: 1940805228
ISBN-13: 978-1940805221

EMPATHY MAPS
Author: Curedale, Robert
Published by:
Design Community College, Inc
March 2016
Paperback: 152 pages
Language: English
ISBN-10: 1940805252
ISBN-13: 978-1940805252

AFFINITY DIAGRAMS
Author: Curedale, Robert A
Published by:
Design Community College, Inc
March 2016
Paperback: 128 pages
Language: English
ISBN-13 978-1940805269
ISBN-10 1940805269

MAPPING METHODS: FOR DESIGN AND STRATEGY
Author: Curedale, Robert A
Published by:
Design Community College, Inc
April 2013
Paperback: 136 pages
Language: English
ISBN-13 978-1940805269
ISBN-10 1940805269

OTHER TITLES
TO ORDER GO TO HTTPS://DCC-EDU.ORG

SERVICE DESIGN

SERVICE DESIGN PROCESS & METHODS 3RD EDITION
Author: Curedale, Robert
Published by:
Design Community College, Inc
2018
Paperback: 532 pages
ISBN-10: 1940805368
ISBN-13: 978-1940805368

SERVICE DESIGN POCKET GUIDE
Author: Curedale, Robert A
Published by:
Design Community College, Inc.
Edition 1 Sept 01 2013
Paperback: 206 pages
Language: English
ISBN-10: 0989246884
ISBN-13: 9780989246880

SERVICE DESIGN PROCESS & METHODS 2ND EDITION
Author: Curedale, Robert A
Published by:
Design Community College, Inc.
Edition May 2016
Paperback: 589 pages
Language: English
ISBN-10: 1-940805-30-9
ISBN-13: 978-1-940805-30-6

SERVICE DESIGN 250 ESSENTIAL METHODS
Author: Curedale, Robert A
Published by:
Design Community College, Inc.
Edition 1 Aug 01 2013
Paperback: 372 pages
Language: English
ISBN-10: 0989246868
ISBN-13: 9780989246866

DESIGN METHODS

DESIGN METHODS 1
200 WAYS TO APPLY DESIGN THINKING
Author: Robert A Curedale
Published by:
Design Community College Inc.
Edition 1 November 2013
Paperback: 396 pages
Language: English
ISBN-10:0988236206
ISBN-13:978-0-9882362-0-2

DESIGN METHODS 2
200 MORE WAYS TO APPLY DESIGN THINKING
Author: Robert A Curedale
Published by:
Design Community College Inc.
Edition 1 January 2013
Paperback: 398 pages
Language: English
ISBN-13: 978-0988236240
ISBN-10: 0988236249

50 SELECTED DESIGN METHODS
Author: Curedale, Robert A
Published by:
Design Community College, Inc.
Edition 1 Jan 17 2013
Paperback: 114 pages
Language: English
ISBN-10:0988236265
ISBN-13: 9780988236264

DESIGN RESEARCH

DESIGN RESEARCH METHODS
150 WAYS TO INFORM DESIGN
Author: Curedale, Robert A
Published by:
Design Community College, Inc.
Edition 1 January 2013
Paperback: 290 pages
Language: English
ISBN-10: 0988236257
ISBN-13: 978-0-988-2362-5-7

INTERVIEWS OBSERVATION AND FOCUS GROUPS
Author: Curedale, Robert A
Published by:
Design Community College, Inc.
Edition 1 Apr 01 2013
Paperback: 188 pages
Language: English
ISBN-10:0989246833
ISBN-13: 9780989246835

INTERVIEWS OBSERVATION AND FOCUS GROUPS
Author: Curedale, Robert A
Published by:
Design Community College, Inc.
Edition 1 Apr 01 2013
Paperback: 188 pages
Language: English
ISBN-10:0989246833
ISBN-13: 9780989246835

OTHER TITLES
TO ORDER GO TO HTTPS://DCC-EDU.ORG

DESIGN RESEARCH

30 GOOD WAYS TO INNOVATE
Author: Curedale, Robert A
Design Community College, Inc.
Edition 1 November 2015
Paperback: 108 pages
Language: English
ISBN-10: 1940805139
ISBN-13: 978-1940805139

INTERVIEWS OBSERVATION AND FOCUS GROUPS
Author: Curedale, Robert A
Published by:
Design Community College, Inc.
Edition 1 Apr 01 2013
Paperback: 188 pages
Language: English
ISBN-10:0989246833
ISBN-13: 9780989246835

INTERVIEWS OBSERVATION AND FOCUS GROUPS
Author: Curedale, Robert A
Published by:
Design Community College, Inc.
Edition 1 Apr 01 2013
Paperback: 188 pages
Language: English
ISBN-10:0989246833
ISBN-13: 9780989246835

BRAINSTORMING

50 BRAINSTORMING METHODS
Author: Curedale, Robert A
Design Community College, Inc.
Edition 1 November 2015
Paperback: 108 pages
Language: English
ISBN-10: 1940805139
ISBN-13: 978-1940805139

DESIGN FOR CHINA

CHINA DESIGN INDEX THE ESSENTIAL DIRECTORY OF CONTACTS FOR DESIGNERS 2014
Author: Curedale, Robert A
Design Community College, Inc.
Edition 1 2014
Paperback: 384 pages
Language: English
ISBN-13: 978-1940805092
ISBN-101940805090

14
BIBLIOGRAPHY

BIBLIOGRAPHY

THE AUTHOR'S PUBLICATIONS

Curedale, Robert. Design methods 1. Topanga, CA: Design Community College, 2012.

Curedale, Robert. Design methods 2. Topanga, CA: Design Community College, 2012.

Curedale, Robert. Service design: 250 essential methods. Topanga, CA: Design Community College, 2013.

Curedale, Robert. 50 selected design methods: to transform your design. Topango: Design Community College Inc., 2013.

Curedale, Robert. Design methods 2: 200 more ways to apply design thinking. Topanga (CA): Design Community College, 2013.

Curedale, Robert. Service blueprints, the tool for service innovation: comprehensive step-by-step guide. Topanga, CA, USA: Design Community College Inc., 2016.

Curedale, Robert. Experience maps: journey maps, service blueprints, empathy maps. Topanga, CA, USA: Design Community College Inc., 2016.

Curedale, Robert A. Affinity diagrams: the tool to tame complexity. Topanga, CA: Design Community College, 2016.

Curedale, Robert A. Empathy maps: stand in your customers shoes. Topanga, CA: Design Community College, 2016.

Curedale, Robert. Design thinking: process & methods. Los Angeles, CA: Design Community College Inc., 2018.

SERVICE DESIGN BIBLIOGRAPHY

Alam, I., & Perry, C. (2002). A customer-oriented new service development process. Journal of Services Marketing, 16(6), 515-534.

Allanwood, Gavin. User experience design: creating designs users really love. S.l.: AVA ACADEMIA, 2018.

Ambrose, Gavin & Harris, Paul (2010). Design Thinking. Lausanne, AVA Academia

Antonelli, Paola, and Patricia Juncosa Vecchierini. Design and the elastic mind. New York: Museum of Modern Art, 2008.

Antonelli, Paola (2009). The People. In Dietrich, Lucas (ed.).

60 Innovators Shaping Our Creative Future. London, Thames & Hudson. pp. 394—399.

Anu, Valtonen, and Miettinen Satu. Service design with theory: discussions on change, value and methods. Rovaniemi: LUP, Lapland University Press, 2013.

Association, Harvard Business School. Service management. Harvard Business School Press, Boston, Mass., 1991.

Balcioglu, Tevfik (ed.) (1998). The Role of Product Design in Post-Industrial Society. Ankara, Middle East Technical University, Faculty of Architecture Press.

Baines, T., & Lightfoot, H. (2013). Made to serve: how manufacturers can compete through servitization and product service systems. John Wiley & Sons.

Baines, T. S., Lightfoot, H. W., Benedettini, O., & Kay, J. M. (2009). The servitization of manufacturing: A review of literature and reflection on future challenges. Journal of Manufacturing Technology Management, 20(5), 547-567.

Banerjee, Maithili. Service design: a comparative study of design and service in UK and India with the idea of introducing service design in India. Saarbrucken: VDM Verlag Dr. Muller, 2010.

Bate, Paul, and Glenn Robert. Bringing User Experience to Healthcare Improvement: The Concepts, Methods and Practices of Experience-Based Design. S.l.: Radcliffe Publishing Ltd, 2007.

Battarbee, K. (2003). Stories as shortcuts to meaning. In Koskinen, I., Battarbee, K., & Mattelmäki, T. (Eds.), Empathic Design. Finland: IT Press, 107-118.

Battarbee, K. (2004). Co-experience: understanding user experiences in social interaction. Doctoral dissertation, University of Art and Design Helsinki.
Berger, Warren. Glimmer: how design can transform your business, your life, and maybe even the world. London: Random House, 2011.

Bettencourt, Lance. Service innovation how to go from customer needs to breakthrough services. New York: McGraw-Hill, 2010.

Beyer, Hugh, and Karen Holtzblatt. Contextual design: defining customer-centered systems. San Francisco, Calif.: Morgan Kaufmann, 2009.

Biemans, W. G., Griffin, A., & Moenaert, R. K. (Forthcoming). New Service Development: How the Field Developed, Its Current Status and Recommendations for Moving the Field Forward. Journal of Product Innovation

Management, 1-16.

Bitner, M. J. (1992). Servicescapes: The Impact of Physical Surroundings on Customers and Employees. Journal of Marketing, 56(2), 56-71.

Bitner, M. J., Ostrom, A. L., & Morgan, F. N. (2008). Service Blueprinting: A practical Technique for Service Innovation. California Management Review, 50(3), 66-94.

Bitner, M.J., "Evaluating Service Encounters: The Effects of Physical Surroundings and Employee Responses," Journal of Marketing, vol. 54, no. 2, 1990, pp 69-82

Bleuel, William H., and Joseph D. Patton. Service management: principles and practices. Research Triangle Park, NC, U.S.A.: ISA Press, 1994.

Blomkvist, J., Holmlid, S., & Segelström, F. (2010). Service Design Research: Yesterday, Today and Tomorrow. In M. Stickdorn, & J. Schneider (Eds.), This is Service Design Thinking. Amsterdam, Netherlands: BIS Publishers.

Blomkvist, J. (2014). Representing Future Situations of Service: Prototyping in Service Design. Linköping, Sweden: Linköping University Electronic Press.

Blomkvist, J., & Segelström, F. (2014). Benefits of External Representations in Service Design: A Distributed Cognition Perspective. The Design Journal, 17(3), 331-346.

Brax, S. (2005). A manufacturer becoming service provider–challenges and a paradox. Managing Service Quality, (15), 142-155.

Brown, Tim. Change by design: how design thinking creates new alternatives for business and society. New York: Collins Business, 2009.

Buchanan, R. (1992). Wicked Problems in Design Thinking. Design Issues. Vol. 8 (No. 2), MIT Press, 5–21.

Buchenau, M. & Fulton Suri, J. (2000). Experience Prototyping. Proceedings of Designing Interactive Systems conference (DIS 2000). New York: ACM Press, 424–433.

Buxton, William, Saul Greenberg, Sheelagh Carpendale, and Nicolai Marquardt.

Carroll, J. M. (2000). Five reasons for scenario-based design. Interacting with Computers, 13, 43-60.

Charter, Martin & Tischner, Ursula (2001). Sustainable Solutions: Developing Products and Services for the Future. Sheffield, Greenleaf Publishing.

Cipolla, Carla (2009). Relational services and conviviality. In Miettinen, Satu & Koivisto, Mikko (eds.). Designing Services with Innovative Methods. Helsinki, University of Art and Design and Kuopio Academy of Design. pp. 232—245.

Clatworthy, S. (2013). Design support at the front end of the New Service Development (NSD) process: The role of touchpoints and service personality in supporting team work and innovation processes. Oslo, Norway: Arkitekthøgskolen i Oslo.

Coates, Joseph F. (2009). Normative Forecasting. In Glenn, Jerome C. & Gordon, Theodore J. (eds.). Futures Research Methodology — Version 3.0. CD-rom. World Federation of United Nations Associations.
Condon, Patrick M. Design Charrettes for Sustainable Communities. Washington: Island Press, 2012.

Cooper, A. (1999). Inmates are Running the Asylum: Why High-Tech Products Drive Us Crazy and How to Restore the Sanity. SAMS, A Division of Macmillan Computer Publishing.

Corsten, Hans, Ralf Gössinger, and Anton Meyer. Service Management. Konstanz: UVK, 2014.

Cottam, H. & Leadbeater, C. (2004). HEALTH: Co-creating Services. UK: Red paper 01. Design Council.

de Bono, E. (1985/1999). Six Thinking Hats. First published in USA by Little, Brown and Company 1985, revised and updated edition published by First Back Bay 199, published in UK by Penguin Books 2000.

De Brentani, U. (2001). Innovative versus incremental new business services: different keys for achieving success. Journal of Product Innovation Management, 18(3), 169-187.

De Jong, J. P., & Vermeulen, P. A. (2003). Organizing successful new service development: a literature review. Management decision, 41(9), 844-858.

Despain, Wendy, and Keyvan Acosta. 100 principles of game design. Berkeley, CA: New Riders, 2013.

Díaz-Kommonen, L. Reunanen, M. & Salmi, A. (2009). Role playing and collaborative scenario design development. Proceedings of International Conference on Engineering Design (ICED'09). Stanford University, Stanford, CA, USA: The Design Society, 79–86.

Doorley, Scott, and Scott Witthoft. Make space: how to set the stage for creative collaboration. Hoboken, NJ: John Wiley & Sons, 2012.

Druin, A. (2002). The Role of

Children in the Design of New Technology. Journal of Behavior and Information Technology. Vol. 21 (No. 1), Taylor and Francis, 1–25.

Duarte, Nancy. Resonate: present visual stories that transform audiences. Chichester: John Wiley & Sons, 2010.

Evenson, S. (2005). Designing for Services. Proceedings of the Designing Pleasurable Products and Interfaces Conference (DPPI 2005). Netherlands, Eindhoven, 149–161.

Edvardsson, B., & Olsson, J. (1996). Key Concepts for New Service Development. The Service Industries Journal, 16(2), 140-164.

Edvardsson, Bo, Anders Gustafsson, Michael D. Johnson, and Bodil Sandén. New service development and innovation in the New Economy. Lund, Sweden: Studentlitteratur, 2002.

Lusch Robert, and Stephen L. Vargo. Service - dominant logic: premises, perspectives, possibilities. Cambridge: Cambridge University Press, 2014.

Fazlagic, Amir Jan. Service design. Warszawa: Akademia Finansów i Biznesu Vistula, 2013.

Fitzsimmons, James A., and Mona J. Fitzsimmons. New service development: creating memorable experiences. Thousand Oaks: Sage, 2000.

Fitzsimmons, Mona J. Service Management. London: McGraw-Hill Education - Europe, 2014.

Fließ, S. and Kleinaltenkamp, M. (2004) "Blueprint the Service Company: Managing Service Processes Efficiently," Journal of Business Research, vol. 57, no. 4, pp 392-404

Frei, Frances, and Anne Morriss. Uncommon Service How to Win by Putting Customers at the Core of Your Business. Boston: Harvard Business Review Press, 2012.

Fulton Suri, J. (2003). Empathic design: informed and inspired by other people's experience. In Koskinen, I., Battarbee, K., Mattelmäki, T. (Eds.). Empathic Design. Finland: IT Press, 51–57.

Gebauer, H., Krempl, R., & Fleisch, E. (2008). Service development in traditional product manufacturing companies. European Journal of Innovation Management, 11(2), 219-240.

Garcia, Fausto. New service development: creating a framework for the management of innovation in experience based firms. Saarbrücken: LAP, Lambert Academic Pub., 2010.

Garrett, Jesse James. The elements of user experience. Indianapolis: New Riders, 2011.

Gaver, W., Boucher, A., Pennington, S. & Walker, B. (2004). Cultural Probes and the value of Uncertainty. Interactions. Vol. 11 (No. 5). New York: ACM Press, 53–56.

Gemmel, Paul, Roland Van. Dierdonck, and Bart Van. Looy. Service Management an integrated approach. Harlow: Pearson, 2013.

Goodwin, Kim. Designing for the digital age: how to create human-centered products and services. Indianapolis, IN: Wiley Pub., 2009.

Gratton, Lynda (2011). The Shift. The Future of Work Is Already Here. London, Collins

Gray, Dave, Sunni Brown, and James Macanufo. Gamestorming: a playbook for innovators, rulebreakers, and changemakers. Farnham: OReilly, 2010.

Gronroos, Christian. Service management and marketing: managing customer relationships for service and manufacturing firms. Chichester: Wiley, 2000.

Grönroos, Christian. Service management and marketing: a customer relationship management approach. Chichester, West Sussex: Wiley, 2005.

Grönroos, Christian, Bo Edvardsson, and Jagdish N. Sheth. Service management. Los Angeles: SAGE Publications, 2013.

Grönroos, Christian. Service management and marketing: customer management in service competition. Hoboken, NJ: John Wiley & Sons, 2015.

Halvorson, Kristina, and Melissa Rach. Content strategy for the Web. Berkeley, CA: New Riders, 2012.

Heapy, Joe. Service design: design for new challenges. Farnham: Gower, 2012.

Heath, Chip, and Dan Heath. Switch: How to Change Things When Change Is Hard. S.l.: Random House US, 2013.

Heskett, James L., W. Earl. Sasser, and Christopher W. L. Hart. Service breakthroughs: changing the rules of the game. New York: Free Press, 1990.

Hohman, L. (2007). Innovation Games – creating breakthrough products through collaborative play. Addison-Wesley.
Hollins, Gillian & Hollins, Bill (1991). Total design: Managing the Design Process in the Service Sector. London, Pitman

Holmlid, S. (2007). Towards an understanding of the challenges for design management and service design. International DMI Education Conference Design Thinking: New Challenges for Designers, Managers and

Organizations, ESSEC Business School, Cergy-Pointoise, France.

Holmlid, S. (2007). Interaction design and service design: Expanding a comparison of design disciplines. Nordic Design Research, NorDes 2007. Stockholm.

Holmlid, S. & Evenson, S. (2006). Bringing design to services. Invited to IBM Service Sciences, Management and Engineering Summit: Education for the 21st century, New York.

Holtzblatt, Karen, and Hugh Beyer. Contextual design: using customer work models to drive system design. New York, NY: ACM, 2000.

Holtzblatt, Karen, and Hugh Beyer. Contextual design: evolved. San Rafael, CA: Morgan & Claypool, 2015.

Horovitz, Jacques, and Gerry Johnson. Service strategy. México: Pearson Educación, 2011.

Iqbal, Majid, and Sharon Taylor. Service strategy ITIL v3 core publications. London: TSO (The Stationery Office), 2007.

ISO 13407 (1999). Human-centred design processes for interactive systems. International Standard EN/ISO 13407:1999.

Johansson, M. (2005). Participatory Inquiry – Collaborative Design. Doctoral Dissertation, School of Engineering, Blekinge Institute of Technology, Sweden.

Johne, A., & Storey, C. (1998). New service development: a review of the literature and annotated bibliography. European journal of Marketing, 32(3/4), 184-251.

Johnson, Steven. Where good ideas come from: the natural history of innovation. Riverhead Hardcover, 2010.

Kankainen, A., Vaajakallio, K., Kantola, V. & Mattelmäki, T. (2011). Storytelling Group – a co-design method for service design. Journal of Behaviour & Information Technology. UK, London: Taylor & Francis, 1–10.

Kalbach, Jim. Mapping experiences: a guide to creating value through journeys, blueprints & diagrams. Beijing: OReilly, 2016.

Kaner, Sam, and Lenny Lind. Facilitators Guide to Participatory Decision-Making: Sam Kaner. Gabriola Island: New Society Publishers, 1998.

Kelley, Tom, and Jonathan Littman. The ten faces of innovation: IDEOs strategies for beating the devils advocate & driving creativity throughout your organization. New York: Currency/Doubleday, 2005.

Key element guide: service

strategy. London: The Stationary Office, 2008.

Kimbell, Lucy. The Service Innovation Handbook Action-Oriented Creative Thinking Toolkit for Service Organizations. Amsterdam: BIS publishers, 2015.

King, Stanley, and Merinda Conley. Co-Design: a process of design participation. New York: Van Nostrand Reinhold, 1989.

Kolko, Jon. Exposing the magic of design: a practitioners guide to the methods and theory of synthesis. Oxford: Oxford University Press, 2015.

Koskinen, I., Battarbee, K. & Mattelmäki, T. (Eds.) (2003). Empathic Design. Finland: IT Press. Leadbetter, C. We-think, 2nd ed. London, England: Profile, 2009.

Koskinen, I. & Battarbee, K. (2003). Introduction to user experience and empathic design. In Koskinen, I., Battarbee, K. & Mattelmäki, T. (Eds.) Empathic Design. Finland: IT Press, 37–50. Lee, Fred. If Disney ran your hospital: 9 1/2 things you would do differently. Bozeman, MT: Second River Healthcare Press, 2004.

Lehrer, M., Ordanini, A., DeFillippi, R., & Miozzo, M. (2012). Challenging the orthodoxy of value cocreation theory: A contingent view of co-production in design-intensive business services. European Management Journal, 30(6), 499-509.

Liedtka, Jeanne, Randy Salzman, and Daisy Azer. Design thinking for the greater good. New York: Columbia University Press, 2017.

Lloyd, Vernon, and Colin Rudd. Service design. London: TSO, 2007.

Lloyd, Vernon, and Sharon Taylor. Service design ITIL v3 core publications. London: TSO (The Stationery Office), 2007.

Lockton, Dan, David Harrison, and Neville A. Stanton. Design with Intent: 101 patterns for influencing behaviour through design. Berkshire, UK: Equifine, 2010.

Lockwood, Thomas. Design thinking: integrating innovation, customer experience, and brand value. New York: Allworth, 2010.

Lockwood, Thomas. Building design strategy: using design to achieve key business objectives. New York, NY: Allworth Press, 2010.

Lockwood, Thomas. Design thinking integrating innovation, customer experience and brand value. New York, NY: Allworth Press, 2011.

Lucero, A. (2009). Co-designing interactive spaces for and with designers: Supporting mood-board making. Doctoral Dissertation. Eindhoven University of Technology, Netherlands.

Lusch, R., Vargo, S. & Wessels, G. (2008). Toward a conceptual foundation for service science: Contributions from service-dominant logic. IBM Systems Journal. 47(1).

Maffei, S., Mager, B. & Sangiorgi, D. (2005). Innovation through service design. From research and theory to a network of practice. User's driven perspective. Proceedings of Joining Forces. University of Art and Design Helsinki.

Mager, Birgit. Service design a review. Köln: Köln Internat. School of Design, 2004.

Mager, Birgit. 10 service design basic cards. Köln: Fachhochsch., Fachbereich Design, 2006.

Mager, B. (2009). Service design as an emerging field. In Miettinen,
S. & Koivisto. M. (Eds.) Designing Services with innovative methods. Finland: Publication series of the University of Art and Design Helsinki, 28-43.

Mager, Birgit. Deep dive: collecting relevant insights. Köln: Service Design Network, 2013.

Mager, Birgit. Touchpoint the journal of service design: vol. 6, nr 3 (2014): Blurring boundaries. Köln: Service Design Network, 2014.

Mager, Birgit (2008). Service Design. In Erlhoff, Michael & Marshall, Timothy (eds.). Design Dictionary: Perspectives on Design Terminology. Basel, Birkhäuser.

Malterud, K. (2001). Qualitative research: standards, challenges, and guidelines. The Lancet. Vol. 358, 483-488.

Manning, Harley, and Kerry Bodine. Outside in: the power of putting customers at the center of your business. Las Vegas: Amazon Publishing, 2012.

Manzini, E. (1993, June). Il Design dei Servizi. La progettazione del prodotto-servizio. Design Management(7).

Manzini, Ezio (1998). Products in a period of transition. In Balcioglu, Tevfik (ed.). The Role of Product Design in Post-Industrial Society. Ankara, Middle East Technical University, Faculty of Architecture Press. pp. 43—58

Manzini, Ezio & Jegou, François (2003). Sustainable Everyday: Scenarios of urban Life. Milan, Edizione Ambiente

Marquez, Joe. Library service design. Place of publication not identified: Rowman & Littlefield, 2016.

Martin, Roger L. The design of business: Why design thinking is the next competitive advantage. Boston, MA: Harvard Business Press, 2009.

Martin, Roger L. The opposable mind how successful leaders win through integrative thinking. Boston, MA: Harvard Business School Press, 2009.

Mathieu, V. (2001). Service strategies within the manufacturing sector: benefits, costs and partnership. International Journal of Service Industry Management ,12(5), 451-475.

Mattelmäki, Tuuli & Sleeswijk Visser, Froukje (2011). Lost in Co-X. Interpretations of co-design and co-creation. In Roozenburg, N. R. M. & Chen, L. L. & Stappers, P. J. (eds.) (2011). Diversity and Unity, Proceedings of IASDR2011, the 4th World Conference on Design Research, 31 October — 4th November 2011. Delft, The Netherlands

Mattelmäki, T. (2006). Design Probes. Doctoral Dissertation, University of Art and Design Helsinki, Publication series A 69, Finland.

Mattelmäki, T., Hasu, M. & Ylirisku, S. (2009). Creating Mock-ups of Strategic Partnerships. Proceedings of IASRD conference. Seoul, Korea.

Mattelmäki, T., Vaajakallio, K. & Ylirisku, S. (2007). Active@work-Design dealing with social change. Online proceedings of the Include conference 2007. London: Helen Hamlyn Research Center, RCA. http://www.ektakta.com/include_proceedings/

McQuilken, Lisa, and Steve Mennen. Services marketing. Geelong, Vic.: Deakin University, 2010.

Menor L.J., Tatikonda M.J., and Sampson S.E. 2002. New Service Development: Areas of Exploitation and Exploration, Journal of Operations Management, 20: 135-157.

Meroni, Anna & Sangiorgi Daniela (2011). Design for Services. Design for Social Responsibility Series. Farnham, Gower Publishing.

Meroni, Anna, and Daniela Sangiorgi. Design for Services. Abingdon, Oxon: Taylor and Francis, 2016.

Miettinen, Satu (2009). Designing Services with Innovative Methods. In Miettinen, Satu & Koivisto, Mikko (eds.). Designing Services with Innovative Methods. Helsinki, University of Art and Design and Kuopio Academy of Design. pp. 10—28

Miettinen, Satu, and Mikko Koivisto. Designing services with innovative methods. Helsinki: University of Art and Design, 2009.

Miller, Luke. The practitioners guide to user experience design. London: Piatkus, 2015.

Moggridge, Bill. Designing interactions. Cambridge, MA: MIT Press, 2007.

Möller, K., Rajala, R. & Westerlund, M. (2008). Service Innovation Myopia? A New Recipe for Client-Provider Value Creation. In California Management review. Vol. 50 (No. 3), CMB.berkeley. edu, 31–48.

Moritz, Stefan. Service design: practical access to an evolving field. S.I.: Lulu.com, 2009.

Morelli, N. (2006). Developing new product service systems (PSS): methodologies and operational tools. Journal of Cleaner Production, 14(17), 1495-1501.

Moser, Christian. User Experience Design. Springer Berlin Heidelberg, 2012.

Nielsen, L. (2002). From user to character: An investigation into user descriptions in scenarios. Proceedings of Designing Interactive Systems (DIS 2002). ACM Press, 99–104.

Norman, Donald A. The design of everyday things. NY, NY: Basic Books, 2013.

Norman, Donald A. Living with complexity. Place of publication not identified: Mit Press, 2016.

Nudurupati, S. S., Lascelles, D., Yip, N., & Chan, F. T. (2013) Eight challenges of the servitization. Frameworks and Analysis. Spring Servitization Conference Proceedings 2013, p8

Oliva, R., & Kallenberg, R. (2003). Managing the transition from products to services. International journal of service industry management, 14(2), 160-172.

Ordanini, A., & Parasuraman, A. (2010). Service innovation viewed through a service-dominant logic lens: a conceptual framework and empirical analysis. Journal of Service Research, 14(1), 3-23.

Osterwalder, Alexander, and Yves Pigneur. Business model generation a handbook for visionaries, game changers, and challengers. New York: Wiley&Sons, 2013.

Osterwalder, Alexander, Yves Pigneur, Greg Bernarda, Alan Smith, and Trish Papadakos. Value proposition design. Hoboken, NJ: Wiley, 2014.

Osterwalder, Alexander, Yves Pigneur, Gregory Bernarda, Alan Smith, and Trish Papadakos. Value Proposition Design: How to Create Products and Services Customers Want. Somerset: Wiley, 2015.

Osterwalder, Alexander, Yves Pigneur, Gregory Bernarda, Alan Smith, and Trish Papadakos. Value Proposition Design: How to Create Products and Services Customers Want. Somerset: Wiley, 2015.

Osterwalder, Alexander, Yves Pigneur, and Greg Bernarda. The big pad of 50 blank, extra-large business model canvases and 50 blank extra-large value proposition canvases: a supplement to business model generation and value proposition design. Hoboken: Wiley, 2017.

Pacenti, E., & Sangiorgi, D. (2010). Service Design Research Pioneers: An overview of Service Design research developed in Italy since the '90s. Design Research Journal(1.2010), 26-33.

Papastathopoulou, P., & Hultink, E. J. (2012). New Service Development: An Analysis of 27 Years of Research*. Journal of Product Innovation Management, 29(5), 705-714.

Pang, S. (2009). Successful Service Design for Telecommunications: A comprehensive guide to design and implementation. Chichester, UK: John Wiley & Sons, Ltd.

Parker, Sophia, and Joe Heapy. The journey to the interface: how public service design can connect users to reform. London: Demos, 2006.

Patel, Raj. The value of nothing: how to reshape market society and redefine democracy. London: Portobello, 2009.

Patnaik, Dev, and Peter Mortensen. Wired to care: how companies prosper when they create widespread empathy. Place of publication not identified: Distributed by Amazon Digital Services, 2011.

Patricio, L., Fisk, R., Falcão e Cunha, J., & Constantine, L. (2011). Multilevel service design: From customer value creation to consumer service experience blueprinting. Journal of Service Research. 14(2). 180-200.

Pine, Joseph B., and James H. Gilmore. The experience economy. Boston: Harvard Business Press, 2011.

Pinheiro, Tenny. The service startup: design gets lean; a practical guide to integrate design and lean startup. S.l.: Amazon.com, 2014.

Pink, Daniel H. Free agent nation: how Americas new independent workers are transforming the way we live. New York: Warner Books, 2001.

Pink, Daniel H. A whole new mind: moving from the information age to the conceptual age. New York: Riverhead Books, 2006.

Pink, Daniel H. A whole new mind: why right-brainers will

rule the future. London: MC, Marshall Cavendish, 2012.

Polaine, Andrew, Lavrans Løvlie, Ben Reason, and John Thackara. Service design: from insight to implementation. Brooklyn, NY: Rosenfeld Media, 2013.

Polaine, Andy, Lavrans Lvlie, and Ben Reason. Service Design: from Insight to Implementation. New York: Rosenfeld Media, 2013.

Pollak, L. (2008). Myths of Service Innovation. International DMI Education Conference Design Thinking: New Challenges for designers, Managers and Organizations. ESSEC Business School, Cergy-Pointoise, France.

Prestes Joly, M.; Cipolla, C.; Mazini, E. (2014) Informal, Formal, Collaborative – identifying new models of services within favelas of Rio de Janeiro. Proceedings from ServDes2014. Lancaster, United Kingdom.

Priestner, Andy, and Matt Borg. User experience in libraries: applying ethnography and human-centred design. Abingdon: Routledge, 2016.

Pruitt, John, and Jonathan Grudin. (2003). Personas: practice and theory. Proceedings of the
2003 conference on Designing for user experiences ACM, San Francisco, CA, USA.

Quesenbery, Whitney, and Kevin Brooks. Storytelling for User Experience. Sebastopol: Rosenfeld Media, 2011.

Raddats, C., & Easingwood, C. (2010). Services growth options for B2B product-centric businesses. Industrial Marketing Management, 39(8), 1334-1345.

Reason, Ben, and Melvin Brand Flu. Service Design for Business. Wiley, 2015. Reichwald, Ralf, and Jessica Scheler. Service Innovation. Leipzig: CLIC, 2009.

Ries, Eric. Lean startup. Place of publication not identified: Portfolio Penguin, 2017.

Rizzo, F. (2010). Co-design versus User Centred Design: Framing the differences. In Guerrini, L. (Eds.) Notes on Design Doctoral Research. Franco Angeli Editore.

Roam, Dan. Unfolding the napkin: the hands-on method for solving complex problems with simple pictures. New York: Portfolio, 2009.
Robinson, Ken, and Lou Aronica. The element: how finding your passion changes everything. London: Penguin Books, 2010.

Säde, S. (2001). Cardboard mock-ups and conversations: Studies on user-centered product design. Doctoral Dissertation, University of Art and Design Helsinki, Publication series A 34, Finland.

Sandén, Bodil. The customers role in new service development. Karlstad: Faculty of Economic Sciences, Communication and IT, Business Administration, Karlstad University, 2007.

Sanders, E. B.-N. & Simons, G. (2009). A Social Vision for Value Co-creation in Design. In Open Source Business Resource, December 2009: Value Co-Creation. http://www.osbr.ca/ojs/index.php/osbr/article/view/1012/973

Sanders, E.B.-N. (2006). Scaffolds for building everyday creativity. In Frascara, J. (Eds.) Design for Effective Communications: Creating Contexts for Clarity and Meaning. USA, New York: Allworth Press.

Sanders, E.B.-N. (2002). From User-Centered to Participatory Design Approaches. In Frascara, J. (Eds.) Design and the Social Sciences. Taylor & Francis Books Limited.

Sanders, E.B.-N. (2001). A New Design Space. Proceedings of ICSID 2001 Seoul: Exploring Emerging Design Paradigm, Oullim. Seoul, Korea, 317–324.

Sanders, E. B.-N. & Dandavate, U. (1999). Design for experiencing: New tools. Proceedings of the First International Conference on Design and Emotion. Delft University of Technology, Delft, Netherlands, 87–92.

Sanders, L., & Stappers, P. J. (2012). Convivial Design Toolbox: Generative Research for the Front End of Design. BIS.

Sangiorgi, D. (2011). Transformative services and transformation design. International Journal of Design, 5(2), 29-40.

Sangiorgi, D. (2009). Building Up a Framework for Service Design Research. 8th European Academy Of Design Conference, (pp. 415-420). Aberdeen, Scotland.

Sarmento, T., & Patrício, L. (2014). Incorporating the customer experience along different iterative cycles of service design. Proceedings from ServDes2014. Lancaster, United Kingdom.

Sato, S. & Salvador, T. (1999). Playacting and Focus Troupe: Theater techniques for creating quick, intense, immersive, and engaging focus group sessions. Interactions. Vol. 6 (No. 5). USA, New York: ACM, 35–41.

Schrage, M. (2000). Serious play: how the world's best companies simulate to innovate. USA: President and Fellows of Harvard College.

Schwarz, Sven, Freimut Bodendorf, and Carolin Durst. Service innovation: research perspective and future roadmap. Nürnberg: Lehrstuhl für Wirtschaftsinformatik im Dienstleistungsbereich, 2012.

Seddon, John. Systems thinking in the public sector: the failure of the reform regime ... and the manifesto for a better way. Axminster: Triarchy, 2008.

Segelström, F. (2013). Stakeholder Engagement for Service Design: How Service Designers Identify and Communicate Insights. Linköping, Sweden: Linköping Electronic Press.

Seland, G. (2009). Empowering End Users in Design of Mobile Technology Using Role Play as a Method: Reflections on the Role-Play Conduction. In M. Kurosu (Eds.) Human Centered Design HCII 2009. Springer-Verlag Berlin Heidelberg, 912–921.

Service design: a toolkit for the design of public services. Brussels: Namahan, 2011.

Service design: Continual service improvement; Service operation; Service strategy; Service transition. London: TSO, 2007.

Servicedesign: vejen til enkle løsninger. Kbh.: Erhvervs- og Byggestyrelsen, 2010.

Shostack, L. (1982). How to Design a Service. European Journal of Marketing(161), 49-63.

Shostack, G. Lynn. "Designing Services that Deliver", Harvard Business Review, vol. 62, no. 1 January - February 1984, pp 133–139

Sleeswijk Visser, F. (2009). Bringing the everyday life of people into design. Doctoral Dissertation, Technical University of Delft, Netherlands.

Sleeswijk Visser, F., Stappers, P.J., Van Der Lugt R. & Sanders, E.B.-N. (2005). Contextmapping: Experiences from practice. CoDesign Journal. Vol. 1 (No. 2). UK, London: Taylor and Francis, 119–149.

Spies, Marco. Branded interactions: creating the digital experience. London: Thames and Hudson, 2015.

Srinivasan, R. Services marketing. Place of publication not identified: Prentice-Hall Of India, 2014.

Stevens, E., & Dimitriadis, S. (2005). Managing the new service development process: towards a systemic model. European Journal of Marketing, 39(1/2), 175-198.

Stickdorn, Marc, Jakob Schneider, and Kate Andrews. This is service design thinking basics, tools, cases. Amsterdam: BIS Publishers, 2011.

Svanæs, D. & Seland, G. (2004). Putting the Users Center Stage: Role Playing and Low-fi Prototyping Enable End Users to Design Mobile Systems. Proceedings of the SIGCHI conference on Human factors in computing systems (CHI 2004). USA, New York: ACM Press, 479–486.

Taffe, S. (2015). The hybrid designer/end-user: Revealing paradoxes in co-design. Design Studies. 40. 39-59.

Tether, B. (2008). Service design: time to bring in the professionals? In L. Kimbell, & V. P. Siedel (Eds.), Designing for Services - Multidisciplinary Perspectives: Proceedings from the Exploratory Project on Designing for Services in Science and Technology-based Enterprises (pp. 7- 9). Oxford, UK: Saïd Business School.

Thackara, John. In the bubble: designing in a complex world. Cambridge, MA: MIT Press, 2006.

Thaler, Richard, and Cass Sunstein. Nudge: improving decisions about health, wealth, and happiness: Rev. and exp. ed. New York: Penguin, 2009.

Tongur, S. and Angelis. J. (2013) Disruptive innovation and servitization - Competitive advantage through product service value propositions. Spring Servitization Conference Proceedings 2013, p.147.

Touchpoint the journal of service design. Köln: Service Design Network, 2009-.

Tufte, Edward Rolf. Envisioning information. Cheshire, CT: Graphics Press, 2017.

Ulaga, W., & Reinartz, W. J. (2011). Hybrid offerings: how manufacturing firms combine goods and services successfully. Journal of Marketing, 75(6), 5-23.

Vaajakallio, K., Mattelmäki, T. & Lee, J-J. (2010a). "It became Elvis" – Co-design lessons with Children". Interactions Magazine. July / August. ACM, 26–29.

Vandermerwe, S., & Rada, J. (1989). Servitization of business: Adding value by adding services. European Management Journal 6 (4): 314 – 324.

Vargo, S. L., & Lusch, R. F. (2008). Service-dominant logic: continuing the evolution. Journal of the Academy of marketing Science, 36(1), 1-10.

Vendrell-Herrero, F., Parry, G., Bustinza, O. F., & O'Regan, N. (2014). Servitization as a Driver for Organizational Change. Strategic Change, 23(5-6), 279-285

Verganti, Roberto. Design-driven innovation: changing the rules of competition by radically innovating what things mean. Boston, MA: Harvard Business Press, 2014.

Viladàs, Xènia. Design at your service: how to improve your business with the help of a designer. Barcelona: Index Books, 2011.

Visser, Froukje Sleeswijk. Service design by industrial designers. Delft: TU Delft, ID Studio Lab, 2013.

Watanabe, Ken. Problem Solving 101: A Simple Book for Smart People. 2013.

Watkinson, Matt. The ten principles behind great customer experiences electronic resou. Harlow: Financial Times, 2013.

Westerlund, B. (2009). Design Space Exploration: co-operative creation of proposals for desired interactions with future artifacts. Doctoral Dissertation, Kungliga Tekniska högskolan, Stockholm, Sweden.

Wener, R.E., "The Environmental Psychology of Service Encounters," in Czepiel, J.A., Solomon, M.R. and Suprenant, C.F. (eds), The Service Encounter: Managing Customer Interactions in Service Businesses, Lexington Books, 1985

Wetter-Edman, K. (2014). Design for Service – A framework for articulating designers' contribution as interpreter of users' experience. PhD Thesis. Gothenburg, Sweden: Litorapid Media AB.

Wright, P. & McCarthy, J. (2008). Empathy and Experience in HCI. Proceedings of the twenty-sixth annual SIGCHI conference on Human factors in computing systems (CHI 2008) Dignity in Design. USA, New York: ACM, 637–646.

Ylirisku, S. & Buur, J. (2007). Designing with video. Focusing the user-centred design process. UK, London: Springer-Verlag.

Ylirisku, S. & Vaajakallio, K. (2007). Situated Make Tools for envisioning ICTs with ageing workers. Online Proceedings of the Include conference 2007. London: Helen Hamlyn Research Center, RCA. http://www.ektakta.com/include_proceedings

Ylirisku, S., Vaajakallio, K., Buur, J. (2007). Framing innovation in co-design sessions with everyday people. Online Proceedings of Nordic Design Research (Nordes07). Stockholm, Sweden: http://www.nordes.org/upload/papers/104.pdf

Vaajakallio, K. (2008). Design Dialogues: Studying co-design activities in an artificial environment. Copenhagen working papers on design. No. 2, Danmarks Designskole.

Vaajakallio, K. & Mattelmäki, T. (2007). Collaborative Design Exploration: Envisioning Future Practices with Make Tools. Proceedings of Designing Pleasurable Products and

Interfaces (DPPI07). University of Art and Design Helsinki, 223–238.

Van Looy, B., Gemmel, P. and Van Dierdonck, R., Services Management: An Integrated Approach, 2nd ed., Esse, UK, Prentice Hall, p.231

Vargo, S. & Lusch, R. (2008). From goods to service(s): divergences and convergences of logics. Industrial Marketing Management. Vol. 37, 254–259.

Young, Indi. Mental models: aligning design strategy with human behavior. Brooklyn, NY: Rosenfeld Media, 2008.

Young, Laurie. From products to services: insight and experience from companies which have embraced the service economy. Chichester, England: John Wiley & Sons, 2008.

Yu, E., & Sangiorgi, D. (2014). Service Design as an approach to New Service Development: reflections and future studies. Proceedings of the Fourth Service Design and Innovation conference, ServDes (pp. 194-204). Linköping, Sweden: Linköping University Electronic Press.

Zeithaml, Valarie A., Mary Jo Bitner, and Dwayne D. Gremler. Services marketing: integrating customer focus across the firm. New York, NY: McGraw-Hill Education, 2018.

THE FIVE MOST CITED AUTHORS AT SERVDES CONFERENCES 2010-2014

- Stefan Holmlid
- Daniela Sangiorgi
- Lucy Kimbell
- Ezio Manzini
- Mary Jo Bitner

www.ingramcontent.com/pod-product-compliance
Lightning Source LLC
Chambersburg PA
CBHW070753230426
43665CB00017B/2343